LEARNING NOWADAYS CONSUMER BEHAVIOR

JOHN LOK

June 2019 Publish

Contents

Preface

Introduction

In this book, it divides three parts. First part explains how environment factor influences consumer behavioral change and second part explains how consumer time pressure factor influences their consumption behavioral change and and third part explains how emotion factor influences consumer behavior and fourth part explains how social factor influence consumer behavior

In first part, it brings these questions: Can environment factors influence consumer behavior changes? How and why environment factors can influence consumer behavior changes suddenly? When the consumer is influenced to change his/her original consumption attitude or consumption choice desire, after the consumer can change his/her consumption desire later. Does how much serious of environment factors influence consumer behavior changes? Does it influence their consumption desire to change in any sudden time or identified time or in any consumption suitation ot identified consumption situation?

In second part, it brings these questions? Does environment factor depend other factors to influence consumer behavior changes? e.g. time pressure feeling factor to the consumer, when one shirt shop has one large discount period, every shirt can be sold less 30% to 50% within this month. Then, it seems that one discount shirt purchase time pressure feeling to let shirt potentient buyers make any kinds of shirt purchase decision immediately when he/she stays in this shirt ship within this month. Also, it seems that this month's crowd environent in this shirt shop, this shirt shop's crowd environment can influence that they feel or believe all different kinds of this shop's shirts worth can let them to choose to buy to compare other shirt shops within this month. So, it seems that time pressure and environment factors both can influence consumers to make consumption choice behavior immediately. My readers can have more unforgetable memory to learn how and why environment factors can influence consumers behaviors after you read this book.

In second part, it brings these cases to explain how consumer time psychological pressure to change their consumption behavior. I explain why and how time factor will bring some product or service to let customers feel time pressure negative emotion or positive emotion. In chapter one, I shall explain how and why Walt Disney theme entertainment park which need to concern long time queue will bring negative emotion to its visitors and how it attempt to solve this long time queue challenge to change their emotion as well as how and why it can apply short time space tourism entertainment facility to let visitors to feel that they can spend short time to catch rocket to go to space tourism. In chapter two, I shall indicate why and how short time cooking factor will be any taste of read cooking meals' main attractive factor to influence food consumers prefer to choose to buy them to replace the fresh uncooked food in supermarkets or food stores. In chapter three, I shall explain how any why long time pressure will influence how to change travellers' shopping behaviors. In chapter four, I shall explain how and why time pressure will influnce consumer behavior. In chapter five, I shall explain how and why airplane's long time air pollution will influence the frequent environment protection traveller change reduce their travelling times. This book is suitable to any readers have interest to research how and why long waiting or consumption time can bring positive or negative emotion to influence their consumption desire.

This book third part explains how to predict consumer emotion to raising any manufactuer product's attraction in competitive product sale market and why emotion may influence consum behavior It concerns how to use face reading technology predicts consumer emotion to predict how to do the acceptable ingredients to produce foods to let them to feel more enjoyable to eat sweet foods or drink soft drinking as well as how to use video camera to investigate to predict customer emotion to find what factors had attracted them to choose to buy the manufacturers' products to use and judge whether how to increase your product more attractive to win your competitors. It concerns how to judge whether the online sale channel is more suitable or is not more suitable to compare to the visiting shop sale channel to let the product manufacturers to decide to choose to concentrate on selling their products from either of these two sale channels. Moreover, I shall indicate how to solve their website weaknesses to attract customers like to visit their websites to make final purchase decision more easily. Finally, I hope manufacturers can learn how to predict consumer emotion to decide how to invent your products to sell in the correct attitude to achieve to increase client numbers and you can learn whether you ought to choose to use which method(s) to predict your clients emotion before you invent your products or manufacture which taste foods to sell.

In my this book, the main important aim, I give examples to explain how to apply psychological and behavioral economic both view point related methods to predict consumer individual behavior to let businessmen learn how to choose the reasonable or right methods to attract consumers to choose to buy whose products or consume whose services to win competitors more easily. In this book final part, I shall indicate clear reasons to explain why I agree behavioral economy method and psychological method can be used to predict consumer behavior in nowadays society.

Prologue

Table of contents

The two categories of behavioral economy.

Explanation what are of Preferences over risky to behavioral consumption and utility function concept to company profit intention or government tax income intention

How can behavioral game theory apply to company income intention?
- Can predict consumer behavior with web search?
- Can firm's conduct and behavior factor influence consumer consumption ?

How to apply behavioral economic principles to assist policy makers or decision makers to make more reasonable decision.

Have behavioral economy and psychology methods close relationship.

How can consumer debt management psychological factors influence consumption behavior?

Can price change influence consumer behavior?

How can constructive consumer choice processes influence consumption behavior?

How can economical environment factor predict consumers consumption?

How can auctions or online experimentation respond to predict consumer behavior and sale forecast accuracy? p.331-350

- Why environment protection product businessmen need to concern what the degree of quality of life to their potential buyers

(i) How environmental risk factor can influence different groups

(ii) How Afria country environmental pollution influences

(iii) How human adult consumption and environmental quality influences future environment for human survival probability of life expectancy.

(iv) Why social and physical environmental factors have close relationship to influence economic growth

(v) How environmental factor can influence any country's house price.

(vi) How environmental pollution can influence social welfare

(vii) What is consumer neuroscientific research method to predict consumer behavior?

Whether design factor can predict consumer behavior for environment protection product

(i) Why environmental pollution and human right abuses has close relationship to influence quality of life and economic growth?

(ii) What is space and environmental technology?

(iii) Why does environment protective product need survey to enquire design questions?

(iv) Can implicit design questionnaire (survey) or /and interview methods can test consumer behavior for measuring consumer response to environment protection product? p.351-360

Face reading technology and video camera recording

- Recommendation of face reading technology is for confectionery food manufacturers and ethnographic consumer behavior video camera recording method to product manufacturers at home
- How constructive consumer choice process measures which attribute factor(s) can influence consumer chooses to buy any product or food in psychological view.

How to evaluate online sale method is more acceptable to sell the product.

- Explaining what situation makes the individual consumer doesn't accept to use internet technology sale channel to buy the product as well as it why internet will cause negative purchase emotion to any consumer to choose to buy any manufacturer's products . p.361-370

reference

Chapter 7
How social factor influences consumer behavior

Human Behavioral network job brings social
economic benefits

What does human network job mean

Why human network job behavior may influence economy

Robots take our jobs behavioral and economy influences

Robot job behavior brings economy influences

Intellectual human economic behaviors
What does intellectual human economic behaviors
mean ?

The relationship between social change and human
behavior

How human productive behavior may influence economic development

- New Zealand farmer individual wine productive behavior
- America high technological productive behavior
- China share market investing behavior

Why has any individual country have many people invest share behavior which can influence the country's macro consumption desire?

Can technology influence human shopping behavioral change?

Why and how human behavior may influence the country's economic growth or recession?

Technology how impacts human behavior changing? p.371-397

ONE

ENVIRONMENT FACTOR HOW INFLUENCES FOOD CONSUMER BEHAVIOR

The demographic and socio-economic factors influence children choose to any less healthy foods to eat

The demographic and socio-economic factors can influence children choose to any less healthy foods to eat, another psychosocial factors, and home, work, and school environments can also influence their less health consumption behavior in global society. In fact, above these environment factors can explain why global many children are influenced to like to buy any less health sugar sweetened , beverage to eat or drink , although they or their parents know any kinds of sugar, sweetened beverage are less health food or soft drink and those sugar sweetened beverage can bring less health when they choose to buy to eat or drink. I shall indicte these environment factors can persuade their sugar-sweetened beverage purchase behavior.

Firstly, for demographic and socio-economic is one important environment factor to encourage or persuade these children , their frequent sugar-sweetened , beverage eating or drinking behavior. This demographic and socio-economic risk factor many include age, gender, race/ethicity and education level four identified aspects as below:

In general, in age, gender, race aspect, makes adult and teenage makes drank over one-third of a -sugar-sweetened , beverage serving more than females on a typical day. The teens, 14 to 15 age also like to drink sugar sweetened beverage one-quarter of a serving more than 12 to 13 year olds. Minority children drank over one-third of a serving more per day compared to white children.

In lower education aspect, as parent education level decreased , their children will like to drink more sugar-sweetened bevereage. Otherwise, high school eduation level parents, their children will drink less sugar-sweetened beverage per day. It may have significant relationships existed between household poverty status and parent's education level status, which can influence their teams children sugar-sweetened beverage drinking behavior in frequency, instead of sugar-sweetened beverage, eating fruits and vegetables was also lower consumption food for children. It may have relationship to children's families eating habits. When, eating fruits and vegetables did not appear in the final adult model, adults who ate fruits , drank sugar-sweetened beverages slightly in daily eating habits. It may be that global parents feel druits and vegetables are not essential foods to their children. So, there are less families number need to buy fruits and vegetables to let their families to eat at home daily in frequency.

For milk and water, it is contrary to high essential food consumption expectations to global families in general. Global children drink one-third of a serving more for every serving of milk and water. Milk consumption included flavored milks and milkshakes which have contributed to the significant relationship between drinking milk. However, water consumption to children is significant lower to compare milk consumption . It may be water has no good taste to let children to feel more than milk.

For high calorie, low nutrient foods, global children , teens and adults have positive cosumption behavior between drinking and eating foods, such as field foods, desserts, pastries, sweets, candy and fast food. It may due to traditional eating cultural habit factor influence, such as western people like to eat fast foods for lunch. Children like to eat sweets, western people like to eat dinner desserts for mix their lunch or dinner habitually. For candy and added sugar foods, global teens who ate candy drink one-fifth of a serving more. Children ans adults who ate sweets like desserts, ice-cream , and candy drank and adults who ate breakfast , pastries , drank nearly one-third of a serving more.

For chips and fied foods, French fries, and deep-fried food were each independently consumption in children, teens and adults respectively. For every serving of chips and fried vegetables reported, children drank about one -fifth to one-third of a serving more. Teens who reported eating French fries drank three-fifths of serving more than teens, who reported not eating any French fries, for Asian teens. Adults deep-fried food consumption was linked to nearly one-third of a serving higher intake and though only marginally significant, adult chip and fried snack food consumption is also high consumption for Western adult . So, it has relationship between the countries' cultures and eating habits and sugar-sweeten beverage consumption.

In addition to dietary intake , child personal attitude and health behavior can influence consumption to child influences consumption to child personality. For parent and teacher behavior example, if children whose parents ate high fat foods that they drank a tenth of serving sugar-sweeten beverage habitually as well as children whose teachers used high calorie, low butrient " treats" as student reward for child's learning performance appreciation, when the child has good learning performance, then whose teacher will bring any high calorie , low nutrient , e.g. chocolate, ice-cream, soft drink to let whom to eat or drink in classrooms habitually. Then, the child's teacher and parent's free sugar-sweeten beverage or food reward behavior will encourage or persuade the child to adapt to eat or drink any sugar-sweeted taste of food or sugar sweeten soft beverage habitually. Also , they will change the " feel quilty" for not eating or drinking healthy food behavioral children to " feel none quilty" for not eating or drinking sugar -sweeten food, when they give free sugar -sweeted taste food or beverage to let them to eat or drink often when they feel any kinds of sugar-seeten food or beverage are their free reward food when they are appreciated for learning performance from their parents or teachers . Otherwise, if the student's school environment, home environment or the young people's work environment discourage and educate them ought not choose high sugar-sweeted beverage or food to drink or eat in preference, because they bring not health food or beverage message for sugar-sweeten beverage or food to let them to know in their schools, homes or workplaces. Then, this social message pressure factor will cause many young people do not choose to eat any kinds of sugar-sweeten beverage or food in preference. Hence, it seems that any environmental factor can change children or young people their eating habits to any kinds of sugar-sweeten beverage or food easily in long time.

- Environment factor influences animal
and plant-based foods consumption

Can animal or plant origin play's role impact human nutrition and diets when weather environment changing their food taste to influence nutrition and taste changing in order to reduce human's consumption desire to eat these animal and plant foods, (excluding beverage), from socio-demographic factor influence. However , I believe any weather changing factor will influence animal or plant food's taste, e.g. animal -based foods, meat products, milk products, egg foods and fish seafoods, (plant- based foods), e.g. grain foods, vegetables , fruits , potato, tomotato foods, margarine / oil, sugar sweets.

So, any weather or temperature or climate environment to the supermarket stores, warehouses, or food stores inside environment changing factor, it will influence the nutrition and diets to the animal or plant -based food's taste or quality to be changed to let people to feel worse taste to buy to eat to compare the kind of animal or plant food prior purchase from the supermarket or food store. For example, when one supermarket or food store its eggs, fruits are kept in one extreme hot or cold temperature environment warehouse longer time. Then, the eggs , fruits ' taste and quality will be influenced to be worse to eat to let people to feel they are needed to be compare to their prior eggs, fruits purchase from this same supermarket or food store before. It seems that this supermarket or food store 's warehouse environment factor will influence its temperature to be changed to worse and it also influences these foods' taste to be worse than before. So, it can influence consumers do not like to choose to buy them to eat from this same supermarket ot food store again.

For another example, this supermarket or food store's cold meats are kept in one not very cold or cool suitable temperature in freeze store. So, these cold meats' tastes and eating qualities are influenced to change to become worse tastes. Then, the cold meat consumers buy cold meats to eat from this supermarket or food store again, but they feel those cold meats tastes are worse to compare their prior cold meats purchase when they cooked to eat at homes. So, this supermarket or food store its warehouse temperature and freeze store temperature to be the most right cool or cold temperature in order to keep its fruits , eggs, cold meats, fishes, seafoods, ice-cream, vegetables etc.animal based or vegetable based foods' eating qualities to be fresh as well as the best taste to let its consumers to buy to eat.

Then, its worse warehouse or worse freeze store inside environment may influence either freeze stores' temperature can not be the most right cold or cool temperature to keep cold meats, ice-cream, fishs, seafoods to be the best taste to let consumers to buy to eat or warehouses' temperature can not be the most right cool temperature to keep vegetables, fruits, eggs, chocolates to let consumers to buy to eat or both influence.

Because this supermarket or food store's consumers can compare this supermarket or food store's animal-based food, vegetable-based food taste to other similar supermarkets or food stores which can sell the similar animal-based foods or vegetable-based foods or compare their prior animal-based foods or vegetable-based foods purchase to present food store animal-based foods or vegetable-based foods their tastes in order to feel whether these foods' tastes are better ot worse.

So, for any supermarkets or food stores businesses, their warehouses or freezers ' inside environment factor is important to influence their food consumers' behaviors indirectly. If their warehouses are kept in the long time variable worse temperature to keep their any animal-based foods or vegetable-based foods in the worse temperature environment. Then, it will may bring its any vegetable-based foods, or animal-based foods' eating qualities or tastes can not be improved better to let every food consumer to feel when he/she buys the supermarket or food store's foods to eat every time. In long time, because any one package of the supermarket or food store's animal-based foods or vegetable-based foods' tastes of eating qualities can not improved to let its consumers to feel good taste to eat, due to worse freezer's temperature or worse warehouse temperature environment factor be caused their tastes or eating qualities to be worse to compare prior. Then, this supermarket or food store will lose many food consumers in possible, due to their animal-based foods or vegetable-based foods' tastes will be compared to their other supermarkets or food stores competitors. If can cause worse consumption behavior to this supermarket or food store. So, for supermarket or food store's food businesses, their warehouses or freezers ' temperature keeping environment factor will have much influence to animal-based food and vegetable-based food tastes and eating qualities to cause food consumers' supermarkets or food stores choices of consumption behavior changing easily.

● Psychological and environmental factor how influences consumer choice

In general, environmental factor can include these aspects to influence consumer behavior, they include cultural, sub-cultural and social class, reference groups, family, roles and statuses, personal age, stage in family life cycle, occupation, economic conditions, consumer personal psychology, learning, perceptions, motivations these aspects.

Firstly, for cultural aspect means that a set of values, ideas, artifacts and other meaningful, interpret and evaluate as members of society. In consumer behavior influence aspect, culture's these components may influence any consumer makes final purchase decision ,such as religion, knowledge to the product, language communication between the consumer and the seller, social customs, food habits etc. of a particular society. Any of one can influence the society's any consumer individual feel how both values and possession to the product and it only influences consumer behavior, but also reflects it.

So, the culture of a society can impact how the society's consumers' buying and usage behavior of products and services . For example, for Asian and Western families' transportation tools culture are different. Western families like to ride bicycles to replace catching public transportation tools or driving cars when they feel the destination's distance is not far away from their homes. They may feel their less frequent driving behavior can reduce air pollution to be serious. Otherwise, Asian families will not prefer to ride bicycles to go to the destination, its distance is not far away from their homes. They need comfortable and enjoyable either they drive themselves cars or catch public transportation tools to go to the short distance destination. So, in general, Western families ' air protection avoiding and envionment protection culture can influence them to prefer to choose to ride bicycles to replace catching public transportation tools or driving themselves cars to go to anywhere short distance destinations in preference. Otherwise, Asian families do not consider environment protection or air pollution issue. So, they won't be influenced to choose to ride bicycles to go to short distance destinations very easily. It is one good example to prove and explain how different culture will bring different consumption behavior for daily transportation needs between Asian and Western people.

For sub-groups or sub cultures example, how they influence consumers behaviors, for example, marketers of cosmetic products need not consider the significant differences among different sub-cultures because use of cosmetic items by women remains more or less the same across the sub-cultures. However, marketers of food items need to take care of feelings and religious sentiments of their different sub-cultural target markets , when designing their marketing programs and product offerings. So, any marketing customer targets mainly depend upon the relevance of a particular product category to a particular sub-culture in order to sell their products to their right sub-culture customer groups more easily.

Secondly, however, age can be identified as sub-cultures by marketers, because of the unique shared values and behaviors are exhibited by them. A generation is a group of persons who have experienced a common social, political , historial and economic environment to influence their consumption behavior changes, e.g. young generation like to choose to buy laptop computer products more than desktop computer products, it may be due to convenient bringing, light weight , small size of laptop computer products characteristics, which can attract to young generation's consideration .

Regional sub-culture concerns the cultural environment and resources, distinct language, social and cultural environment, which can influence consumers behaviors. For example, in eating cultural aspect, sub-groups can be identified as having distinct and homgenous needs, tastes, lifestyles and values. For example, Western and Asian's eating and dressing cultures are different, their consumption pattern , especially in cases of dresses, food and drink consumption are different . Asian like to drink tea habitually, but, Western like to frink coffee. Asian like to cook vegetarian to eat, but Western like to eat not cook vegetarian , fresh delicacies. Asian like to dress chinese long shirt. Western like to dress T-shirt, suit, they feel polite attitude. They feel dressing can represent their Chinese and Western culture. So, regional sub-cultures can influence Asian and Western food habits and dressing habits are different as well as Asian and Western people's lifestyle is different , it can cause their food habits and dressing habits have much different.

Thirdly, also, the social class will influence consumption behaviors difference between high social class and low social class. For example, the high social class consumers, e.g. lawyer, doctor, architect, teacher etc. professional occupation consumers, they tend to be more fashional tend conscious as compared to their middle class counterparts. Similarly, when buying middle or high social class people often look for the price tag first, where as those belonging to upper class look for brand name and style first, price being the last priority. This shows that in majority it cases that norms, values ans buying patterns indicates that social classes act as a frame of reference for high, middle and low social class of consumers‘ buying behavioral difference in a particular social class.

Finally, another interesting environment factor is every shop's location choice. Does the shop's location environment can influence consumers shopping choices or consumption choices in preference indirectly? For the selection of the favourite location , such as the distance to the nearest public transport stop. So, customers can catch any public transport tools to arrive the shop in the short time, amount of fashion and luxury ships, they are close to the transport stop. So, consumers can feel to choose to buy any the kinds of products, the shop is located in the crowd location, daily shops and restaurants, leisure outlets are close to the shop. So, consumers can buy the product to close to the transporation stop from the shop easily as well as when they may feel hungry , they can go to restaurants to eat food immediately when they had bought any products from the shop or they can find any kinds of leisure activities to close to the ship easily after they bought any products from the shop conveniently.

Moreover, instead of concerning the most preferred location , the shop's owner also needs to regard whose shop's internal environment , because it can influence consumers' purchase desire in possible. For example, how the shape and color of the facades, amount of light, background noise and width of the street. Hence, the shop's internal designs and feeling environment whether it can let consumers have comfortable or enjoyable feeling to persuade to buy any of its products easily as well as whether the shop's location is close leisure places, public transportation stop stations, restaurants, etc. These external environment factor, which will may influence how many customers choose to enter the shop to choose any kinds of products to buy or raise their shopping desire in possible.

In conclusion, environment facto can include customer individual psychological factor or shop location visable or feeling or touch internal and external environment factor, which can influence any customer individual shopping desires to be raised or decreased from the shop's itself store design and shop external environment influence.

● How hospitality environmental factor influences patients service feeling

Does hospitality environment relate to patients‘ feeling to doctors and nursed services performance? Some patients need to live in hospital patient rooms, if the patient rooms sizes are too small or not clean or not comfortable to satisfy their living feeling, when they need to live in the hospital. some patients may need to live more than one month, even three months, even more than half year time in the hospital. If the hospital's patient rooms are small size and patient rooms number is less even, patient rooms' inside environment is not clean to let patients to walk, lacking any air conditions number, or none of air conditions to be provided to some or all patient rooms to let them to feel cooler or more comfortable in summer time , when they need to sleep in the hospital's patient rooms. Then, even the hospital's doctors and nurses , their performances are excellent, the hospital's patients won't feel very satisfactory from their medical service in possible, because they still feel the hospital patient rooms' living environment is very poor when they need to live in the hospital's patient rooms for a long time. Hence, hospital patients' medical satisfaction can include the hospital patient rooms' living quality level, instead of its doctors and nurses ' medial service performance.

In fact, hospital patients are same to consumers experiences, they may take place at different environment settings, such as shows, operas, restaurants, cimemas, hotels and others . So, hospital service environment seems to be similar any product consumption service entenvironment. If the patient feels he/she is living in a dirty patient room in a long time, he /she will feel not comfortable to compare to live his /her home. Although, the hospital has professional doctors and nurses to serve him/her every day, but the hospital 's dirty environment feeling will let he/she feels dissatisfied or dissatisfactory living feeling in the hospital's environment quality can bring poor memory to let the patient to remember in long time after he /she recovers his/her health and leaves the hospital to go back home.

Hence, if the patient feels the hospital's patient room living environment is satisfied to live or poor living quality during his/her living period in the hospital. The poor hospital patient room living feeling won't only influence the patient to feel when he/she is living in the hospital , even, his/her poor living hospital's room memory won't be forgotten when he/she go back home to live. It is one poor living hospital patient room living experience occurs as a result of suffering, or simply living in the hospital.

Hence, hospital's environment factor is one tangible aspect , instead of medical services let all patients to feel satisfactory when they visit the hospital in order to the hospital's patient rooms living environment can provide comfortable, clean furniture, bed and air conditions provision of cool temperature in summer as well as warmers or heaters provision of warm temperature in winter; free television, free mobile provision, independent bathroom , kitchen and toilet facility provision in the hospital's patient rooms; clean floors , clean bowls and chopsticks, forks, plates provision for patients' eating tools needs.

All of these eating, entertainment and living facilities in any hospital patients' rooms which ought provide to be provided to let patients to feel comfortable to live in his/her hospital living period in the hospital. Thus, it implies that any hospitals' patient rooms' facilities will bring indirect influence to every patient medical service living satisfactory feeling, insteda of doctors and nurses' medical service . So, all hospitals ought calculate their hospitals' environment living quality whether they can or can not satisfy their patients' long term or short term patient rooms living needs effectively.

- How the indentified environment impacts the identified consumer behavior

Can any consumption environment impact consumer behavior? Can only some identified consumption environment impact the identified consumer behavior to some identified products? For example, can the direct or indirect environment impact the country household's consumption pattern? It may be every household consumption pattern is different , every country household's consumption pattern will be influenced different to compare other countries' household consumption pattern?

The different indirect and direct environmental factors will impact every country household consumption pattern in difference, they can include these elements as below:

The country's environment profile of the households' calculation how they calculate their families household expenditure, how the country's different household products' life cycle assessment to evaluate how to spend to buy ay household using products, e.g. every house's kitchen cooking tools, furniture, electronic products, such as, radio, television, fan, air condition, cooler, heater, air condition, warmer to every household , how every household makes buying decision for families to use in frequent time or in not frequent time, e.g. every month or every three months or within one year changing new household using products , or every one year to two year changing new household using products for the country's household's habitual spending. So , every country's household's budget spending expenditure of families new products chaning habit, it will be influenced to general households' consumption behavior in the country in general.

Hence, the country's any household product manufacturers' themselves products life cycle and consumer's budget to families' using expenditure monthly both factors , they will influence the country;'s general households' consumption pattern or behavior in generally . The country's product manufacturers' products life cycle can be one indirect environment factor to influence the country's households' consumption pattern. For example, if the manufacturers' television products' life cycle can be used longer time, when it can raise more price to sell because it can have longer useful time to compare other brands of televisions to be sold to the country itself local households to use. For another example, if the car manufacturer can manufacture more reliable driving cars to let the country's household can buyers feel have more condfidence to drive safely on road and their machines can be used to drive longer time to compare other brands of car manufacturers' cars in the country. Then, these above two different household products' indirect environment life cycle factor can influence the country's household consumers to choose to buy them to use in preference or not.

For the country household expenditure budget direct environment factor aspect, this country indirect economic varied can be changed to either be better or worse, which can influene this country's environment influenced expenditure budget to consume in the month directly. For example, if the country had many employers did not decide to increase staffs number in this year, then this country will have more young people can not find any jobs to do , even they may be university graduate in this year. So, it will cause this year unemployment ratio raising to this country in this year. Then, this country will have many household's family income will reduce in possible because any household families will have young people to lose jobs to work to earn enough income to spend in this year, e.g. spending the entertainment household products,such as car. Then, the country will have many families will make budget not to buy any cars to drive for this year. So, the country's household budget expenditure will be direct influenced by every family's income and it wil be indirect influenced by the country's economic environment changing factor to bring poor household consumption desires in this year. For example, the country's households rise or reduce in the real family income (producing income) can influence to the country's every household's budget consumption expenditure pre month. The country's household consumers face trade-off in their purchase decisions, since their income are limited and choices are numerous. In order to make choices, the country's household consumers must combine every month consumption expenditure budget constraints. So,, it explains that why and how the country's indirect economic environment and direct every household budget expenditure and the product manufacturer's product life cycle factor will influence this country's household consumption desires indirectly in the year.

What can they afford and preference? What would they like to consume in preference for their family to use ? Do they feel urgent needing to buy to use for their family? So, the country household's every month budget consumption expenditure budget constraint, means what the country's a household consumer can purchase is constrainted by the month's real income.

The slope of the consumption budget, measures the rate at which the country' is a household consumer can trade off one brand of home not purchase product for replace another when the original using home product is needed to be replaced to use by another new one, and the relative prices of between the current using home product and the not using home product. So, the country's any one household's every month expenditure consumption budget constraints are determined by both the country's every household's every month real family income and the product's current relative sale price.

So, it seems the country's household per month consumption expenditure budget can influence to whethe what kind of home product(S), which are the country's individual household consumer's pruchase choice in preference in the month. It has direct relationship to influence every country's hosuehold consumption behavior.

TWO

QUEUE FACTOR INFLUENCE THEME PARK VISITOR EMOTION

Disney long time queue
pressure and short time
space tourism entertainment factor

- Disney short time space tourism entertainment facility

Disney can attempt to design space tourism entertainment facility to let visitors to feel they can enjoy to catch long time rockets to go to space to tourism, but in fact, they only spend short time to catch rockets to go to space to travel. Nowadays, Disney provides traditional entertainment to visitors to play. It is too common and it is not very attractive or unique to let visitors to feel entertainment satisfaction. So, it needs to provide unique theme park entertainment to let visitors feel it's entertainment is very different to other similar theme park competitors.

In the past Disney background history, Disney had encountered human resource and strategic management etc. different challenges about ten years. Then, Disney had applied knowledge management strategy to solve any challenges to attract many overseas and US local visitors who choose to visit to Disney theme park to play its entertainment facilities successfully. However, nowadays, Disney will encounter other challenges, such as, how to design its entertainment facilities to attract many visitors to visit, due to global entertainment theme park competitors are increasing, how to change its image to let visitors to feel it has much different image to compete its competitors. In this chapter, I shall explain how to apply space tourism knowledge management concept to raise Disney attraction as below:

First, what is a tourist destination and space tourist destination difference? e.g. space trip routes, Disney trip routes. Because any Disney visitors can not play all entertainment facilities and visit any entertainment destination in one day as well as any space travellers can not catch the space ship to fly all routes in space in one day. Hence, any Disney entertainment theme park and space tourism companies need provide any suitable space tourism destinations or Disney entertainment facilities destinations to let consumers to choose to entertain.

A tourism destination has many different characteristics. It is one product but also many,
involves many stakeholders with differing objectives and requirements, is both a physical entity and a socio-cultural one, is a mental concept for potential tourists, is subject to the influence of current events, natural disasters, terrorism, health scares etc.is subject to historical, real and fictitious events,
is evaluated subjectively in respect of its value-for-money (based on reality compared with expectations), and differs in size, physical attractions, infrastructure, benefits offered to visitors and degree of dependence on tourism ? In fact no two tourism destinations can be treated the same. Disney ought to choose space travel feactures to attract many visitors, so it ought no choose general earth tourism features because space tourism features are more attractive and fresh ideas to attract visitors, e.g. space toursim related entertainment facilities, space tourism 3 D to 5 D movies to provide visitors to watch to feel who are sitting in space flying boats to travel during they are staying Disney theme park any time. So, they will feel Disney theme park is one space tourism boat similarly.

Second, what are between space tourism impacts and Disney entertainment impacts difference ? Tourism has a far wider range of direct and indirect impacts than other economic sectors. At its simplest tourism can be seen to be a temporary addition to the population of a given location, with tourists having all the needs and impacts that the permanent population does, plus a few more besides. Government planning, regulation etc. is therefore needed; yet tourism is an economic sector executed by the private sector. Tourism activity involves direct contact with the local population. Tourism, then, involves a triumvirate of destination interests ?state, private sector and community.

As such, Disney must let visitors to feel that it can provide space tourism service , it is not general tourism servic to satisfy their space toursim entertinment theme park difference.

Space tourism planning for development and marketing is unlike any other economic sector and requires special approaches, procedures and institutions. Thus, Disney needs to know that space tourism features are different to general earth tourism as well as what factors will influence whose consumers do not choose to find their entertainment service. e.g. expensive air ticket, too cold or too hot weather, expensive space ship tickets or Disney admission fee , crowd in Disney or space ship etc. different factors to influence whose customers‘ choices.

Third, what is the difference between general earth tourism and space travel tourism perception? ?what is reality? How between space and earth tourism difference between a destination, or commercial tourism organisation, promotes its products and/or services is a key factor in the realisation of developmental or economic/financial objectives. In an activity like earth tourism where the customer is so far to live from the place he/she is considering to visit. Othwise, on space tourism perception and reality hand, such as spending long time to catch plan to arrive Disney or space ship destination or what entertainment service he/she is thinking to buy, such as Disney entertainment facilities or space ships facilities. Disney space entertainment tourism marketing is a central component of tourism. Two of the adages of tourism marketing arising from this situation are that:

1.Can Disney test drive a earth holiday only ?

2.Does it let its visitors to feel space tourism hoilday?

3. On Disney space tourism, is the perception the reality to its visitors' feeling?

Disney and space tourism entertainment businesses can consider how marketing policy and strategy might be incorporated in a destination overall Disney space tourism theme park development approach, Disney needs to consider those basic characteristics of space tourism that have implications for the marketing function.

● Fragmentation of space tourism supply

The space tourist product is a composite one, a combination of attractions, transport, accommodation, entertainment and other services. In most countries, there are many separate suppliers of these various components ? Disney theme park needs to supply these unique space toursim characteristics to feel visitors to feel, such as Disney own airlines to be supplied to overseas visitors to fly to Disney by cheap airline ticket fees, Disney supplies space unique characteristics hotels which can let visitors to live in space , space tour excursion organisers supply to let visitors feel Disney is one space entertainment theme park to provide space facilities entertainment services etc.

It is an important feature of Disney space tourism concept that, though an Disney individual supplier of different Disney space entertainment tourist services may serve unique similar space entertainement facilities and space entertainment service than other similar entertainment theme park competitors market, rarely, if ever, does a single space entertainment supplier provide the entire range of Disney space similar products /space similar services required by a tourist on a visit to any destinations in space theme park. Whether sold as a Disney space entertainment cheap package or assembled by the tourist himself or by a Disney space travel agent to give cheaper Disney admission fee price to compare to other travel agent Disney ticker prices , the Disney space tourist product is in practice a composite one. It is apparent, then, that given the fragmented nature of supply on one hand, and the demand for a combined set of Disney space tourism products on the other, a fundamental challenge for a destination is to achieve coordination and integration of all components across all sub-sectors of the Disney theme park entertainment tourism industry - that is, of only one supply to Disney space tourism entertainment theme park only. So, global theme park visitors only feel only Disney theme park can provide unique space toursim feeling when they choose to enter Disney theme park. It means that other global theme entertainment theme park can not provide space tourism experiences to attract them to visit.

CHARACTERISTICS OF SPACE TOURISM WITH IMPLICATIONS FOR DISNEY SPACE ENTERTAINMENT THEME PARK

Disney and space tourism entertainment businesses can consider how marketing policy and strategy might be incorporated in a destination overall Disney space tourism theme park development approach, Disney needs to consider those basic characteristics of space tourism that have implications for the marketing function.

● Fragmentation of space tourism supply

The space tourist product is a composite one, a combination of attractions, transport, accommodation, entertainment and other services. In most countries, there are many separate suppliers of these various components ?

Disney theme park needs to supply these unique space toursim characteristics to feel visitors to feel, such as Disney own airlines to be supplied to overseas visitors to fly to Disney by cheap airline ticket fees, Disney supplies space unique characteristics hotels which can let visitors to live in space , space tour excursion organisers supply to let visitors feel Disney is one space entertainment theme park to provide space facilities entertainment services etc.

It is an important feature of Disney space tourism concept that, though an Disney individual supplier of different Disney space entertainment tourist services may serve unique similar space entertainement facilities and space entertainment service than other similar entertainment theme park competitors market, rarely, if ever, does a single space entertainment supplier provide the entire range of Disney space similar products /space similar services required by a tourist on a visit to any destinations in space theme park. Whether sold as a Disney space entertainment cheap package or assembled by the tourist himself or by a Disney space travel agent to give cheaper Disney admission fee price to compare to other travel agent Disney ticker prices , the Disney space tourist product is in practice a composite one. It is apparent, then, that given the fragmented nature of supply on one hand, and the demand for a combined set of Disney space tourism products on the other, a fundamental challenge for a destination is to achieve coordination and integration of all components across all sub-sectors of the Disney theme park entertainment tourism industry - that is, of only one supply to Disney space tourism entertainment theme park only. So, global theme park visitors only feel only Disney theme park can provide unique space toursim feeling when they choose to enter Disney theme park. It means that other global theme entertainment theme park can not provide space tourism experiences to attract them to visit.

- Short time Disney space tourism entertainment feeling

It follows from the fact that Disney space entertainment theme park tourism demand is for a composite product that the various general earth tourist products and services are interdependent and complementary. Disney needs to supply the unique space tourism experience to let theme park visitors to feel. The supply of one (for example Disney space tourism theme park international air transport to/from a destination) depends on the supply of another (such as hotel accommodation) and they complement each other. I means that Disney can build one airport which can let visitors to feel it has space travel feeling during they arrive the Disney country.

A Disney space tourism theme park destination reputation can be set by the weakest link in the tourist product chain. This leads to the marketing policies and actions of one enterprise directly influencing other enterprises. A country with a liberal charter policy and/or an airline with an aggressive pricing policy may result in the attraction of low budget tourists, something that could damage the high quality image central to the marketing of a five-star hotel chain in the Disney destination. There is again then the need for coordination and cooperation in order to enhance the effectiveness of individual marketing and promotional efforts of the various tourism suppliers. Due to Disney can have any space tourism airports in every country to let visitors to feel that it is only Disney visitors have qualification to enter to Disney space tourism airports only. So, any non visiting Disney theme park visitors won't have chance to enter Disney space tourism airports when they fly to the owned Disney theme park countries.

In consequence of the intangibility of Disney and space entertainment businesses are tourist entertainment service products, when a supplier of a tourist services considers the potential market, the essential thought process should be: expectations ?experiences ?memories. This is the same whether the supplier is a destination promotion authority seeking to attract tourists to a specific country or location within that country, or the operator of a fixed-site facility like a hotel, restaurant or attraction, or a provider of tour excursion.

Each Disney tourist is a set of expectations. The Disney space tourism product cannot be test driven or known about with certainty in advance of being consumed. The Disney space entertainment tourist therefore builds mental images of the destination and of the facilities and other components of the tourism product of that destination. He/she has a set of expectations about the place to be visited.

Disney space tourism experiences is because the intangibility of tourism products means that the tourist engages in a series of activities ?typically, for example, riding on Disney transport is supplied between airport and Disney theme park, Disney space entertainment facilities visiting attractions, staying in some form of space tourism accommodation, eating, drinking, recreating, interacting with other people ?none of which produce a final physical product to take home. Each Disney space tourism tourist trip, therefore, is a combination of various experiences.

At then end of the trip the tourist is left with nothing more than memories ?the derivation of the word souvenirs - and proxies of the trip ?such as supplying Disney space tourism photos or videos to let visitors who can remember when they visit to Disney to play to feel space tourism experience.

The key for the Disney space tourism marketer is that the expectations created achieve the fine balance between attracting the Disney space tourist while not promising more than can be delivered. The Disney space tourism entertainment experiences are assessed by the tourist against his/her pre-trip expectations. A major determinant of success is how well the experiences match or exceed these expectations. This assessment has relative as well absolute dimensions. A destination may have a perception in the marketplace of being expensive or offering poor service, something which will limit its drawing power. If the Disney tourist finds it is not so costly or that service is better than expected, his/her level of satisfaction will be higher. Of course, the reverse can also be the case with more damaging consequences for the destination.

The intangibility of the Disney theme park tourist product and the consequent need for the marketer to address the potential market perceptions of the tourist product has two dimensions: first, the need to offer unique space tourism psychological benefits to the prospective Disney tourist; and, second, to recognise that the perception is the space tourism reality - with each Disney tourist having sovereign power over his/her destination decision making ?and that Disney space product sale marketing activities should be designed to alter the market prevailing images in line with the marketer desired position.

● Seasonality of Disney space tourism experience period.

It is a characteristic of most tourism markets that demand fluctuates over the course of the year, Disney will have many visitors in holidays, e.g. Christmas, school public holidays, new year holidays. The principal determinant is climatic ?either in the destination or the tourist generating markets. Residents of northern parts of the European and

North American continents tend mostly to take domestic or intra-regional holidays in the summer months of June ?September whereas they take long haul, inter-regional holidays more in the winter when the climate at home is generally cold and wet. As a result, tourist operators have periods when demand is near capacity and others when the level of utilisation can be 30 percent or even less, with the remaining months ?the shoulder season ?falling in between these two extremes. Thus, the country's season will influence Disney visitor number.

These demand variations are all the more acute because of the fact that any tourism product cannot be stored ?the perishability factor ? Disney needs let visitors to feel that they can play space entertainment facilities and let them to feel space tourism experience in Disney and the concern of marketers is to generate as much demand in the trough periods as possible since the fixed cost element of any tourism operation do not change between seasons. The Disney space tourism entertainmet marketing response to seasonality can range from the reduction of prices in order to induce people to travel in periods other than would be their normal preference to targeting geographic markets with different seasonal patterns of travel so that the demand for the destination from one group complements that of the other group. Thus, the country's tourism attraction can influence Disney visitor number indirectly, due to whether the period is holiday travelling seasonality or not.

● Disney short time space tourism influences to visitors' long time catching rockets feeling

In fact, space tourism and Disney theme park both businesses which have similar characteristics. Such as they are entertainment business, Disney provides different kind of entertainment facilities to let visitors to play to feel exciting satisfaction as well as space tourism provides one space ship to let travellers spend less time to sit in the space ship to fly to space to see any space stars and let them to feel exciting in the black space environment. They have these similar aspects:

They need have high technological machine facilities to supply, e.g. Disney needs different kinds of machine entertainment facilities to let visitors to sit down to play, Space tourism needs space ships to supply to travellers to sit down to fly to space. They needs to provide high quality of entertainment service to satisfy consumer individual need, e.g. Disney needs often to change its entertainment facilities to let visitors can play any different kinds of new entertainment machines more satisfactory. Otherwise, space tourism needs often to change new design of space ships to let travellers to sit as well as chooses different space trip routes to let travellers to see different space sightseeing when their space ships enter to any different space trip route every time. Due to Disney and space tourism have these kind of similar entertainment factors to cause their business can be success or failure. Thus, I believe Disney knowledge management strategy is similar to space tourism business. I shall indicate these knowledge management strategies which can be applied to space tourism business as below:

When discussing the advancement of space science and space technology, most people think about deep space flights, lunar stations, and thrilling outer space adventures. The fact is that the majority of the human technology in space, which consists of interconnected satellites, points towards Earth, and is used to provide services for and fulfil the goals of people on planet Earth. Over the next decade, there will be an increased need for innovative Earth information systems to support the international space community's efforts to provide a robust infrastructure.

However, space exploration requires vast sums of money. Is the amount of money spent on space research justifiable? Could the money be cheaper spent to let every space travellers? Thus, space tourism will have the effective knowledge management strategy to let every space traveller to feel every space trip fee is very reasonable to satisfy their space trip needs. The space trip service includes many different kinds of space good tasty foods supplies, comfortable and good design and safe environment of space ship facilities, exciting different space trip route choices, the reasonable space trip time length, space flight timetable arrangement, space ship service attendant attitude and performance and space tourism professional technical knowledge. Thus, space tourism business needs have these unique space knowledge management knowledge: Such as space tourism service attendant staff individual space ship service knowledge and space ships safe flight and trip space science tourism knowledge, space foods manufacturing knowledge, space ships repair and crisis management knowledge. If any space tourism company expected whose space travelers have confidence to choose to sit their space ships to go to space to travel safely. Otherwise, even although if the space tourism ticket fee is cheap in common , global space travelers won't prefer to choose to catch any space ships to go to space to travel if who felt any space ships were unsafe and dangerous transportation machine to let they lack confidence to sit safely. Thus, space tourism operators need to consider how to apply knowledge management strategy to let space travelers feel more safe and satisfactory needs more than Disney visitor.

Disney and space tourism entertainment businesses , both of them have long time entertainment development history as below:

First, for entertainment theme park industry development history. The development of the theme park entertainment travel and tourism industry had been beginning from USA , it changed customer needs and expectation to cause amusement park industry development after world war II in USA.

Wiig, k.(1993) showed that The economic activities associated with travel as is measured by the wide variety of current and capital expenditures made by or for the benefit of the traveller before, during and after the trip. Since the Second World War the Travel and Tourism Industry has developed. After Second World War, these main factors that have led to the economic growth and socio-economic circumstances of the Travel and Tourism Industry to cause amusement park industry development indirectly to USA are as below:

Firstly, the greatest single transport factor that has increased for travel and tourism is the car ownership. There was an increase in the number of cars on the road between 1951 and 1970's and an even bigger increase between 1951 and mid 1990's. Also, increased car ownership has now been a major factor of visits to tourist's attractions and leisure facilities nowadays. Then, people now don't have to work as much so more time to have holidays in the USA and abroad to spend whose leisure time. Before second war, the average working week was 50 hours but after second war, the typical hours in a normal working week ranges from 37 – 40 hours in USA. So, nowadays, there are many developed countries people who have more time to go to travel, such as USA, UK, France etc. countries.

Also, after second war, the global employees' salary are risen largely, who can have afford income to provide to go to travel at least one time every year . It will cause travel industry develops quickly. On the other side, Jet Aircrafts Developed , the breakthrough of the Jet Engine first started after the Second World War. It brought dramatic planes travel between countries, such as France or UK travellers who can catch air plans to travel to visit USA Disney amusement park in the most short time and distance fast. Then in the 1970s the jet aircraft really started being able to carry more passengers and increased profit and made flights cheaper to attract different countries travellers to go to different countries often. The last twenty years tour operators have also created hotel and Disney visiting and cheap air ticket price travel packages for the needs to attract to raise further new travellers numbers. Moreover, Many travel retailers use to rely on pen and paper to do the work but attitudes started changing as technology started to improve by the early 1990s. View data was the first industry-wide booking system, first introduced back in the 1980s. View data is more than 20 years old and out of date but still the trade's favourite reservation system. Global distribution systems (GCDs) were known as a computer reservation computer in the late 1980s. These were set up by competing airlines to distribute their fares electronically to business travel agencies. Also now you can book online, over the phone and on teletext.

Over the years the technology has improved all through the travel and Tourism industry with better transport, computerised reservation systems at travel agents and airports and better packaged holidays. Even more, over the last couple of years the low cost airlines have made a big development in the business. Low cost airlines like Easy jet, Ryan air and BMI Baby make it easy for people to travel to places in Europe for cheap prices, then cheap price travel is popular. Also, long Haul destinations have changed the travel industry a lot most holidays started just to Europe travellers and other travellers like Australia and New Zealand and France and Japan etc. countries doesn't take to long time to travel to USA by air plants very convenient. This gives people to travel around the whole world and go somewhere different. Moreover, package holidays have made a big improvement in the business. Thus, travel convenience can cause Disney visitors had been increasing many numbers.

Finally, on the weather and diseases both aspects can cause many overseas travellers like to choose to go to USA to travel. Over the years the weather has been getting warmer so snow will melt in the ski tourist places will start to lose money and tourist because of the weather also some places will have increased tourist for the weather being warmer as well as some countries are also loosing tourist because of diseases like foot and mouth because people don't like to travel to somewhere where they could catch something and can't even go there. For example, Britain lost a lot of tourists a couple of years ago through foot and mouth. After world war II, peoples needs and expectations have changed a lot in recent years. People are now fitter, healthier and more prosperous and are seeking more different and exciting types of leisure and tourism experiences. This, these environment and air ticket and travel package cheap price and warm weather and overseas countries' diseases increasing factors had assisted USA Disney traveller numbers rose.

Second, for space tourism entertainment industry development. Since the early 1970 year, the social sciences concern the process of globalization. Brennan (2011) explained " that globalization means the new international division of labor, changing forms of industrial organization and processes of urban-regional restructuring to transformations in the nature of state power, civil society, citizenship, democracy, nationalism, localities and architectural forms among many others. However, globalization research includes geographical concepts, such as space-time compression, space of flows, space of places, globalization , localization and scape, among many other terms ." Hence, the conceptualization of space exploration can relate to globalization by the channel e.g. the internet, a symbol that we are all connected and nobody is quite in charge as well as everyone in the world is affected, directly or indirectly. Also by this new Global investment in satellite navigation systems was extensive in the 2000 year. The USA with the GPS system. In particular, the space exploration means the space market has expand into new niche sector: Space tourism and travel, mining of resources, manufacturing opportunities , satellite technology all represent a shift toward privatization of the sphere. The new century is an important time in the history of space, not just for science, but in the opportunities it offers for business enterprise and commercialization. Human being are no longer in pursuit of progress and dreams of a high technological, science fiction life, they will use space technology to solve problems on Earth and to improve their quality of life despite limited financial resources.

Again, Brenna (2011) showed "Today, USA, Russia etc. countries are the world's super-powers at the time were engaged in the space race. They believe exploration and application of Earth orbital space become serious resources of national development and real advancement of people's living standards." The present day space industry has evolved from the romanticism of the 1960s and 1970s, when putting a human being on the moon captured the imagination of the world. Now, a multi-pronged approach to space exploration is attempting to address environment issues, advance technology and industry, and cater for the next generation of holiday makers the space tourists. A number of factors have contributed to the globalization of the space industry. Political changes in the 1990s and the end of the space race meant that almost all trading nations, function with market based economies and their trade polices have tended to encourage free market between nations. The globalization of the space industry has been further encouraged by technical standardization between countries. Most governments actively seek to encourage global operators to base themselves in their countries (namely, the USA space infrastructure, Russian know how, Brazilian lower launch costs). Yip (2003) cities "decreasing costs, globalization, scale economies, sourcing efficiencies as offering the potential for competitive advantage to some countries." A recent report from the Futron Corporation (2009) addresses strategic private questions about space power and competitiveness:

- What are the core measure of space competition?
- Is space nationalism on the rise, and if so, what are the implications?
- What are the implications of multi-polar space community?
- What are the economic consequences of a commercial space environment based on multiple international providers of key technologies, systems and services?

Hertzfeld (2007) has described how space power can be viewed from a commercial perspective in two ways. "The first is economic: Encouragement of USA space ventures to be dominant in the world marketplace, either through the creation of a monopoly by market dominance. The second is aggressively denying others access or interfering with the operations of foreign space assets. " Thus, it is possible that space exploration can stimulate the economy via job creation and the possibility of products entering future potential economic aspect of two civilian application of space technologies: communications and meteorology.

Another author's opinion, Taraseko (1996) has classified "Russian space systems according to the missions performed. These systems can be sub-divided into space weapons, space surveillance and intelligence systems, support systems and scientific systems ." He implied Russian will concentrate on manufacturing space weapons , then it will also sell space weapons to global finally. I think space exploration will have military and civil two aspects, instead of space tourism. Thus, on space system military aspect, it includes space weapons, space to Earth anti- satellite, early warning. Beside, on space system civil aspect, it includes support and applied communications, navigation, mapping, meteorological remote sensing and scientific research. It implies 'Globalization' will be cooperated by different main space leaders who will be carrying on space exploration activities in the future.

Thus, theme park and space tourism entertainment industry which have long time history development till to nowadays. They have been experiencing from old traditional technological facilities to innovate change to new unique technological facilities development. However, Disney and space tourism businesses whose knowledge management strategies concentrates on satisfying staff service and customer entertainment and foods needs and entertainment facilities and space ships facilities needs, so Disney and space tourism both businesses need have these similar knowledge management strategies to satisfy whose customers' needs importantly.

- Disney long time queue challenge

Disney has wrong judgement to operate its business in USA and overseas Disney operation wrongly. Such as Disney estimated the demand of employee numbers wrongly. It only employed an additional 200 experienced Disney managers were located in the other three centres. In addition, some 4000 employees were unable to find suitable positions. It caused management lacks optimistic assumptions to know who ought to be provided training to its staffing to dealt cultural difference challenges. Moreover, it also had external threats and internal weakness challenges. It included high bank investment interest rates charge , unreasonable working conditions, poor communication and lack of cultural awareness because managers and it caused staff turnover increasing finally. The most failure, before Disney had not carrying on research whether whose visitors feel happy and satisfactory to enjoy its entertainment facilities when who are staying in Disney. Otherwise, who feel unsatisfactory and unhappy , even who need to complaint whose service quality. Hence, Disney numbers of visitors was decreasing before. Such as, visitors felt unhappy because who need to spent much time to queue. It also caused Disney visitor numbers was declining. Thus, Disney will need to consider how to change human resource activities to adapt clients' needs, such as reducing bad emotion to cause visitors who needed to spend much time to queue to wait to play entertainment facilities.

Disney had attempted this traditional knowledge management strategy to solve its human resource and daily business operation challenges successfully. As Harriet Griffey (2010) stated that "sometimes, boredom can give disadvantages to reduce staffs' ability to motive to work and reduces positive emotion , such as happiness. Thus, it causes people (staffs) lack motivated reasoning to unconsciously evaluate evidence in ways consistent with whose preferences. This type of bias can hinder a company's ability to learn from mistakes and to build successful strategies."

However, Disney chose to implement knowledge management strategy to satisfy visitors demands and needs to let who feel more satisfactory when who entered Disney to play its any entertainment as below:

For first example, Disney demanded cleaners to repeat to remember any information to prepare to answer visitors' enquiries. It will train every cleaner memory to remember any information to be long term from short term memory successfully and every cleaner won't feel bore to do only cleaning job duty. When every one feel places are clean, who will concentrate on answering any visitors enquiries as the same time. Even, if they can give excellent service performance to serve visitors to let who to know how to go to any places in the short time. It is possible that visitors will appreciate whose service performance to let their manager to know, so that every cleaner will have chance to raise salary.

Besides for second example, waiting time and queues are daily problem for Disney theme park. Fast lines or priority queues appear as a solution of efficient queues for clients. Disney understood fast ticket line system affected visitor attendance numbers. Disney entertainment facilities long waits leaded to lower service evaluations and greater customer dissatisfaction. Efficient queue waiting time management can improve Disney visitor satisfaction and the willingness to recommend the service. Disney analysed of theme park visitor behaviour in relation to pay the higher ticket price to select to pay more for fast queuing line ticket than common queuing line ticket. In fact, Disney fast queuing line ticket system choice gave potential queues to any waiting clients . In general, Disney visitors don't like to wait long time in every entertainment facilities queuing line, who will feel a waste of time and waiting can lead to negative emotional response like frustration, impotence, tension or irritation .

In fact, Disney amusement theme park needed visitors wait long queues and delays which were a frequent occurrence in every entertainment facilities line. Disney theme park as sets of rides, spectacles and leisure mechanisms are intended to entertainment and spark the imagination of clients, allowing visitors to escape their daily routing. In result, waiting is often a problematic issue that can influence Disney visitor experience and that can appear as one of the principal motives for complaining. As Disney visitor demand fluctuates constantly and demand patterns are often difficult to predict. It caused extra staff needed for the extra line. Finally, priority services such as fast line system facilities segmentation of its amusement park. When Disney offer the possibility of purchases a fast line, which are creating two different group. Disney visitors who are highly sensitive to waiting times are willing to pay to avoid or reduce lines or visitors that are highly sensitive to price that prefer to wait rather than to pay extra money. Also, Disney provides extensive training opportunity for participants through its own Disney university. The question of whether their training opportunity can lead the improve human resource activities. On the third hand problem, Disney are also worried that employees may leave it and join other competitor to serve their parks after training. Disney shows a trend of increasing depending on human capital other than physical capital. It thinks human capital is the knowledge, skills, ideas and commitment of its employees. It explains that investing in training and development is essential to its client service growth. In fact, Disney had owned enough entertainment facilities, restaurants, hotels, shopping centres within theme park, but its visitor numbers are increasing to need to be served satisfactorily. However, it needs to train cleaners, entertainment facilities service staffs, queuing service staffs, hotels, restaurants, shopping centres service staffs, instead of it's entertainment facilities attraction.

For the final example, Disney observes that spending on training and development is typically regarded as consumption, instead of investment. On job training usually can't be replaced by formal education, therefore Disney chooses to make contribution on providing further training and development to employees. Disney paid salary for staff training, which included classroom, seminars, symposia or conferences; computer based training, on site training, book and periodicals reading, formal mentoring and informal mentoring program opportunities to meet its old staffs and new staffs both needs of motivate factors to achieve advancement , achievement, personal growth responsibility and achievement and recognition to raise its business performance effectively and efficiently.

However, Disney's amount of training has a positive influence on intrinsic motivation of its employees. Job satisfaction, salary, working condition, its policies, administration, relationship with supervisors, peers and subordinates are Disney factors to influence it's human resource activities performance. Disney training contents include these functional area: Raising excellent service performance include that hotel food and beverage service delivery, shopping center, merchandise sale, restaurant service, entertainment facilities queuing waiting service, cleaning and enquiring how to go different locations in Disney, cashier service etc. They are very important to influence visitor numbers. Disney implementation of knowledge management solution to improve queuing waiting line process. The use of Disney front line service staffs as human capital combined with knowledge of customer preference has made the fast pass an innovation solution to enhance queuing in the Disney theme parks. Disney ability to capture customers in virtual queues when giving them a pleasurable waiting experience has made them a leader in knowledge management initiatives in the service industry. Disney's emphasis on human capital within their theme parks, combined with traditional queuing theory to create more pleasurable waiting environments. Hence, Disney showed the value of tacit employee knowledge integrated with traditional queuing theory to reduce loss of customer satisfaction to enhance, goodwill and profitability. Knowledge management expresses itself as human action in form of evaluation, attitudes, points of view, commitments, motivation etc. It seemed that Disney agreed that human capital (people, knowledge, ideas, creativity) maybe today's most valuable commodity.

- How to solve Disney long time queue challenge

Knowledge Management Strategy was used to queue control from Disney. Disney managers have long understand the pressure of waiting time and revenue; who know that every minutes spent waiting in queuing is a minute that the client is not generating revenue. So, Disney managers have processed with design of a reservation system recognizes that guests can be freed from physically standing in the actually and perception of waiting by allowing guests to engage has arrived. Cope et al., (2008) showed that" the system was first tested at Disney in 1998. Managers assessed the system by surveying guests who used it. Results were positive and indicated that guests spent substantially less time in queuing, spent more per capita, and saw significantly more attractions, satisfaction level sky rocketed.The system was expanded in 1999 to include five of the most popular park attractions and was named FASTPASS. The system has since been expanded to all Disney theme parks worldwide, and is now in use by over 50 million guests per year .That guests have two options .Namely, they can choose to Obtain a FASTPASS ticket and come back a later, designed time or Wait in a traditional queuing. Guests are assisted in making their choice by information regarding estimated waits of both options. Thus, can decide to wait in the traditional queuing, or take a FASTPASS ticket and return it a later time with no further wait. Once an assigned FASTPASS time is generated and provided to a guest, it is valid for the 60 minutes beyond that time, creating a window in which guest can return."

There are numerous benefits in allowing park guests to return to an attraction within a designed time frame. Queue Waits involve managing two major client issues:

1.How long Disney visitors actually wait every time queue.

2.How long Disney visitor think they are waiting by whose psychological feeling every time queue.

Thus, if they feel that who spend much time to queue, it will cause they feel angry and they also feel admission ticket price is paid too high to them unfairly. In general, clients were allowed the ability to see two attractions during the time they would have previously been able to see only one. This can viewed as an implementation of a multi-phased system, depending on the attraction picked, each queuing may be single channel attractions, the guest creates whose own multi phase system. Obvious, results, were that guests were able to engage in more revenue producing activities, saw more of the popular attractions and began to par take care, in other less utilized attractions .

Wiig defined(1993)" Knowledge management in different ways and from different perspective. The emphasis is on human know how and how it brings value to an organization. Intangible asset contributes to corporation objective may be immeasurable and isn't simple to evaluate the impacts of knowledge management."

However, Knowledge management may not be only factor influencing organizational performance. In fact, Disney refined technology utilization to improve the user design of all human resource related systems, improving timeliness (queue waiting time deduction), setting elapsed time goals and monitor performance towards those standards, considering to use of automated fast queue waiting system, evaluating staffing levels, a close examination of adequacy of current staff level is warranted, beyond to improve visitors satisfaction. Clients holding fast pass tickets may choose to visit a gift shop or any park concessions. Thus, Disney has ability to co-branded products and service.

Disney's approach combining queuing and human capital. Dunn, J et al., (2002) showed "The use of fast pass provides an insightful application of the combination of techniques of queuing and human capital to strategically leverage knowledge management principle .When waiting lines are an part of the Disney experience, park guests build magical memories through innovation. It is Disney's recognition of front line service staffs that transforms that employees into knowledge who multi task in their roles. For example, an attraction host or a street sweeper may be a valuable Source knowledge to park guests. In addition to their primary roles, they may have a wealth of information about attractions for guests. They may be able to give directions, provide schedules, and offer helpful suggestions from their daily observation. This is the first stop to increase knowledge management . Next, Disney improves its clients' perception by minimizing the perception of waits. The use of the fast pass enables Disney not only to enhance the psychological aspect of waiting lines, but also to capitalize at the same time." Instead, Disney needed to give people specific tools designed to help them to do their job and solve specific business problems. Thus, after Disney learned how it applied the knowledge management method to solve its challenges, e.g. Human capital and queuing theory provide two very different valuable assets to raise its competitive ability. Then, its visitor numbers was increasing largely and quickly.

In conclusion, Disney need to change it's strategy to adapt any the business environmental situation change in different time. For example, in the past, due to Disney had encountered operation challenge and human resource management challenge. So, it apply fast queue knowledge management strategy to solve visitors' spending long queue time is needed to wait to play any Disney entertainment facilities to let them feel satisfactory and feel no angry to compaint Disney. It seems that it is more successful to attract many visitors prefer to pay admission fee to visit Disney to play.

However, nowaday, Disney is encountering another kind of challenge, such as how to increasing its entertainment facilities more attration to compete its theme park entertainment facilities competiors. I shall recommend that it can apply space tourism strategy to design its entertainment facilities are similar to space tourism entertainment facilities to let its visitors feel its entertainment facilities are more attractive to win its similar theme park competitors in future theme park entertainment industry development. So, it needs to change its entertainment facilites to let visitors to feel that they can spend short time to stay in Disney theme park in order to satisfy their entertainment feeling more than other similar entertainment theme park competitors.

Bibliography

Ansoff, H.I. (1987) Corporate Strategy. Penguin, London

Bahandin, G. & Guerganna, K.S. United States, (Jan. 2009).Strategic human resource management and global expansion lessons from the Euro Disney challenges in France. International business & economics research journal, vol. 8, no.1.

Barnard, Bruce: Business is booming in the world's biggest tourist market, March 1999, p.22, Journal of Commerce, Brucells.

Barnard, Bruce: Business is booming in the world's biggest tourist market, March 1999a, p.24, Journal of Commerce, Brucells.

Benesch, Dieter, 1989: " Theme parks in Florida-Eine Analyse von Angebot und Nachfrage sowie Regionalwirtschaftfliche Auswirkungen" , Master 's Thesis at the University of Economics and Business

Administration, Vienna. AAdvisor: Prof. Dr. Karl Sinnhuber, Library.

Brennan, L. & Vecchi, A., (2011). The Business Of Space, The Next Frontier Of International Competition. Palgrave Macmillan Press: USA, New York.

Charles B. (2012) Curiosity Takes Us Back to Mars the
WHITE HOUSE Available at: Date Of Publication: 6 Aug.
https://www.whitehouse.gov/blog/2012/08/06/curiosity-takes-us-back-mars

Cope, R. R. Cope and H. Davis (2008). Disney's virtual Queues: A strategic opportunity to co-brand services ? Journal of Business & economics research, vol. 6 no10, 13-20.

Dickson, D., R. Ford and B. Laval (2005). Managing real and virtual waits in hospitality and service organizations. Corncell hotel and restaurant administration quarterly, vol. 45 no1, 52-68.

Dunn, J & A Neumsister (2002). Knowledge management in the Information age. E. business review, Fall , 37-45. Jounral of service, spring 2011, vol. 4, no1, De Grovte (2009).

Edinger Tourismberatung GmbH: Study: "Die Entwickling von Freizeitparks in Osterreich, 1998, for: Bundeministerium fur wirtschaftliche Angelegenheiten, wien" Innsbruck.

ERA (Economics Research Associates) 1998: " The Future Role of Theme parks in International Tourism" , Clive B. Jones & John Robinett, Los Angeles, p.5

ERA (Economics Research Associates) 1998a: " The Future Role of Theme parks in International Tourism" , Clive B. Jones & John Robinett, Los Angeles, p.13

Foden, harry G. 1996, " Destination attractions as an economic development generator", Economic Development Review, Fall 1996, 10., American Economic Development council

Friedmann, David:" Status Report of the Los Angeles County Economy", Vol.1, prepared for the "Los Angeles Board of Commerce, 1999.p.78

Futron Corporation (2009) Resource Centre. Available at:
http://www.futron.com/resource_centre/resource_cemtre.htm.

Gartrell, R.B. (1994) Destination Marketing for Convention and Marketing Bureaus. Kendall/Hunt Publishing, Dubuque, Iowa

Harriet Griffey. (2010) The art of concentration, enhance focus, Reduce, stress and achieve move. Macmillan publishers ltd,Basinastoke and Oxford, London UK.

Hertzfeld, H.R. (2007) Globalization, Commercial Space And Space Power In the USA, Space Policy, Vol.32, no 4. November.

IAAPA: International Accociation of Amusement Parks and Attractions (http://www.iaapa.prg), " Theme Park Industry at-a-a glance" (Brochure), 1999, Atlanta, Georgia.

Kotler, P., Bowen, J. and Makens, J (2003) Marketing for Hospitality and Tourism. Prentice Hall ?Pearson Education, New Jersey

Kotler. P., Hamlin, M.A., Rein, I. and Haider, D.H (2002) Marketing Asian Places: attracting investment, industry, and tourism to cities, states & nations. John Wiley & Sons (Asia) Pte. Ltd., Singapore

Kotler, P., Haider, D.H. and Rein, I (1993) Place Marketing. Free Press, New York

Kyriazi, Gary, "Amusement Parks: A Pictorial History" Secaucus, NJ: Castle Booka, 1997.

Lundberg, Donals E. (ph.D.): " The Tourist Business", 1995, 5. Edition-Published by Van Nostrand Reinhold Company, New York.

Middleton, V.T.C. & Clarke, J. (2001) Marketing in Travel & Tourism. Butterworth Heinemann, Oxford

PKF consulting, 1997: " Study of the Projected Future Tax for: The City of Anadheim, the Anaheim Public Financing Authority, Nov. 13, Collections From Designated Sources to be Received by the city of Anaheim", 1997, prepared -1997.

Tarasenko, M.V. (1996) Evolution Of The Soviet Space Industry, Acta Astronautica, Vol. 38, no. 4-8, pp. 667-73.

The Economist 1997: "The Los Angeles economy: Bigger than South Korea", Feb, 4. 1997 page 25-26, London.

Wiig, k.(1993). Knowledge management foundations: Thinking About thinking. How people and organizations create, represent and use knowledge vol.1 , of knowledge management series schema press: Arlington, TX.

Yip, GS. (2003) Total Global Strategy II: Updated For The Internet And Service Era (Upper Saddle River, NT: Presentice-Hall).

THREE

Time factor influences supermarket ready-food consumer need

Ready-food meal short

time cooking attractive factor

Ready-food meal can be attractive to change food consumers' long time cooking behavior. Because they can buy the ready cooking meal to heat to eat at home in short time. So, the short time cooking factor will influence many food buyers to choose to go to sumpermarkets to buy any taste of ready food to eat when they are busy to work ever day. I shall explain why an how shot time ready-food can change food consumer's choice to go to supermarkets to buy these any taste of ready-cooking food to replace the fresh food at food stores. Short time cooking factor is the major influence their food choice buying behavior.

Although, previously dismissed and a poor substitute for real cooking and ready meal sales have grown rapidly in recent years in many western developed countries, such as UK, France or Germany. But, Ready meal manufacturers ready to respond to a changing marketing environment. Due to one big change in recent year has been growing demand for ready prepared meals bought from a supermarket. An analysis of the reasons for the growth in the ready prepared meals markets indicates the effects of boards factors in the marketing environment on the size of a particular market. In fact, this food market is changing to drive the growth in the ready meals market, but there are differences in the food market potential between countries. The effect of change in the marketing environment on sales of ready meals, such as technology has played a big role in the growing take up of ready meals and new technologies have allowed companies to develop ready meals which preserve taste and texture, which still making them easy to use by the consumer. Furthermore, great advances in distribution management, in particular the use of information technology to control inventories, has allowed fresh, chilled ready meals to be effectively and efficiently distributed without the need for freezing or added preservatives. Ready meals particularly appeal to single householders, which individual family members tend to eat at different times, so family meals together remains stronger in many continental European countries than in the UK individual ready meals.

Young people have lost the ability to cook creatively, as cookery has been reduced in importance in the school, so young clients group will rise to buy ready meals from supermarket. Marketing can be seen as a system that must respond to environmental change. A food market can be defined as a meeting place for stakeholder (consumers) and sellers. Food market can be set up in a supermarket or restaurants. A food market consists of the individual's target taste, such as older group, family group, young group or business clients who are actual or potential caters of a restaurant meals or supermarket package of foods. Grocery stores (supermarkets) have an influence of meals (fast cooked food) outlets in low income urban areas, which has contributed to the income in access to healthy foods. An organization's marketing environment means the individuals, organizations, and forces external to the marketing management's ability to develop and maintain successful exchanges with its customers. The marketing environment to ready meal manufacturers had three levels.

Firstly, it includes the micro environment, it describes those elements that impinge directly on the ready meal manufacturers themselves, so the micro environment of ready meal manufacturers which include business clients who have direct contact, such as restaurants, supermarkets and individual clients who have direct contact. Otherwise, supermarket shoppers, restaurant clients and food supply competitors who have no direct contract to ready meal manufacturers, so who won't include in food market micro environment to ready meal manufacturers.

Secondly, it includes the macro environment, it describes things that are beyond the immediate environment but can nevertheless affect an organization, so the macro environment of ready meal manufacturers which include the export countries' economies forces, such as unemployment ratio, GDP; technological forces, such as the export countries' factories food productive technology; social/ cultural forces, such as the export countries' people taste acceptance; political/legal forces, such as the export countries' import food quota numbers.

Thirdly, it includes the internal environment, it describes ready meal manufacturers' employees and equipment and finance and functional responsibilities. Environment means everything outside influences the person, in contrast with individual or personal variables . The effects of change in the marketing environment on sales of ready meals can be analyzed by creating healthy food and eating environment changing factor and supermarket technological changing factor as below:

The ready meal manufacturers could not ignore threats to the natural ecological environment change Due to the food companies could have technology to manufacture good taste cooked ready meals to provide to supermarkets to sell. Thus, it might influence the consumers to decide whether restaurants or supermarkets or ready meals suppliers who could provide the most reasonable price and taste to satisfy whose eating needs every day. Thus, it caused the growing demand for ready prepared cooked meals bought from supermarkets. Due to it was possible that consumers felt to eat ready cooked meals in expensive restaurants or who did not like to buy foods to cook from food suppliers or who could not feel which could supply more good food taste and health food quality to compare supermarkets specially. Otherwise, although, supermarkets could provide cheaper ready cooked meals to satisfy who to feel good food taste and health food quality. Due to ready meal manufacturers had new techniques to develop ready meals which preserve taste and texture, which still making them easy to use to eat by the consumers. Furthermore, great advances in distribution management, in particular the use of information technology to control inventories, has allowed fresh , chilled ready meals to be effectively and efficiently distributed to supermarkets or restaurants without the need for freezing or added preservatives.

Creating healthy food and eating environments view describes an ecological framework for conceptualizing the many food environments and conditions that influence food choices, with an emphasis on current knowledge was been regarding the home, child care, school, work site, retail store and restaurant settings. The status of measurement and evaluation of nutrition environment and the need of action to improve health are highlighted in marketing environment. More processed and convenience foods are available in large portion sizes and which were supplied at relatively low prices at supermarkets. Parents are working larger hours, there are fewer family meals and more meals are eaten away from home. The school food environment is remarkably different. It seemed that it would be changed in the marketing environment on sales of ready cooked meals to supermarket more easily. Due to supermarkets' cooked meals should focus on selling high calorie and low nutrition foods are available in multiple venues throughout the school student client group target because it was possible that supermarkets could sell ready cooked ready meals prices were more cheaper to compare to restaurants or school canters' cooked meals provided prices.

The effects of change in the marketing environment on sales of ready meals which indicated that consumers chose prefer to buy ready cooked meals from supermarkets. It seemed that a restaurant market failure could be caused to arise. For example, there was poor information on the part of food (ready cooked meals) to provide to the restaurant about the foods that consumers in a location(place) would demand for a given price to compare to the supermarket sale prices. The restaurant would lose clients if which cooked the kind of meals to sell higher price to compare to the supermarket sale of the kind of cooked ready meals price possibly. Large size supermarkets could sell cheaper ready cooked meals to low income group clients. It could cause competition to constitute a market failure to small size supermarkets. If the small size supermarkets lacked good information on the true food (ready cooked meals) with concentrations to sell cheaper prices, then this ready cooked meal market failure was one potential reason why small size supermarkets did not locate to close to the large supermarkets. Due to supermarkets grew in size would influence clients' choice to buy the numbers of cooked foods (ready meals) products. Moreover, The advent of computerized logistics and inventory systems were integrated with the large size supermarkets themselves occurred between the 1980 years and 1990 years .

So large size supermarkets were reliance on their own distribution and cooked food (ready meals) inventory systems along with larger supermarket sizes to allow super center to change to sell ready cooked meals at lower prices. Supermarkets marketing can promote healthful eating by increasing availability, affordability or restricting / de-marketing unhealthy foods to sell cooked Food (ready meals) marketing strategy at supermarkets, including labelling, packaging, pricing and point of sale advertising. Consumers' cost saving efforts and income and ready cooked meals prices increasing or decreasing factors can drive the choice of supermarkets as well as cooked meal products use of coupons and loyalty cards bargain shopping is another factor to influence their choice. Private label or store (supermarket) brands are taking an increasing share of consumers shopping dollars as the importance of brands. Supermarket shoppers stated priorities are cooked food (ready meals) quality or taste and price and healthy cooked food (ready meals) choices.

However, supermarket shoppers' buying behaviors don't always reflect on favor healthful foods. Due to demand for locally grown cooked food is increasing. Anyway, restaurant meals are changed to supermarket to sell, which decide what kinds of meals to stock and how many of different kinds of meals to stock and how much variety of kinds of meals to offer to any one supermarket as well as supermarket shoppers prefer fewer options, provided that their preferred brand or cooked food (ready meals) products are available. The designs of supermarket ready cooked meal products and packaging to supermarket to sell is the focus of unusual colors or shape which can be used to increase interest and is specially pervasive among fun foods to compare to restaurant meals. Package design, including where text and images are placed, which can influences cooked foods (supermarket ready meals repurchasing again).The influence of design differs by the type of display consumer segments seek (convenience, information or images) and ready cooked meals package sizes have a relatively strong influence on consumption; larger ready cooked meals packages might increase per-use consumption ,but smaller packages might not improve self regulation and might not actually increase total consumption. In conclusion, I suggest that this ready meal manufacturers need to give more attention to be paid to food sellers, such as supermarkets' competitive differentiation and understanding the way in which customers attribute value to its ready meal products choice. Moreover, many consumers have become increasingly concerned about the health implication of the food they eat, so ready meal manufacturers will need to continue responding to such concerns. For example, who have responded with a range of low calorie meals, and addressed specific, sometimes transient, health fads, with respect to trans-fatty acids and omega 3 supplements of these cooked meal ingredients. Many consumers have also become concerned about the ecological environment and some supermarket suppliers, such as Marks and Spencer have incorporated sustainability agendas into their ready meals, for example by reducing packaging and sourcing supplies from sustainable sources. Thus, it caused ready meal manufacturers why who needed to give more attention to concern how supermarkets helped them to sell cooked ready meals in this foods market.

● Busy workers will be fast short time ready cooking meal consumer in supermarket

The macro environment, it describes things that are beyond the immediate environment but can nevertheless affect the organization. Such as the ready meal manufacturers in its macro environment, including the economic environment which can cause the manufacturers sell ready meal numbers whether which can sell more or less to different exported countries due to the exported countries' unemployment ratios, GDP and Government policies etc factors influence. Economic theory can help to explain why it can influence consumer behavior. In food sale market, it can include consumer behavior and demand side as well as retailer behavior and supply side two issues. Consumer behavior and demand side issue, such as the exported countries' consumer whose knowledge of the nutritional benefits of foods whether which prices were raised to choose to buy reasonably as well as retailer behavior and supply side issues, such as investing for developing a restaurant or supermarket in an underserved area whether the types of meals choices which are valued or which are not valued to buy to offer to clients from imports. On the other hand, economic environment factor, individual income can influence who chooses the type, quantity and quality of food that is purchased for a house holder and it also influenced the cooking and storage facilities available in a household to influence food choice.

On the other way, economic environment variation factor can also influence food access across areas. It is important to understand the economic conditions that may contribute to food deserts, that is the costs that food retail businesses face and the choice available to consumers who want to buy foods. Economic environment factor considers the consumer and demand factors, business and supply factors and the market conditions that interact to create differences in the food retail environment across areas and subpopulations. In general, high income meal client group can accept to choose to go to supermarkets or restaurants to spend than low income meal client group. The impact of the economic environment on sales of ready meals is such as an individual get richer, who can afford to buy ready prepared foods, rather than spend time and effort to prepare to cook them at home. It seemed that low income consumers were decreasing to eat meals at expensive restaurant to the alternative of relatively cheap ready prepared meals at home.

Research could also consider how consumer knowledge and preferences and the time cost tradeoffs affect consumer decisions of which foods to eat and whether to make or to buy prepared foods from supermarkets or to eat at restaurant meals . Travel costs and time costs of acquiring foods as well as the time costs of preparing foods (meals) are also likely to affect demand for particular foods. Research on price variation at the local level and demand models could also be used to help determine which factors contribute to differences in access to food retailers. Price is also major determinant of food (meal) demand. The higher, the price of a food(meal), the lower the meal quantity demanded. On the other hand, the higher the price of a substitute food (meal), the higher demand will be for that food (meal) item. Given the budget constraints of low income consumers and the price of some specific foods (meals), low income consumers may substitute higher priced foods (meals) with lower priced foods(e.g. hamburger for steak or canned fruits for fresh fruits). Considering restaurants foods purchasing choice, such as economies of scale, which is when the costs of operating a restaurant decreases as restaurant size increases and economies of scope, which is when the costs decrease as more meals variety increases, suggests that larger restaurants that offer greater variety can offer lower meal prices. Both factors may account for the ability of larger restaurants to survive more easily than smaller restaurants. Considering supermarkets foods purchasing choice, it is possible that food retailers (supermarkets) actually have some market power, especially in setting where there are few competitors to close.

It would have an incentive to increase food (ready meal) price and restrict foods(ready meals) supply quantities to increase profit. Supply side conditions, such as economies of scale, it could lead to (ready meal) food retailers (supermarkets) to have more market power, if it was not close between supermarkets. Individual behavior to make healthy choices can occur only in a supportive economic environment with accessible and affordable healthy food choices. Hence, food environment and sale strategies is needed to consider to adopt the exported countries‘ economic change.

Food marketing client target groups can include home parents, students and working people groups mainly and marketing and economic environment factors would cause food choices and

these factors impact health and nutrition and the focus on the connections between people and their environments. In conclusion, macro level economic environmental factors play a more indirect role but have a substantial and powerful effect on what people eat. Macro level factors operate within the larger society, include food marketing, social norms, food production and distribution systems, agriculture policies and economic price structures as well as social environmental to influence within the home, such as model of healthful dietary intake by parents feeding style, frequent family meals may promote healthful food consumption among children.

● Short time fast ready cooking meals will be Hong Kong busy food consumers market

Hong Kong people can choose to go to restaurants to eat or go to supermarkets to buy foods to cook to eat. Although, ready meal manufacturers had increased the sale numbersof the ready prepared meals in many western countries in recent years. However, there still had any factors to limit it's sale numbers to Hong Kong market over the next five years, so it needed to aware of what was changing in Hong Kong food market environment and appreciated how change in this Hong Kong food environment to lead to change patterns of eating cooked ready meals demand to attempt to win its similar food competitors in Hong Kong market next five years. Hong Kong food environment related to Hong Kong people eating behaviors, include social environments and physical environments and macro level environment.

The cooked meal quality and quantity of available can influence food numbers to produce meal to supply to Hong Kong food market. Hence, Hong Kong natural climatic change can influence the overseas food supply numbers to be imported to cause meals prices to go up or go down. If next five years, Hong Kong climate was good to grow plants and feed animals e.g. pigs and cows etc. meats. The restaurant meals or supermarket meals sale prices can be cheaper due to farmers who have much foods and vegetables to supply , so who can sell cheaper price to these restaurants or supermarkets to cause whose production cost to be decreased next five years in my country. Hence, ready meals prices could not sell more higher than Hong Kong meals prices. Hong Kong people eating behaviors are often changed over a lifetime. In general, Hong Kong people want to eat to satisfy physical hunger and psychological desires and yet want to be healthy, which may enquire adopting eating patterns that conflict with these desires. My country people make decisions about food several times a day: when to eat, what to eat, with where to eat and how much per meal prices and how much per meal numbers .

In general, Hong Kong people like to eat Chinese foods , but who also like to go to restaurants to eat or supermarkets to buy western foods, such as liking of specific tastes are important influences. However, these can be modified by experience with food from various intrapersonal and interpersonal factors to influence Hong Kong people to choose to buy uncooked or cooked meals from Hong Kong supermarkets. The next five year, food retailer behavior and supply factors of food access might affect overseas sales of ready meals numbers imported to my country. In general, supply is driven by the costs of input foods. The land, materials, machines and labor costs are needed to build and operate a restaurant or supermarkets. If these costs are increased to these food suppliers in my county next five years, overseas food demand shall be caused to be decreased if Hong Kong economy had changed to be worse and the new restaurants and supermarkets which costs were changed to be higher to much as well as Hong Kong unemployment was caused to be raised and many people lost jobs to have efforts to go to supermarkets to buy higher prices ready meals or go to restaurants to eat higher price ready meals.

My country's social environment and physical environment which also might affect sales of ready meals numbers next five years. Social environment includes interactions, with family, friends, peers and others in the community to impact food choices through mechanisms as well as physical environment includes the different places where people eat or buy food, such as whether the supermarkets or restaurants locations which are close to the buyers, e.g. schools, offices, houses. Hence, food suppliers' locations choice can influence who (target client groups) choose to buy more or less ready meals numbers. Foods prepared at home factor there may be relatively greater time costs than those to buy cooked foods(ready meals) from supermarkets or takeout foods. Hong Kong consumers may value the convenience of a fast food or takeout cooked meal more because it doesn't require spending much time to prepare to cook at home. Hence, Hong Kong people whose taste is for different kind of cooked foods (ready meals) and who feel the food suppliers' locations whether are convenient and Hong Kong economy whether is better or worse to cause unemployment numbers next five years, these factors can affect sales of imported ready cooked or uncooked meal numbers to my country Hong Kong next five year.

FOUR

TIME FACTOR INFLUENCES TRAVEL LEISURE NEED

I shall explain how time pressure influences airport passengers consumption behavior and travel agents choice behavior. Nowadays, travellers enjoy to go to different countries to travel. In consumer psychological view, instead of the travelling agents' travelling e-ticket cheap and fast seats online booking service or walk in travelling travel agents travelling paper ticket purchase or attractive trip arrangement service to attract travelling consumers' choice.

In any countries, whether attractive airport appearance design, airport convenient public transportaton tools service, e.g. enough airport bus, taxi, train, tram , underground train , ferry etc. number supplying , which can let any foreign travellers find and choose any kinds of public transportaton tools to catch to arrive destinations when they arrive any countries' airports easily, different kinds of varoety of attractive product shops or food courts/shops which can let airport passengers to sit down and choose any kinds of food to eat or they can choose any books, magazines, or stationerys or cigarettes, wine, toys , electronic products, e.g. desktop, laptop computers etc. products to consume for reading or using need in the airport's any restaurants or ships conveniently.

All these airports' intangible or tangible factors whether they can influence consumers' shopping desires in airports, even whether these both factors can attract or persuade many travellers prefer to choose to go to the country to travel and increase the country's travellers number. Concerning these two questions, my readers can earn more useful opinions to analyse whether any country's airport's image will have relationship to influence travellers' tourism choice and tourism consumption choice behavior , due to the country's airport's facility management , service, appearance design , convenient transportation, safety etc. important factors influence in order to assist to develop the country's tourism industry success in possible.

Nowadays, global travelling entertainment activities are popular. Some travellers like domestic travelling or some travellers like to catc airplanes to go to other countries travel. In consumer behavioral view point, when the consumer discovers the product's price is higher than the another product's price. Then, he/she will usually to choose to buy the cheaper product, such as travel agent travelling entertainment activities arrangement service case, whether the travelling provider charges higher travelling entertainment activities arrangement service fee to compare the another similar travelling entertainment activities arrangement service provider. Does this travelling entertainment activities similar fee comparison factor influence any travellers choose to find the cheaper travelling entertainment activities arrangement provider? If travelling entertainment activities arrangement price is not the main factor to influence traveller individual choice. What other factors can influence traveller individual travelling entertainment activities arrangement choice? I shall explain what the other factors are influcenced traveller individual travelling entertainment arrangement choice.

The factors include that the cultural distance on satisfaction and travel intention factor, the lifestyle concept in travel behavioral factor, the business travellers motivation behavioral factor, the impacts of peer-to-peer accommodation use on travel patterns factor, factors influence local tourists decision-making be on choosing a destination factor, transportation, shopping centers, travelling destination facilities supplying factor, social media travelling networking sites promotion factor, traveller's travelling experience psychological factor, travelling service for disabled people's travelling need factor, green travel entertainment service for environment protection travelling environment need factor the impact of travel blogging on the tourist, traveller individual vacation destination choice factor, economic impact to the traveller individual sudden changing factor.

Therefore, it brings these questions: How any why traveller individual travelling choice won't be influenced by travelling entertainment service price only? Does it mean the travelling entertainment service providers will not reduce their traveller number when they can respect or consider above factors to avoid to bring negative influence to traveller consumers, but they still change higher travelling entertainment arrangement service fee to them?

This final part , such as travel entertainment industry, nowadays global travelling entertainment activities are popular, some travellers like domestic travelling or some travellers like to catch airplanes to go to other countries travel. In consumer behavioral view point, when the consumer discovers the product's price is higher than the another product's price. Then, he/she will usually to choose to buy the cheaper product, such as travel agent travelling entertainment activities arrangement service case, whether the travelling provider charges higher travelling entertainment activities arrangement service fee to compare the another similar travelling entertainment activities arrangement service provider. Does this travelling entertainment activities similar fee comparison factor influence any travellers choose to find the cheaper travelling entertainment activities arrangement provider? If travelling entertainment activities arrangement price is not the main factor to influence traveller individual choice. What other factors can influence traveller individual travelling entertainment activities arrangement choice? I shall explain what the other factors are influenced traveller individual travelling entertainment arrangement choice.

The factors include that the cultural distance on satisfaction and travel intention factor, the lifestyle concept in travel behavioral factor, the business travellers motivation behavioral factor, the impacts of peer-to-peer accommodation use on travel patterns factor, factors influence local tourists decision-making be on choosing a destination factor, transportation, shopping centers, travelling destination facilities supplying factor, social media travelling networking

sites promotion factor, traveller's travelling experience psychological factor, travelling service for disabled people's travelling need factor, green travel entertainment service for environment protection travelling environment need factor the impact of travel blogging on the tourist, traveller individual vacation destination choice factor, economic impact to the traveller individual sudden changing factor.
Therefore, it brings these questions: How any why traveller individual travelling choice won't be influenced by travelling entertainment service price only? Does it mean the travelling entertainment service providers will not reduce their traveller number when they can respect or consider above factors to avoid to bring negative influence to traveller consumers, but they still change higher travelling entertainment arrangement service fee to them? In my this part, I shall explain above factors how to influence traveller individual behavior to let readers can predict traveller individual behavior more accurately.

- Time pressure influences airport actual functionality and passengers consumption behavior

Instead of airport is one arrical and leaving terminal station place main function for any travelling passengers after the airplances had landed on the country airport's subway. I feel that airport has also another main functions. It can help the country to attract more travellers to choose to go to the country to travel as well as it can persuade them to raise consumption desire in their whole journeys after they leave the travelling country's airport if they feel the country airport's service performance can satisfy their short time staying need. I shall explain why any countries' airports can influence travellers' travelling destinations and travelling shopping choices to be increased or decreased. The future airport will be the assistance role to assist tourim industry development. The factors include, for example, safety and terrorism control, when the travellers feel the country's airport is safe to stay when they catch air planes to arrive the coutry first time. Then, the country's airport can build safe image to let them to feel the country is safe to travel indirectly, traditional cirport service providers will need to seek new service way to deliver value, such as subscription based service models can let travellers to feel the country's airport can provide one comfortable and enjoyable short term travelling staying environment in the country's airport. Then, they bring pleasant emotion to prepare their journey trip after they leave the airport in the foreign country.
So, if the country's airport can let the travellers feel safe and comfortable , then it can bring new exciting and enjoyable feeling to the country's image. Because airport will be any travellers' first time arrival place after they catch airplanes to arrive another country. So, positive or negative airport's image will influence travellers how they feel whether the country , it is worth to choose to travel indirectly. However, airports need have good facilities to satisfy any related airplane service employees or any airport food or product businesses need, instead of travellers' need. For example, it needs have good allocation of terminals and access to facilities , they will be managed and regularly reviewed and regarded their good facility availability , capacity constraints and the best use of available facilities to satisfy any food or product sale shops' sale need and airport passengers' purchase need both in airports or airplane pilots, airplace service employees, irport security employees' comfortable working environment need.
However, airport inside and outside also needs to be arranged enough parking space facilities to let any aircraft

parked or stored at the airport from the place where it is parked or stored in order to let any vehicles to be parked in airports or ouside airports easily and conveniently. When any sudden emergency matters occurred, the aircraft subjects to unforeseen operational delays , it should need to contact airport operations control centre to indicate when the expected time of arrival and departure is, there is no need to request a new slot in cases of unforeseen operational delays where the operation will take place within 24 hours of the agreed slot time. For example, of unforeseen operational delays include aircraft technical issues or weather conditions that could not have been planned for. Hence, operationally delayed aircraft must utilise slots in the same manner as originally agreed. If any change to the original slot agreement is required, e.g. a slot must be requested immediately. Moreover, when aircraft subjects to non-operational delays must request new slots immediately, following the correct process in those conditions of use, an example, of a non-operational delay may include delay caused by late running passengers or poor schedule planning. Hence, airport needs have good facilities and communication system to coordinate to any departments to avoid aircraft unforeseen delays to cause airport passengers feel nervous and brings negative and poor emotion to the airport's service performance.

On airport baggage handling function aspect, airport operators must comply with the baggage policy made available to all operators with the airline business management team. For example, where a flight destination or carrier is identified as being at significant or high risk, the operator will pay a charge as notified by management, equating to the cost of any policing cost additional to the services normally provided at the airport for carriers or destinations at lower levels of risk. In fact, airport baggage management needs be checked and delivered in order to help any airplanes' passengers to transport their baggages to follow their airplanes to be delivered to their same destinations when their airplanes are flying with the passengers and whom baggages to arrive the same country's airport at the same time absolutely. So, barrage management operators need submit or demand and in agreed format the already fleets absolutely, such as fleet detail to report these data to include aircraft type and registration, number of seats maximum take off weight kilogrammes of each aircraft owned or operated by the operator, in order to avoid any passengers' luggages wrong delivery occurrence in possible.

Hence, any airports must need to consider above basic passenger service operation in order to avoid any accident occurrences to bring poor airport service attitude feeling. If airport management expected that they have good service performance to satisfy travellers' short term staying needs in themselve countries' airport.

- How airport strategies solve passengers
feeling time pressure challenge

Any countries' airports expect to increase passenger movements, they must have effective strategies to carry on reviewing any errors and improve performance effectively. For instance, how to keep cost effective measures to lower operating costs and keep good performance on quality, such as for maintenance and cleaning airport cost reducing measures to introduce variable, performance -based elements to encourage productivity gains, how to manage and implement new technological systems to improve information flow and work processes within the country's airport, e.g. airport e-immigration system can allows to receive real-time alerts on any airport building faults. It can reduce airport reliance on manpower in these areas, thus reaulting in better productivity and cost savings for long term airport expenditure. So, high technological strategy system is needed to implement to any country's airport in order to facilitate the handling of more aircraft movements to optimise aircraft handling on runways. Their benefits include reduction of departure flights separation times, reconfiguration of flight routes, and improvements in runway inspection processes.

These new measures can bring effective in improving any country's airport's runway efficiency, developing new infrastructure including the extension of the taxiway, roadway and power supply networks. It aims to satisfy travellers' convenient transportation needs when they arrive any countries' airports and prepare to find suitable transportaton tools to arrive their destinations more easily (airport transportation roadway, taxiway building network strategy).

Hence, any countries' airports need have good strategy to manage a wide range of activities and risks, which are broadly classified into strategic , financial operational, regulatory and investment. Any countries' airports also need to seek how to reduce the occurrence of risks and to minimum potential adverse impact as much as possible, uch as airport risk management strategy. Because when the country has many people are living and they need often to catch airplanes to leave their countries to travel as well as there are many foreign travellers choose to travel the country. Then, the country's airport must need to expand size and raise good facilities, e.g. more automated immigration gantries are needed to be installed, taxi waiting areas are also needed to be explanded with additional taxi bays constructed to accommodate the higher number of arriving passengers , even increasing airplane subways number to satisfy many airplanes need to fly away from the country's airport or coming airplances fly to the country's airport's landing on runway needs often.

So, airplane subways number expanding strategy and cutomated immigration gate fast checking system is needed when the country has many travellers choose to go to the country travel and/or many local people need to leave themselves countries to travel. For instance, departure and arrival immigration control as well as pre-boarding security screening will be controlled for more efficient deployment of manpower and equipment. Moreover, in the line will the trend of self-service options of airports arrived the world, provisions will be made to have more kioslls for self check in,self-bag -tagging and self bad-drops. The increasing use of these options will help airlines and ground handling agents reduce processing times and staffing requirement. For example, a fully automated to reduce reliance on scare manpower baggage check in and check out system, the baggage handling system will also be equipped with ergonomic lifting aids to enable heavy and odd-sized bags to be handled with ease, even by older workers.

Then, the country's airport must need to increase subways number and immigration fast checking service facility to avoid handling passengers crowd queueing problem often occurs every day. When any airports often let passengers feel time pressure to queue to spend long time to wait immigration checks and leave the airport. It will bring their negative emotion feeling to the country's airport. Then, it is possible to influence they choose to go to the country to repeat travel again. Hence, the country's different airport strategies are needed when the country has increasing travellers number trend as soon as possible.

Another strategy concerns airport emergency service on safe aspect. Any countries' airports need have a highly trained specialist wait that is positioned to provid fast action rescue and fire protection for passengers' life safety ,e .g. aircraft rescue and fire fighting vehicles are needed airport. An incident command and control simulator which provides realistic and interactive simulations of emergency scenarios for the purpose of any sudden accident occurrences in any countries' airports.

So, any countries' airports need to develop an internal digital system to ease labour-intensive work processes like fire safety inspection, incident reporting, logistic management and recording of its personal fitness results, with the new safe system , data entry is needed mobile enabled with the use tablet computers. For example, the airport safe unit can continue to enhance its emergency preparedness and rescue capabilities with the successful staging of two drills, simulated aircraft crashes on land and at sea, as well as any exercises validated crisis contingency plans are recommended to earn strong capability in coordinating rescue efforts involving both the airport community and mutual aid agencies in order to carry on rescuing passengers and airport pilots and service attendants whom life safe service when air planes are crashed on land and at sea.

Another strategy is now aviation facilities strategy, it can support fly, cruise and fly-coach initatives, important options to a rising number of interm travellers, if it can be implemented successfully. It can bring enhancement measures benefits, includes the reduction of departure flight separation times, reconfiguring of flight routes and implementation of aircraft speed control for increased runway use efficiency.

Hence, one successful airport operation , the airport management needs to know how to implement the traveller check out or check in service functions when they arrive the airport or leave the airport and to satisfy its passengers' short term terminal station staying or transfering another airplane's flying need as well as it also needs to know how to implement its different strategies to improve its service performance and to let passengers have more confidence to the country's airport service operators' behavior and they also feel safe when they are staying the country's airport. Hence, any travellers' short term staying feeling in the country's airport , whether the country's airport can bring either positive or negative emotion , which will influence they choose to go to the country to travel again in possible. Hence, airport management can not neglect how to improve airport service performance to satisfy any first time or more time airport visitors' short term staying need.

- Long time airport staying bring passengers

positive consumption emotion

It is an interesting question: Can the country's airport service performance influence passengers consumption desire? Nowadays, travelling is a kind of popular entertainment whn working people have holidays, retired people have more savings and students need to go to holiday to feel rest time after they had hard to study. They will choose go to other countries to travel. So, " freguent travelling times" which will increase to any travelling consumers. If the traveller often chooses to go to the country to travel, he must need to permit to enter the country from its airport immigration. If his every visiting time to the country's airport, he feels the country's airports' staffs services are poor performance and he feels that they are not polite or rude attitude to treat him when he needs to check out or check in from the country's airport immigraton gates, even he feels difficult to enquire any airport service staffs, either he feels difficult to find them or they need to spend long time to let him to queue to wait enquiry, even he also needs to spend long time to queue to wait check in or check out in airport immigration gates when he arrives the country's airport or he leaves the country's airport.

All of these negative airport staffs' service attitudes and poor service behavioral feeling, they will cause the frequent traveller doubts whether the country is a worthy travelling place and it is possible to led his negative consumption desire in the country's airport. Then, all of these negative emotion will influence the frequent traveller reduces consumption in the country's airport , even wothut any consumption in the country's airport, when he visits the country to travel every time. So , it seems that airport's service performance will influence travellers carry on more or less consumption in the country's airport. Then, it will influence all the country's airport related retail and restaurant businesses' sales to be reduced indirectly in the country's airport.

Instead of airport service performance intangible factor aspect, the airport's clean, airport itself appearance attractive design, large size and shops and restaurants' suitable locations and internal environment design etc. these tangible factors will also influence travellers' consumption desires in the country's airport. For example, in one special day, e.g. Olympic Games day, the Olympic Games country's airport may complete in record time and its airport can successfully handle a estimate record 85,000 minimum departing passengers a day during the Olympic Games period, twice the number on normal days. Travellers and media will describe the Olympic Games country's airport retail shops and restaurants consumption experience as seamless, magical and unforgettale airport staying experience, if the Olympic games country's airport can provide an excellent service performance on the Olympic games period. Then, it will influence the increasing sale amount in the Olympic Games country airport retail stores and restaurants during period. So , when the country is experiencing special day, such as "Olympic Games " is chosen to carry on competition in the country. Then, in this Olympic Games period, it will attract many travellers to choose to go to this country to travel, due to they have interest to watch Olympic Games competition in this country. This country's airport will represent this country's image. If it 's airport service staffs can provide excellent service to let any one of travellers to feel when they are staying in this country's airport short time and this country's airport itself appearance and design can also be changed more attractive and beautiful and the airport's retail stores and restaurants also design more attractive and beautiful. Then, the travellers' consumption desires will be possible to raise , when they visit this country's airport in first time in this Olympic Games travelling period.

- Global air transport network attractive strategy

In the future, if the country has a strong and affordable global air transport network, it will bring more advantages. Due to many travellers expect to catch air planes which can fly to another country in short time , it can reduce accidents occurrence chance on sky or on sea. So, short time flying can be more attract to compare long time flying. So, it explains that why many travellers prefer to choose one way flying more than transfering another /other air plane(s) flying. Although, they need to pay more air ticket fee. So, if the country's airport can have more subways number and large subways areas to let many arrival air planes and leaving air planes need to fly from land or fly to land in the country's airport frequently. Then, the travellers can buy any air tickets to book same day or next day or later day flught time to fly to any country to travel more easily, when the country's airport has large area size and many subways to let many airplanes can stay in its aircraft subways in same time. Then, the country's airport flight frequency will increase , it means that there are many travellers can catch airplances to fly to other countries in any time very easily from themseleves country's airport. It is time-sensitive feeling to let the country's travellers, they can feel to fly to other countries to travel in short day. They do not need delay to fly to any countries, when the flight airline is either full seat or the time can not permit any air places land on the country's subways.

So, none delaying time sensitive travelling frequent flught model will be one attractive flight flying method to influence the country's travellers choose to frequent travelling behavior. Because they do not change their travelling day, due to airplanes have no enough seats supply or the country's airport has no enough land subways to let any airplanes to stay to cause delaying their flight travelling booking seat day expectly.

So, airport is similar to airline to need to use different customer relationship management to attract returning travelling customers . It brings this question: What are the most attractive motivation factors in airport travel market? I believe that factors may include airport loyalty, various flight time arrangement distribution channel, passenger check in or check out, laggage safe delivery, airpor security service. Moreover, flight schedules are also a main factor influences the travellers' final travelling country choice decision among different travelling countries. However, if the country's airport can build good loyalty image when passengers are staying in the country's airport in short time, it can show a more attractive motivator to increase travellers' consumption desires when they are staying in the country's airport in short time.

Hence, airport 's loyalty seems have relationship to influence travellers' consumption behavior when they are staying in the country's airport. For example, when the different countries' travellers feel enjoyable and happy to stay in the country's airport longer time. Then, their airport long time staying behavior will raise their consumption desire and chance to find any right restaurant to eat food or drink or find any right retail shop to buy right products in airport. Hence , when the country's airport can buil loyal customers relationship. Then, it will bring the advantages or benefits to the airport's any retail shops or restaurants on sale growth aspect, such as : their retention rates will go up easier, their customer referrals will go up easier, the country airport retail shopd and restaurants travelling customers whom spending rates will go up easier, the country airport retail shops and restaurants customers will be loss price sensitive, the costs of retail and restaurant servicing then will go down easier. Hence, if the country's airport customer service performance can maximize travellers' loyalty. It will influence travellers to feel the country airport's retail shops and restaurants have more loyalty to compare other countries airports' retail shops and restaurants loyalty.

So, it implies that any any country airport's loyalty will have relationship to influence its travellers how they feel the country airport's retail shops and restaurants' loyalty. Due to loyalty is intangible and it is obly feeling. So, when the travellers have positive emotion and wheh they are staying in the country's airport long time. Then, they will have positive emotion to spend more time to walk around in the country's airport as well as when they are passing any airport's retail shops or restaurents. Their pleasant emotion may encourage their consumption behaviors to have interest to find any right restaurant to eat food or drink or find any right retail shop to buy any right product in the country's airport in preference easily. Because they had been accepted to spend long time to stay in the country's airport, when they feel interest and surprise to visit the country airport when they arrive. Moreover , the long airport staying time will increase their purchase chance to any the country's airport's retail stores or restaurants in the country 's airport in first time visiting.

- How to satisfy customer expectation

for long time staying passenger service at airport

When one country's airport can satisfy passengers expectation to accept its service demand, then profitability and passenger number will be influenced to increase. So, airport management needs to focus on how to satisfy any passenger individual need or expectation when he/she needs to stay in whose country's airport for wait to either transferinf another airplance need to carrying on check in or check out in the country's airport immigration gate need in short time.

However, because if the country's airport service can let its passengers feel happy , then they will be super spenders to spend airport staying longer time to consume or entertain in the country's airport. Moreover, it will bring any the country airport's retail shops or restaurante to earn more sale growth indirectly. So, any country airports need to consider how to bring excellent customer services for any passenger individual need in airport. Because its service behavior or performance will have indirect relationship to impact the county airport's any businesses and itself any parking , entertaining services income in airport.

" The concept of managing airport customer expectation on passenger service quality" will be any country airport's main aim. Basically, airport passengers' perception concern how the airport service staffs' service attitudes or performances influence how they feel either negative emotion, such as anger, dissatisfaction, irritation, neutrality or positive emotion, such as happy, satisfaction, pleasure, delight. So, when the airport passenger individual perception is better , then his expected to the country airport individual service staff level will be at the highest level, but if his service expectation is less than his expectation standard, then the airport passenger will dissatisfy with the lowest satisfaction level to be influenced the country airport's other any one service staff by the one airport service staff whose poor performance. Because any one of the country airport's service staff , every one will influence the country airport's image. Of every one has excellent service performance, then, it will let many different counties' passengers feel sympathetic emotion from their every one's behavior. Otherwise, if every one has or most service staffs have poor or not considerate ot not sympathetic service attitude to be let them to feel, then any one of them will let many itself airport's countries' passengers feel the country airport's image is poor. They won't like to spend long time to stay in the country airport, even their short time airport staying behaviors will influence the country airport's any retail shops or restaurants businesses sale growth to be reduced from their short staying time influence.

In general, airport service staffs need to spend some time to answer any passengers' enquiries. So, how they answer their enquiries will influence how their achievement in order to raise the country airport's passengers satisfactions.

It may lead a rise in different countries'passengers' loyalty and retention, therefore the country airport can increase many different countries passengers number when the repeating airport visitors , they prefer to choose to go to the country to travel again , due to its airport is attractive reason in possible.

So, any country airport management ought have a policy from how the airport established desirable standard performance, measure it against actual performance to action taken once and revise any unachieved acceptable service level to the acceptable excellent passenger service performance in the country airport. For example, any country airport needs to manage and identify the target passenger segmenation target groups and to make bettwe understand the key elements that have the greatest impact on meeting every different target passenger segmentation group individual expectations and needs from their services in themselves country airport. So, any country airport will have relationship to any one of airline, as well as any one airline will have direct relationship to every passenger when he/she stays in the country airport in short time.

However, instead of restaurants and retail shops; sale relationship will be influenced by the country airport's service performance, airport management also bring more empahsis on non-aeronautical (non related airlined and retail business) revenues, such as shops rents, concessions, car parking service income, consultancy and property developed diversified service incomes. So, airports need to focus directly to enterainment travelling airlines' passengers, meeters, and greeters, business-travelling passengers , users of general aviation services and transfer air plane short time staying visitors, or lone time staying visitors, e.g. the passengers need to live airport hotel for on night or more than one night sleeping before they catch the airplane on the day. So, all these different target passenger segmentations will have different service needs in any country airports.

However, airport passengers' behaviors and expectations of the airport experience depend highly on the types of traveller, they include: demographic characteristics, (i.e. gender, age group, income, sex, occupation) , purpose of trip (i.e. leisure, business), and their circumstances. In general , the passenger can be divided into different group, such as arriving, departing and transfer with different expectation and need, in the way they will be using the airport services and facilities different need and will also influence the behavior of individuals when in the commercial area. For example, passengers who are departing and arriving will require all airport facilities including: car rental, rail, buses access, pre-booking taxi service, check in or check out service, bad processing and security check and vertical and horizontal moving in passenger terminals. Otherwise, transfer passengers will have a short waiting time in airport and their needs will be likely different from those of origin and destination passengers. Some of the transit passengers will need to spend one hour, even more than four hours or half day in the airport. By providing airport facilities that can accommodate their needs, such as a place to lie down and take a short sleep time, free shower, free email public service will mostly give than an enjoyable airport experience. Evem some handicapped people or old people who feel difficult to walk in the airport corridor. Then , the airport will need to arrange the auto -wheel chairs and auto airport vehicle facilities to let service staffs to provide electronic auto wheel chairs to let them to sit down or drive the auto airport vehicle to sit down with them to go to their destination in the airport's any places immediately. For passengers travelling with families may want children play areas, where kids can have a great time when waiting to board the aircraft. They also want the availability of rooms of families travelling with badies equipped with changing facilities, baby crib, microwaved and hot water need. When passengers are on business trip, may want a lounge, with all the business, facilities that they can feel free to use, such as free internet access and other services , such as fax, scan and photocopy machine. Hence, any airport managements need to develop the strategic customer facilities providing service in order to improve the design and delivery of all the facilities and services need by understanding expectation of each passenger segmentation group in their airport staying time.

Finally , in airport unique design aspect, our global airports will need have different unique design to let any travellers to feel that the country's airport can have its unique design to let themm to feel the country airport has itself own airport culture or entertainment features to attract they observe its appearance in order to achieve the increase more travelling visitors number when they feel enjoy to stay in the country airport longer time before they leave the airport. I shall indicate different countries' airports how they will perform themselves different airport cultures and unique design as below:

For China and Hong Kong Chinese airport design example, their airports need have Chinese cultural feeling to let Western travellers to feel their airports' designs and cultures are different to any Western countries' other cultures. So, China anf Hong Kong airports' designs can increase many old big size building photos number in their airports to let foreign visitors can walk on the long glass walkway corridor , when they enter walkway coddidor to walk through different 100 more airplane leaving and arriving gates number and the ground floor is built from heavy glass material. So , any one foreign traveller need to walk through on the long glass walkway corridor to pass any one gates to arrive his/her airplane leaving and arriving gate location and catch airplance to fly. Also, the glass walkway ground floor can let them to see the airport's vehicles and airplanes and people and trees outside environment clearly when they are walking on the airports' all glass material manual made ground floor. It will let foreign travellers feel China and Hong Kong airports building designs are different to the foreign countries' themselves airports' designs as well as Hong Kong and China airports' old building photos will let all leaving passengers feel difficult to forget their old building historical photos and they will know hoe their architectural skills are developed to imprved to build nowadays unqiue desing method from traditional building design method in Hong Kong and China airports. Otherwise, for US, Uk etc. foreign countries their airports designs can increase underground floor fish pool architectural design outside to their airports in order to let any passengers feel that they can see many different kinds of various fishes are swimming. So, their outside large fish pool can let them to feel surprise when they are staying in their any airports, e.g. one beautiful large size fish pool, it can be built to close to their airports and the fish pool can have various kinds of big and small fishes swim in the pool to let passsngers to see, or their airports can appear suddenly and unexpected of a gaping hole in the airport's outside ground, known as a sinkhole. Sometimes, the airport's outside sinkhole will fill up with fresh water to become deep , shaped manual made sinkhole to let passengers to feel they need to enter to the sinkhole and then they can enter the airport. So, the outside large size sinkhole will attract many passengers to stat to observe how the fresh water is entering to the sinkhole interestingly. Then, they will feel surprise when they need to pass though the sinkhole , then they can enter the airport.

In conclusion, attractive airport architectural design will let any passengers can not forget that they had ever visit the country to travel in their travelling experience as well as they can be influenced to like to stay longer time in the country airport by the airport's attractive design and environment influence. The most important influnece, it can influence airport related business income when they like to stay longer time in the airport.

● Long time cultural distance factor on satisfaction respects travel intention

Every country cultural difference is different. How and why cultural difference has a real impact on tourist satisfaction and it can also influence to repeat travel. Is cultural tourism one major factor to influence tourist to repeat travelling intention or choice to the country in international tourism choice market? For example, China and India have similar culture. Their cultural difference is not much, e.g. eating cultural habit is similar , entertainment cultural habit is similar. These both countries people do not want to spend much money in eating and entertainment both aspects. Hence, these two countries people do not consider how to consume to enjoy entertainment and eat expensive food. Hence, it is based on cultural similar reason. These both countries tourists will prefer to choose to repeat travelling either China or India. When the Indian tourists had chosen to go to China to travel in the first time. Then, the Indian tourists will choose to go to China to travel in second time again. Also, the Indian tourists had chosen to go to China to travel in first time. Then, the Chinese tourists will choose to go to India to travel in second time again. What factors influence China and India tourists respect to travel between these both countries. The factors will include cheap air ticket price, cheap hotel living price , less economic cost factor. However, I believe the similar cultural factor will be the major factor to influence many Chinese and Indian tourist prefer to choose to repeat travelling between these both countries.

As my indication to these both countries people have similar eating habits, choosing foods, low health foods, common foods choice eating at cheap restaurant habitual consumption. Also, they have similar entertainment habits, their entertainment demand is not high. They like to ride bicycles to go to anywhere to travel. They like to go to swim, play basketball, football etc. sports. These all sports are cheap sport consumption. So, it based on similar individual low enjoyment demand and low health, food quality demand similar cultural factors. Chinese and Indian people have no long distance cultural difference between eating and entertainment habitual factor will include them to choose to repeat travelling between these both countries. Due to China and India have many restaurants can provide cheap food or sport service providers can provide different kinds of cheap sport entertainment consumption to satisfy their cheap food and cheap entertainment needs in their journey in China or India anywhere. So, it explains that why these both countries tourists will repeat to travel these both countries again after they had visited China or India to travel in first time. So, the similar cultural factor can impact these both countries tourists to repeat to go to these both countries to travel again. Hence, if these two countries' cultural distance is far or different, then themselves countries' tourists won't choose to repeat travel between themselves when these two countries for cultural distance tourists had visited to another country in first time. Hence, culture has been continuously considered as a much factor which tourists consider in terms of choice of the destination travelling place. Also, it explains cultural distance which can make tourist individual has less satisfaction to concern to tourists to repeat travels.

Otherwise, for far cultural distance two countries case example, such as Chinese and American , these two countries people's eating habit and entertainment cultural needs are different. For eating habit difference example, American like to eat pork, beefs, chickens, potato to replace rice and other foods. Otherwise, Chinese like to wat rice, vegetables more than potatoes, pork , beefs for lunch , dinner . So , their eating habits are very different. Also, American like to drive boats on the season drive cars to go to anywhere to travel on holidays for sports or holiday entertainment activities . Otherwise, Chinese like to play basketball, football, ride bicycle of cheaper sport entertainment on holidays. So, American entertainment activities are more expensive to compare Chinese. Also, US and China , like families whose power distance is different, such as every per family powerful member is parents, who have more power to give opinions to choose anywhere to travel for whose sons and/or daughters whole family members travelling arrangement.

Therefore, if the Us family powerful members, such as at least one son or/and daughter members who need t choose to go to which country to travel if the family powerful members, such as the child/ children's parent feel China's food taste or entertainment activities are totally different to be similar to their country's food taste and entertainment activities habitually after their whole family members had travelled to China in first time before.

Although, their son(s) and daughter(s) will hope to go to China to repeat travel again. But, due to the US family parents are their son(s) and daughter(S) powerful decider to make any travelling decision to choose which country will be next time travelling destination. If their parents feel China's eating and entertainment culture is totally different to their countries. Then, the US family will not choose to repeat travel to the China country again any more easily, because this US family can not feel satisfactory when they visited China in their first time before, due to they feel China 's food and entertainment cultures are totally different to their US country. So, the cultural distance factor will influence the US family don't choose China to go repeat travel again.

Consequently, different countries' similar or different cultural factor will influence the country's tourists choose to repeat travel to the country again. So, any country needs to know what its culture is in order to attract the similar cultural countries tourists to repeat travel to itself country more easily.

- Long time lifestyle factor influences travel behavior

Whether do different countries tourists' different lifestyle which can influence their travel consumption behaviors? Even, which countries that they will choose to go to travel. For example, when one tourist who owns himself/herself often to drive to go to anywhere habitually. The tourist's driving car habital behavior which will influence that he /she will feel need to rent car to travel to anywhere habitually , when he/she selects to go to the country to travel. Hence, if he/she feels the tourism destination has no any rent car service providers to provide him/her to rent any car to travel anywhere in the country's travel destination. Does the country lack rent car service factor which will influence that he/she will still choose to go to the country to travel in preference? For example, when one New Zealander's family who own at least one car at home. So, the New Zealand whole family every member can often drive car to go to anywhere , even, one family member had driven one car to leave his/her home. So, driving own car activity or behavior has been one habitual activity to influence the New Zealand every member to feel the travelling destination needs have rent car service provider supplies cars to let them to rent to travel. The driving car lifestyle has caused the whole New Zealander family driving habit. When the family's sons) and/or daughter(s) need(s) to go to school or go to shopping as well as their parents also need to drive their cars to go to office to work in themselves home town often. In common, there are many New Zealanders who will have at least one car at home because they feel that they can drive their themselves cars to go to anywhere in New Zealand more than waiting bus or tram or train or ferry etc. public transportation tools more conveniently. So, New Zealanders' driving own car habit will influence their lifestyle to feel that they also need to rent cars to travel to go to any where to travel to replace to wait public transportation tools choice in the travelling destination during their journey.

For shopping trips is more influenced by their driving car activities. So, it seems that this New Zealander families will be influenced to their tourism destination need, they need the tourism destination has car renting service provider to be supplied anywhere to let them can drive the renting cars to go to anywhere in tourism destination. It means that when the tourism destination has less rent car providers can provide renting car services to drive anywhere or it has none any renting car service providers are existing in the tourism destination. Then, the renting car service providers number shortage or none any renting car service providers to be provided to the country's tourism destination, which will cause the New Zealander families do not prefer to choose to go to the country to travel generally, e.g. Hong Kong, China, Korea these Asia countries have no many rent car service providers in these countries. So, the New Zealand families won't prefer to choose to go these countries to travel when they discover these Asia countries lack enough rent car service providers to let them to drive to travel in themselves conveniently. Otherwise, America, England, Japan etc. countries have many rent car service providers. So, these countries will be this New Zealander families' preferable tourism countries. Thus, the New Zealand families' driving ownership car lifestyle will influence their travel behaviors to choose to go to the country which can have many rent car providers in the tourism country any where tourism destinations in preference.

Thus, whether the country has renting car service providers , it will be variable factor to influence any country's car ownership families' driving car travel behaviors in their journey in order to let they feel that they can drive themselves ownership cars to go to anywhere to travel conveniently, even when they leave their countries. Hence, these countries' car ownership driving habitual families' behaviors will be influenced their tourism destination or location decision choice when the country has many renting car service providers in preference as well as this renting car service provider supplying factor will be more important to influence the habitual driving own car traveller to be preferable choice to compare other factors, e.g. cheap entertainment consumption providers factor which include cheap hotel living fee, cheap food price consumption etc. expenditure in the travelling country.

Thus, it explains that different countries' car ownership tourists , whose driving own car activities will cause their daily lifestyles, then their daily driving own car lifestyles will influence their tourism destination choices indirectly. So, it seems that lifestyle can be a outcome variable (or dependent variable) factor to influence travel behavior in any travelling built environment. The travelling built environment characteristics can include density measures (

population density, job density), job-housing density). These travelling built environment factor can represent what the city resident's lifestyle. For example, where the location in relation to local center or regional center to the country's residents are living. This country resident's living location will cause this country resident's lifestyles , e.g. holiday or leisure whether it is low budget, active and adventurous or frequent traveller with second place or self-organized , family oriented or close to home. Hence, the country's living built environment will influence the country's resident's lifestyles. Due to different countries' residents will have different lifestyles. Hence, built environments and life styles have relationship to influence every country's residents when they need to go to other countries to travel in their holidays. For example, frequent travellers are usually living in big and busy cities, otherwise, non -frequent travellers are usually living in the country sides, where there are less offices or factories are built to let people to work. So, big city will bring busy feeling to the country's residents, then they will be influenced to feel need to often to go to travel for leisure intention in their holidays. Otherwise, countryside will bring not busy or quiet environment feeling to the country's residents, then they won't feel working feeling when they are living in county side. So, they won't feel need to go t o anywhere to travel in their holidays often.

Hence, built environment will bring either busy or not busy (quiet environment feeing) to the both different country residents when they are living in the places. Their living places will cause their lifestyles are different. Then, they will be influences to feel have more frequent travelling needs or less frequent travelling needs to explain why every country people will have more or less frequent travelling needs.

- Long time peer-to-peer staying
accommodation need impacts
business tourism pattern

I shall explain how any why peer-to-peer accommdation can attract business tourisms to choose business tourism intention? Usually , employees or employers buy business trips, why they choose one particular travelling company over another and why the business tourists choose to travel when the peer (more than one business tourists) who will choose to peer-to-per accommodation business tourism pattern more than the more expensive hotel living comfortable feeling business tourism pattern.

Business travel agents need to know or understand what reasons the employer or employee feels peer-to-peer accommodation business tourism motivation is more suitable or better to compare hotel living comfortable feeling business tourism pattern. Why can business tourism accommodation choice factor influence the business tourist's business trip choice.

Business trip means work related travel to an irregular place or work and it represents that one employee or more than on employees business tourists whose expenses are paid by the business ,he or she or they work(s) for. So, in employer's business trip expense view point, he/she expects the employee or employees can choose the most cheap expenses for whose business trip. It also means that the employer does not expect that it is a high quality journey for the employee's or employees' business trip. The business tourism is year-round, peaking in spring and autumn , but still with high levels of activity in the summer and winter months. It may be long time or short time, e.g. less than one month or more than one month, even more than half year for the business trip. When the employee is employees are working permanent full time employment. It is not for leisure intention, it means that the employer does not hope employee or employees spend(s) extra more expense to spend any leisure or goes (go) to any destinations to visit in their/her/his whole business trip.

Hence, it is based on the cheap expenses for the business trip aim, employer usually demands employees or employees to choose the peer-to-peer be cheaper accommodation to live or the employer will help its employee(s) to choose the peer-to-peer cheaper accommodation to live. So, it seems that expensive hotel living facilities won't be the preferable accommodation choice for employer because the business trip pay or reimburse the employee. Hence, business travel agencies ought not help the business tourists to choose expensive travel package, e.g. expensive hotel accommodation on the trip, expensive transportation tools, e.g. taxi renting service to get to business meetings, the cheap peer-to-peer cheap hostel accommodation and cheap transportation tool, e.g. travel buses pre-booking service, or cheap restaurant choice vacation incentives package is more attractive to let them/him/her to choose for their/her/his business trip.

A business person or a peer-to-peer business people also have /her expect to take advantage of frequent flyer schemes which allow him/her/them to take leisure trip with airlines when they/he/she is /are accumulated sufficient miles in the cheap or air ticket(s) to catch air plane for business trip. Hence, he/she /they expect(s) to earn airlines expenses from whose frequent flyer schemes when they/he/she can claim to original air ticket price from whose employer, but in fact, peer-to-peer business tourists or individual business tourist pay lesser air ticket charge from whose frequent flying program accumulated sufficient miles, even no any payment. So, airlines can benefit the business traveller, such as improved in competition millages programs, quick check in and online check in, lounges with broadband connection etc. service.

Why does peer-to-peer accommodation living factor is the most influential to any business tourist(s) to choose the travel agent? In employer's business trip expensive view point, if it has many employees need to go to other countries business trips for long days frequently. Then, the employer will consider whether the every day accommodation living cost is expensive or not. So, comparison hotel and peer-to-peer hotel price, hotel accommodation price is usually higher than small accommodation rent price. When peer-to-peer accommodation has been shown to positively impact to business trip employers in popular. Because any business spending will be one important considerable factor to influence employers to choose. However, the accommodation renting price will be more influential to impact business tourism cost. Hence, employers will estimate every whole business trip expenses how it can impact peer-to-peer or hotel accommodation choice. So, the living budget factor will be one important influential factor to influence any employers how to choose where are the suitable destination for every individual business tourist or peer-to-peer group business tourists to live. So, it seems small size peer-to-peer accommodation are compared to large size expensive hotels more suitable for business tourists.

Although, it is possible that individual employee or a group peer-to-peer employees will feel peer-to-peer accommodation is not more safe than hotel accommodation. But, their/his/her employer usually does not consider safety, comfortable environment issue for their/his/her every business trip. They only consider lose accommodation price issue. So, the accommodation choice will be one critical factor to influence employers how to help their individual employee or a group peer-to-peer employees to choose where he/she/they will live when he/she/they arrive(s) the destination for whose every business trip. Hence, it seems that accommodation will be one critical factor to influence anywhere to be chosen to live for any business trips to their individual employee or group peer-to-peer employees' needs.

● Long time social , cultural , personal psychological factors influence local tourists'destination choice

What are the main internal and external factors to influence local tourist's domestic travelling choice behaviors and destination choice decision making? What are the social , cultural , personal psychological factors to influence the decision-making of local tourists to travel to different types of tourism destinations in domestic travelling destinations, e.g. attractions, available amenities, image price external factors. They can influence local tourist's destination choice behaviors. Does the individual occupational reason can influence local tourist's local destination travelling choice? So, any travel agents need to develop and promote of domestic destination need to determine the factors influencing tourist's destination choice.

In a local destination tourist individual productive way, how local tourism agents can bring what factors to influence or charge whose local destination travelling behavioral changes. For example, tourist individual behavior and destination choice factor, the comparison between the current local tourism destinations choice and the past local tourism destinations choice factor. Instead of local different travelling destination prices comparison, journeys comparison . What are the other internal and external factor to influence the local tourist's travelling destinations choices behaviors, e.g. attending local festivals, events, taste local cuisine and be part of unique features of a destination. These will be valuable external or internal factors to influence the local tourist's local destinations choices. So, different countries‘ local travelling destinations will need have a number of key elements that attract visitors and meet their needs. The key elements may include , for example, primary activities, physical setting and social / cultural attributes primary external activities elements, and secondary elements may include catering and shopping, and addition elements/accessibility and tourists information providing to local tourists.

Due to local destination tourism must be cheaper than overseas or foreign destination tourism. So, the local tourist travel agents need to provide their travelling services to local tourists, more attractions, accessibility , amenities, excellent available packages activities and ancillary services to compare overseas tourism destinations. Because the local tourists will compare the overseas different destinations travelling places to decide whether they ought choose to travel overseas or local different destinations at the moment. So, any entertainment activities concern local destinations which will be local tourists' preferable comparative travelling services to the local travel agent and the overseas travelling service in order to decide whether he/she ought choose local travelling or overseas travelling at the moment.

Hence, local different travelling destinations attractive factor will be one important influential factor to influence local tourist's travelling choices. However, a tourist's attitude, decisions, activities, ideas or travelling experiences evaluating and searching of any tourism service behaviors will influence the final travelling destination choice decision whether he/she ought choose to go to overseas or local travel. He/she will consider how to spend time and money and effort to carry on any kinds of entertainment activities in whose local or overseas journeys. So, the different destination local and overseas internal travelling price and spending entertainment time in journey and spending effort to arranging every travelling entertainment which every will be one considerable issue to compare budget to overseas and local different travelling destinations. If the tourist feel whose country , e.g. American's local travelling destination budget is spend less than overseas travelling destination too much. Then, the American will choose to local travelling destinations more than overseas travelling destinations and the moment. So, travelling budget will one factor to influence the tourist to choose whether overseas or local travelling.

So, it seems that time, money and effort will be another factor to influence the tourist will be another factor to influence the tourist chooses to go to overseas or local travelling destinations, instead of different travelling entertainment provider choices factor in the local or overseas travelling destinations . Moreover, the tourist's individual income, the local and overseas living condition, formation of cultural and aesthetic tastes, price of local and overseas travelling service and discounts, local and overseas travelling destinations' temperature or weather viable, e.g. number of sunny days, geographical condition, cultural and natural resource, medical tourism etc. external factors will influence the tourist individual final travelling decision to choose either local tourism or overseas tourism entertainment decision.

- Long time tourist individual driving behavior

impacts travel behavior

Does every tourist individual driving behavior influence whose travel behavioral choice? However, individual mobility decisions are possible difficulties for measures aiming at tourist individual travelling behavioral changes and links them to the transport need aspect when the tourist arrives the destination to travel. For example, whether the travelling destination has bus public transportation tool supplies or ferry transportation tool supplies or taxi transportation tool supplied or train or tram etc. different public transportation tools to influence the tourist individual travelling destination choice.

When every country decides to develop travel industry. It needs to understand how to arrange what kind of public transportation tools to be supplied to satisfy any countries' tourists mobility needs in whose journeys in order to achieve tourism planning for public transportation system to attract different countries' tourists to choose to arrive itself different destinations to travel more easily. So, the country's transportation services supplies will have permanently impacted to every tourist individual travel behavior towards more mobility when he/she arrives to the country to travel.

Can transportation system factor influence tourist individual travelling destination decision? it depends on the tourist individual attitude or transport needs of decisions. For example, if the city , e.g. New York has many tourists, who are high income, young gender, high education level tourists. Then, they will choose more expensive and comfortable train more than cheap and not comfortable bus transportation tool. So, I assume that the year has many high income, high education , high social class occupation tourists arrive US , New York city . Then, they will choose train more than bus transportation tool to go to anywhere to travel in New York city. So, it is not represent that the city has many cheaper public transportation tool, such as many buses number to be supplied , the bus public transportation tool can bring more income to attract overseas tourists to come to New York travel. It depends on whether the tourist individual characteristics, e.g. high or low income, more or less comfortable transporation tool supplies needs or high or low educational level, alone tourist or family tourist or friend relationship tourist. Any one of these tourist individual psychological factors will influence the tourist to choose either cheap and less comfortable public tool system or expensive and more comfortable public tool system to be supplied to the city to travel. So, the city's comfortable or not comfortable public transportation tool supplies which will influence the overseas tourists how to choose the city to travel.

However, on the tourist's habitual behavior of catching which kind of transportation tools, this factor will bring to influence how to choose the kind of transportation tool(s) whether the city can provide choice to let the overseas tourist to make where travelling decision when he/she arrives to the country. However, his/her transportation tool catching habit will be possible to influence whose travel times for public transport use, instead of which kind of transport tool(s) he/she will choose to catch when he/she arrives the country to travel.

In conclusion, the tourist's age, income, occupation, education level will influence how the tourist's transportation choice in himself/herself country, then it also bring this question: will influence the tourist individual destination choice if the country can provide or can not provide the kind of public transportation tool(s) to let the tourist to choose to catch in his/her journey in the country's city. Hence, it explains that why every country's pubic transporation tool supplies will influence the tourist to choose where to travel in the country.

- Long time disabled habits

and attitudes influence to disabled tourists' behaviors

What factors can affect the travel behaviors of people with disabilities by ages and lifestyle variable factors? When one person is disable, he/she will have different behaviors to satisfy whose needs in whose whole travelling journey. In special , the older age and younger age disable tourists who will have different travelling needs. In fact, the disabled tourists won't easy to go anywhere travelling destinations in whose whole travelling journey. So, it seems that the travelling entertainment needs won't be very much to these younger or older disabled tourists. Moreover, people with disabilities travel will be compare with people without disabilities. So, it is one key to explain why the travelling entertainment purposes or needs to disable people which are lesser than the people without disabilities.

In negative or problematic experience of travel to disabled tourists aspect, I believe that it is one travelling experiences problem is considered to need to be solved to any younger or older age disabled tourists, because they are handicapped people, they will feel walk in difficulty, even they need wheel chairs to help them to walk. So, the moving disabled problem will influence how they feel unsafe on public transport in any strange travelling countries considerable. In special, the older aged 50 and over disabled people need to catch any public transport when they need to sit on wheel chairs to go to anywhere destinations in any strange travelling countries. They will feel not convenient and unsafe when they need to sit on wheel chairs to go to anywhere destinations. These travelling places are their first time arriving places. Hence, transportation tools will be consideration problem to any disabled tourists. It seems that renting car travelling providers will be one popular or preferable choice to any younger orolder age disabled tourists. Because disabled tourists won't need to catch public transport tools, such as buses, trains, trams, taxis in unsafe, notconvenient natural travelling environment. They can drive themselves renting cars to go to anywhere travelling destinations easily or conveniently. Thus, I believe that the renting cr travelling service which is very attractive to any young or old age disabled tourist nowadays.

In general, instead of renting cars to drive behavioral change to disabled tourists usually ,renting cars behaviors which will replace to choose to catch any public transportation tools behavior to disable tourists. What kinds of other behavioral changes will impact to disabled tourists? Other aspect consideration is disabled tourist individual health problem . For example, if the disabled tourist is driving himself/herself renting cars to go to anywhere destinations in long term in the travelling country. The long distance of driving miles travelling and driving long hours spend travelling behaviors will influence the disable tourist individual nervous health to be more poor, because he/she needs to spend more time and nervous to drive whose renting car to go to anywhere in whole travelling journey. So, it is very dangerous and unsafe to the disabled tourist when he/she needs to concentrate on nervous to drive himself/herself renting car to go to anywhere destinations to travel in whose travelling journey or trip.

In consideration of the older age disabled tourist groups will be more unsafe and dangerous when he/she needs to spend much time to drive whose renting car to arrive any travelling destinations. So, it is based on this long time unsafe driving factor, the older age disabled tourist groups will choose to spend lesser time to drive to go to anywhere destinations to travel alone or with their friends and/or families in general. Similar patterns are evident in the numbers of miles travelled and the time spent to driving renting car behavior to any older age disabled tourist groups will be lesser than the younger age disabled tourist groups . Due to the long time unsave renting car self-driving feeling to the older age disabled tourists. It will impact to influence the older age disabled tourists to choose to catch any public transport or walking to replace renting car self-driving behaviors in their trips, when older age handicapped tourists loss hearing, sight, memory, recognizing physical danger, personal care difficulties disabled characteristics.

Thus, the long time renting car driving behavior which will influence the old age disabled tourists to choose to catch public transport tools to replace to rent car to drive in whose trip persuasively. So, the renting car providers will have lesser old age disable tourist number to compare to young age disabled tourist number in common. Also, the old age disable tourists will prefer to choose the travel destinations where have many public transport tools to let them to catch for their travelling journeys.

● Long time social internet networking behavior
impacts traveller individual behavior

Can web site online internet networking influence traveller individual behavior changes? If web site can influence every online traveller user individual behavior change, how it influence every online user individual behavior change in order to impact his/her travelling service or arrangement change choice. For example, when the traveller walks in one travel agent's shop to find the most suitable travelling package for whose trip.

At the moment, he/she plans to find the travel agent to help him/her to arrange any travelling package. But when he/she goes back his/her home, he/she turns on his/her computer to link online travel agent website. Then, he/ she discovers this online travel agent can provide more attractive travelling package similar service and he/she will compare the walk in travel agent's travelling package to this online travel agent travelling package. Although, the walk-in travelling agent can provide lesser service fee to compare this online travel agent. But , he/she feels this online travel agent can provide more attractive and enjoyable travelling entertainment and trip arrangement service to satisfy his/her travelling need. So, he/she decides to choose this online travelling agent's travelling package and it seems that the online travel agent web site can influence his/her original travelling agent target choice.

Nowadays, the most famous online development reshaping traditional marketing methods of tourism business will be possible to replace the traditional walk-in travel agent business. Because travelling consumers like to turn on computer to link to different travelling agents' websites to choose which travelling package is the cheapest or it can provide the most attractive or enjoyable entertainment arrangement in the trip. So, online travel agents will influence travelling consumers to reduce to spend time to walk in to visit any travel agent shops. The traveller prefers to spend much time to find which travelling agents' websites to find the most right online travelling agent to help him/her to arrange the trip service to replace to find the most right walk-in travelling agent at home conveniently. So, travelling agent website development can impact every traveller individual planning behavior to be changed influentially because when he/she plans to walk in to visit the identified travel agent shop, but when he/she has one desk top computer to be installed at home. Then, he/she will have another choice to buy the travelling package service. So, he/she will change his/her walk in to visit the travel agent planning behavior to change to clicking on any travel agent's website behavior.

Moreover, travelling website characteristics or attractive point is easy communication. When the traveller feels any worry or trouble, he/her need to enquire the online travelling agent immediately. He/she can send email to enquire the travelling agent to arrange travelling package similar service to walk in travel agent and he/she will compare the walk in travel agent's travelling package to this online travel agent travelling package. Although, the walk-in travelling agent can provide lesser service fee to compare this online travel agent. But, he/she feels that this online travel agent can provide more attractive and enjoyable travelling entertainment and trips service to satisfy his/her travelling need. So, he/she decides to choose this online travelling agent's travelling package and it seems that the online travel agent website can influence his/her original travelling agent target choice.

Nowadays, the most famous online development reshaping traditional marketing methods of tourism business will be possible to replace the traditional walk-in travel agent business. Because travelling walk-in consumer like to turn on computer to link to different travelling agents' websites to choose which travelling package is the cheapest or it can provide the most attractive or enjoyable entertainment arrangement .

Thus, online travelling information search tool can attract travellers to choose to find any travel agents' websites from internet to replace walk-in travel agents' shops influentially. Also, it seems online travelling service will be popular to replace walk-in travelling service in possible.

● Long time cultural distance on satisfaction and respect travel intention

Every country cultural difference is different. How and why cultural difference has a real impact on tourist satisfaction and it can also influence to repeat travel. Is cultural tourism one major factor to influence tourist to repeat travelling intention or choice to the country in international tourism choice market? For example, China and India have similar culture. Their cultural difference is not much, e.g. eating cultural habit is similar , entertainment cultural habit is similar. These both countries people do not want to spend much money in eating and entertainment both aspects. Hence, these two countries people do not consider how to consume to enjoy entertainment and eat expensive food. Hence, it is based on cultural similar reason. These both countries tourists will prefer to choose to repeat travelling either China or India. When the Indian tourists had chosen to go to China to travel in the first time. Then, the Indian tourists will choose to go to China to travel in second time again. Also, the Indian tourists had chosen to go to China to travel in first time. Then, the Chinese tourists will choose to go to India to travel in second time again. What factors influence China and India touists repect to travel between these both countries. The factors will include cheap air ticket price, cheap hotel living price , less economic cost factor. However, I believe the similar cultural factor will be the major factor to influence many Chinese and Indian tourist prefer to choose to repeat travelling between these both countries.

As my indication to these both countries people have similar eating habits, choosing foods, low health foods, common foods choice eating at cheap restaurant habitual consumption. Also, they have similar entertainment habits, their entertainment demad is not high. They like to ride bicycles to go to anywhere to travel. They like to go to swim, play backetball, football etc. sports. These all sports are cheap sport consumption. So, it based on similar individual low enjoyment demand and low health, food quality demand similar cultural factors. Chinese and Indian people have no long distance cultural difference between eating and entertainment habitual factor will include them to choose to repeact travelling between these both countries. Due to China and India have many restaurants can provide cheap food or sport service providers can provide diffent kinds of cheap sport entertainment consumption to satisfy their cheap food and cheap entertainment needs in their journey in China or India anywhere. So, it explains that why these both countries tourists will repeat to travel these both countries again after they had visited China or India to travel in first time. So, the similar cultural factor can impact these both countries tourists to repeat to go to these both countries to travel again. Hence, if these two countries' cultural distance is far or different, then themselves countries' tourists won't choose to repeat travel between themselves when these two countries for cultural distance toutists had visited to another country in first time. Hence, culture has been continuously considered as a much factor which tourists consider in terms of choice of the destination travelling place. Also, it explains cultural distance which can make tourist individual has less satisfaction to concern to tourists to repeat travels.

Otherwise, for far cultural distance two countries case example, such as Chinese and American , these two countries people's eating habit and entertainment cultural needs are different. For eating habit difference example, American like to eat poks, beefs, chickens, potatos to replace rice and other foods. Otherwise, Chinese like to wat rice, vegatables more than potatoes, porks , beefs for lunch , dinner . So , their eating habits are very different. Also, American like to drive boats on the seasor drive crs to go to anywhere to travel on holidays for sports or holiday entertainment activities . Otherwise, Chinese like to play backetball, football, ride bicycle of cheaper sport entertainment on holidays. So, American entertainment activities are more expensive to compare Chinese. Also, US and China , like families whose power distance is dfferent, such as every per family powerful member is parents, who have more power to give opinions to choose anywhere to travel for whose sons and/or daughters whole famililly members travelling arrangement.

Therefore, if the Us family powerful members, such as at least one son or/and ond daughter members who need t choose to go to which country to travel if the family powerful members, such as the child/ children's parent feel China's food taste or entertainment activities are totally different to be similar to their country's food taste and entertainment activities habitually after their whole fmily members had travelled to China in first time before.

Although, their son(s) and daughter(s) will hope to go to China to repect travel again. But, due to the US family parents are their son(s) and daughter(S) powerful decider to make any travelling decision to choose which country will be next time travelling destination. If their parents feel China's eating and entertainment culture is totally different to their countries. Then, the US family will not choose to repeat travel to the China country again any more easily, beause this US family can not feel satisfactory when they visited China in their first time before, due to they feel China 's food and entertainment cultures are totally different to their US country. So, the cultural distance factor will influence the US family don't choose China to fo repeat travel again.

Consequently, different countries' similar or different cultural factor will influence the country's tourists choose to repeact travel to the country again. So, any country needs to know what its culture is in order to attract the similar cultural countries tourists to repeat travel to itself country more easily.

- Long time lifestyle habit influences travel behavior

Whether do different countries tourists' different lifestyle which can influence their travel consumption behaviors? Even, which countries that they will choose to go to travel. For example, when one tourist who owns himself/herself often to drive to go to anywhere habitually. The tourist's driving car habital behavior which will influence that he /she will feel need to rent car to travel to anywhere habitually , when he/she selects to go to the country to travel. Hence, if he/she feels the tourism destination has no any rent car service providers to provide him/her to rent any car to travel anywhere in the country's travel destination. Does the country lack rent car service factor which will influence that he/she will still choose to go to the country to travel in preference? For example, when one New Zealander's family who own at least one car at home. So, the New Zealand whole family every member can often drive car to go to anywhere , even, one family member had driven one car to leave his/her home. So, driving own car activity or behavior has been one habitual activity to influence the New Zealand every member to feel the travelling destination needs have rent car service provider supplies cars to let them to rent to travel. The driving car lifestyle has caused the whole New Zealander family driving habit. When the family's sons) and/or daughter(s) need(s) to go to school or go to shopping as well as their parents also need to drive their cars to go to office to work in themselves home town often. In common, there are many New Zealanders who will have at least one car at home because they feel that they can drive their themselves cars to go to anywhere in New Zealand more than waiting bus or tram or train or ferry etc. public transportation tools more conveniently. So, New Zealanders' driving own car habit will influence their lifestyle to feel that they also need to rent cars to travel to go to any where to travel to replace to wait public transportation tools choice in the travelling destination during their journey.

For shopping trips is more influenced by their driving car activities. So, it seems that this New Zealander families will be influenced to their tourism destination need, they need the tourism destination has car renting service provider to be supplied anywhere to let them can drive the renting cars to go to anywhere in tourism destination. It means that when the tourim destination has less rent car providers can provide renting car services to drive anywhere or it has none any renting car service providers are existing in the tourism destination. Then, the renting car service providers number shortage or none any renting car service providers to be provided to the country's tourism destination, which will cause the New Zealander families do not perfer to choose to go to the country to travel generally, e.g. Hong Kong, China, Korea these Asia countries have no many rent car service providers in these countries. So, the New Zealand families won't prefer to choose to go these countries to travel when they discover these Asia countries lack enough rent car service providers to let them to drive to travel in themselves conveniently. Otherwise, America, England, Japan etc. countries have many rent car service providers. So, these countries will be this New Zealander families' preferable tourism countries. Thus, the New Zealand families' driving ownership car lifestyle will influence their travel behaviors to choose to go to the country which can have many rent car providers in the tourism country any where tourism destinations in preference.

Thus, whether the country has renting car service providers , it will be variable factor to influence any country's car ownship families' driving car travel behaviors in their journey in order to let they feel that they can drive themselves ownship cars to go to anywhere to travel conveniently, even when they leave their countries. Hence, these countries' car ownship driving habitual families' behaviors will be influenced their tourism destination or location decision choice when the country has many renting car service providers in preference as well as this renting car service provider supplying factor will be more important to influence the habitual driving own car traveller to be preferable choice to compare other factors, e.g. cheap entertainment consumption providers factor which include cheap hotel living fee, cheap food price consumption etc. expenditure in the travelling country.

Thur, it explains that different countries' car ownship tourists , whose driving own car activities will cause their daily lifestyles, then their daily driving own car lifestyles will influence their tourism destination choices indirectly. So, it seems that lifestyle can be a outcome variable (or dependent variable) factor to influence travel behavior in any travelling built environment. The travelling built environment characteristics can include density measures (population density, job density), job-housing density). These travelling buit environment factor can repreent what the city resident's lifestyle. For example, where the location in relation to local centre or regional centre to the country's residents are living. This country resident's living location will cause this country resident's lifestyles , e.g. holiday or leisure whether it is low budget, active and adventurous or frequent traveller with second place or self-orgnized , family oriented or close to home and unadventurour. Hence, the country's living built environment will influence the country's resident's lifestyles. Due to different countries' residents will have different lifestyles. Hence, built environments and lifestlyes have relationship to influence every country's residents when they need to go to other countries to travel in their holidays. For example, frequent travellers are usually living in big and busy cities, otherwise, non -frequent travellers are ususally living in the countrysides, where there are less offices or factories are built to let people to work. So, big city will bring busy feeling to the country's residents, then they will be influenced to feel need to often to go to travel for leisure intention in their holidays. Otherwise, countryside will bring not busy or quiet environment feeling to the country's residents, then they won't feel working feeling when they are living in counryside. So, they won't feel need to go t o anywhere to travel in their holidays often.

Hence, built environment will bring either busy or not busy (quiet environment feeing) to the both different country residents when they are living in the places. Their living places will cause their lifestyles are different. Then, they will be influences to feel have more frequent travelling needs or less frequent travelling needs to explain why every country people will have more or less frequent travelling needs.

- Time factor influences travel behavioural consumption

How to predict travel consumption by time factor? It is one question to any travel agents concern how to use past time and future time to predict how many numbers of travelers where who will choose to go to travel more accurately. I think that who can consider how to predict travel behavioral consumption from psychology view and computer science view both.

On the psychology view, It has evidence to support the relationship between self-identify threat and resistance to change travel behavior to any travelers, controlling for whose past travelling behavior, resistance to change if a psychological phenomenon of long standing interest in many applied branches of psychology. Past travelling behavior has been acknowledged as a predictor of future action. Such as travelling behavior that is experienced as successful is likely to be repeated and may lead to habitual patterns. Some psychologists differentiate habit between two concepts, such as goal oriented and automatic oriented both. Although repeated past travelling behavior is addition goal oriented and automatic oriented. Further non-deliberative nature of habit may make appeals to judge and to predict future individual traveler's behaviour accrately. However, repeated travelling behavior without a necessary constraint of goal orientation and automatic oriented both. So, it seems that the traveller's past travelling experience time psychological factor can influence any individual traveler why and how who choose to decide whose travelling behaviour.

- Can the country's past travel time climate change factor influence travelling behaviours?

The flexibility of human travelling behavior is at least the result of one such mechanism, our ability to travel mentally in time and entertain potential future. Understanding of the impacts is holidays, particularly those involving travel. Using focus groups research to explores tourists' awareness of the impacts of travel own climate change, examines the extent to which climate change features in holiday travel decisions and identifies some of the barriers to the adoption of less carbon intensive tourism practices. The findings suggest many tourists don't consider climate change when planning their holidays. The failure of tourists to engage with the climate change to impact of holidays, combined with significant barriers to behavioral change, presents a considerable challenge in the tourism industry.

Tourism is a highly energy intensive industry and has only recently attracted attention as an important contributions to climate change through greenhouse gas emissions. It has been estimated that tourism contributes 5% of global carbon dioxide emissions. There have been a number of potential changes proposed for reducing the impact of air travel on climate change. These include technological changes, market based changes and behavioral changes. However, the role that climate change plays in the holiday and travel decisions of global tourists. How the global tourists of the impacts travel has on climate change to establish the extent to which climate change, considerations features in holiday travel decision making processes and to investigate the major barriers to global tourists adopting less carbon intensive travel practices. Whether tourists will aware the impacts that their holidays and travel have on climate changes.

When, it comes to understand indvidual traveler's behavioral change, wide range of conceptual theories have been developed, utilizing various social, psychological, subjective and objective variables in order to model travel consumption behavior. These theories of travel behavioral change operate at a number of different levels, including the individual level, the interpersonal level and community level. Whether pro-environmental behavior can be used to predict travel consumption behavior in a climate change. However, the question of what determines pro-environmental behavior in such a complex one that it can not be visualized through one single framework or diagram.

Despite the potentially high risk scenario for the tourism industry and the global environment, the tourism and climate change ought have close relationship. Whether what are the important factors and variables which can limit tourism? e.g. money, time, family problem, extreme hot or cold weather change, air ticket price, journey attraction etc. variable factors. Mention of holidays and travel were deliberately avoided in the recruitment process, so as not to create a connection factor to influence traveler's individual mind. However, the dismissal of alternative transportation modes can be conceived as either a structural barrier, in the sense that flying is perhaps the only realistic option to reach long-haul holiday destination, or a perceived behavioral control barriers in that an individual perceives flying as the only option open to whom. The transportation tool factor will be depend to extent on the distance to the destination. This can also be interpreted in a social perspective as an intention with the resources available where much international tourism is structured around flying. To increase the availability of different transportation modes, tourists could choose holiday destination closer to home.

Finally, also how to predict future travel behavioural consumption. I feel that travel agents need to predict whether any country's random daily variation of weather factor is also important to influence travel behaviour. e.g. in weather, temperature, rainfall adn snowfall with traffic accidents factors will have relationship to cause travel demand. Some scientists estimate suggest that when warmed temperatures and reduced snowfall are associated with a moderate decline in non-fatal accidents, they are also associated with a significant increase in fatal accidents. Thus increase in fatalities and temperature. Half of the estimated effect of temperature on fatalities is due to changes in the exposure to pedestrians, bicyclists and motorcyclists as temperature increase. So, if any countries have rainfall, snowfall and low temperature to cause traffic accidents, whether this accident occurrence will influence the travelers who liking climb snow hills, riding bicycle, running sports who will avoid to travel to these countries' bad weather after occurs. So, why I feel that this natural climate factor will also be one serious factor to influence travel behavioral consumption.

- Can the traveller's past travelling time entertainment experience factor predict future travel consumption behavior?

Whether individual habitual behaviour can influence travelling behaviour : e.g. renting travel transportation tools

Whether habit can be intended to predict of future travel behavior to people are creatures of habits. Many of human's everyday goal-directed behaviors are performed in a habitual fashion, the transportation made and route one takes to work, one's choice of breakfast. Habits are formed when using the some behavior frequently and a similar consistency in a similar context for the some purpose whether the individual past travel consumption model will be caused a habit to whom. e.g. choosing whom travel agent to buy air ticket or traveling package; choosing the same or similar countries' destinations to go to travel ; choosing the business class or normal (general) class of quality airlines to catch planes. Does habitual rent traveling car tools use not lead to more resistance to change of travel mode? It has been argued that past behavior is the best predictor of future behavior to travel consumption. If individual traveler's past consumption behavior was always reasoned, then frequency of prior travel consumption behavior should only have an indirect link to the individual traveler's behavior. It seems that renting travel car tools to use is a habit example. So, a strong rent traveling car tools useful habit makes traveling mode choice. People with a strong renting of traveling car tools of habit should have low motivation to attend to gather any information about public transportation in their choice of travelling country for individual or family or friends members during their traveling journeys.

Even when persuasive communication changes the traveler whose attitudes and intention, in the case of individual traveler or family travelers with a strong renting travel car tools habit. It is difficult to change whose travel behaviors to choose to catch public transportation in whose any trips in any countries. However, understanding of travel behavior and the reasons for choosing one mode of transportation over another. The arguments for rent traveling car tools to use, including convenience, speed, comfort and individual freedom and well known. Increasingly, psychological factors include such as, perceptions, identity, social norms and habit are being used to understand travel mode choice. Whether how many travel consumers will choose to rent traveling car tools during their trips in any countries. It is difficult to estimate the numbers. As the average level of renting travel car tools of dependence or attitudes to certain travel package policies from travel agents. Instead different people must be treated in different ways because who are motivated in different ways and who are motivated by different travel package policies ways from travel agents.In conclusion, the past and present and future travelling entertainment time experience factors can influence whose traveler's individual behavior either who chooses to rent traveling car tools or who chooses to catch public transportation when who individual goes to travel in alone trip or family trip. It include influence mode choice factors, such as social psychology factor and marketing on segmentation factor both to influence whose transportation choice of behavior in whose trip.

● How to determine future travel behavior from past travel time experience and perceptions of risk and safety for the benefits to travel consumers?

How to determine future travel behavior from past travel experience and perceptions of risk and safety for the benefits to travel consumers? Why does individual traveler avoid certain destination(s) is(are) as relevant to tourist decision making as why who chooses to travel to others. Perceptions of risk and safety and travel experience are likely to influence travel decisions. If travel agents had efforts to predict future travel behavior to guess whether travelers will feel where is(are) risk and unsafe to cause who does not choose to go to the country to travel. Then, the travel agents will avoid to choose to spend much time to design the different traveling package to attract their potential travel consumers to choose to travel. The reason is because in the case of individual traveler's tourism experience, the traveler whose past disappointment travel experience (psychological risk) will be a serious threat to the traveler's health or life (health, physical or terrorism risk). The past safety or unhealthy risk to the country(countries) will influence the traveler decides to choose not to go to the countries(country) to travel again in the future.

● What is past travelling experience time push and pull factors influence any traveler who chooses where is whose preferable travelling destination

How to predict individual traveler's behavioral intention of choosing a travel destination. Understanding why people travel and what factors influence their behavioral intention of choosing a travel destination is beneficial to tourism planning and marketing. In general, an individual's choice of a travel destination into two forces. The first force is the push factor that pushes an individual away from home and attempt to develop a general desire to go somewhere, without specifying where that may be. The other force is the pull factor that pull an individual toward in destination, due to a region-specific or perceived attractiveness of a destination. The respective push and pull factors illustrate that people travel because who are pushed by whose internal motives and pulled by external forced of a destination. However, the decision making process leading to the choice of a travel destination is a very complex process. For example, a Taiwanese traveler who might either choose new travel destination of Hong Kong or another old travel Asia destinations again or who also might choose any one of Western country, as a new travel destination. The travel agents can predict where who will have intention to choose to travel from whose past behavior and attitude, subjective and perceived behavioral control model.

The factors influence where is the traveler choice, include personal safety, scenic beauty, cultural interest, climate changing, transportation tools, friendliness of local people, price of trip, trip package service in hotels and restaurants, quality and variety of food and shopping facilities and services etc. needs. So, whose factors will influence where is the individual travel's choice. It seems every traveler whose choice of travel process, will include past behavior. e.g. travelling experience, travelling habit, then to choose the best seasoned travelling action to satisfy whose travel needs. This process is the individual traveler's psychological choice process, who must need time to gather information to compare concerning of different travel packages, destination scene, climate change, transportation tools available to the destination, air ticket price etc. these factors, then to judge where is the best right destination to travel in the right time.

- Why past travelling time expectation, motivation and attitude factor can influence travelling behaviour?

Social psychology is concerned with gaining insight into the psychological of socially relevant behaviors and the processes. For instance, on a global level bad influence to global warming, it influences some countries extreme cold or hot bad climate changing occurrence, then it ought influence some travelers' behavioral decision to change their mind to choose some countries to go to travel at the moment which do not occur extreme hot or cold climate (temperature). e.g. above than 40 degree in summer or below than 0 degree in winter. Due to the extreme climate changing environment in the countries, it will cause them to feel uncomfortable to play during their trips. So, the global warming causes to climate changing factor will influence the numbers of travel consumption to be reduced possibly. This is global climate changing environment factor influences to bad or uncomfortable social psychological feeling to global travelers' mind of traveling decision. What is individual traveler expectation, motivation and attitude? Tourism sector includes inbound (domestic) tourism and outbound (overseas) tourism both incomes to any countries. According to recent article, a tourist behavior model has been developed, called the expectation, motivation and attitude (EMA) model (Hsu et al., 2010).

This model focuses on the pre-visit stage of tourists by modeling the behavioral process by incorporating expectation, motivation and attitude. Travel motivation is considered as an essential component of the behavioral process, which has been increasing attention from the travel; industry. The economic approach defines "tourism" is an identifiable nationally important industry. It includes the component activities of transportation, accommodation, recreation, food and related service. So, tourism behavioral consumption is concerned the individual tourist's usual habituate of the industry which responds to whose needs, and of the impacts that both the tourist and the tourism industry have on the socio-cultural, economic and physical environment.

However, travel motivation means how to understand and predict factors that influence travel decision making. According to Backman and others (1995, p.15), motivation is conceptually viewed as " a state of need, a condition that services as a driving force to display different kind of behavior toward certain types of activities, developing preferences, arriving at some expected satisfactory outcome." So, motivation and expectancy which has close relationship to any tourist before who decided to do any tourism of behavior. Some economists confirmed motivation and expectancy which has relations, such as expectation of visiting an outbound destination has a direct effect on motivation to visit the destination; motivation has a direct effect on attitude toward visiting the destination; expectation of visiting the outbound destination has a direct affect on attitude toward visiting the destination and motivation has a mediating effect on the relationship in between expectation and attitude.

How can apply past travelling entertainment experience time factor to predict future travel behavioural consumption?

I also suggest to use qualitative of travel behavioural method to predict future travel consumption. Methods such as focus groups interviews and participant observer techniques can be used with quantitative approaches on their own to fill the gaps left by quantitative techniques. These insights have contributed to the development of increasingly sophisticated models to forecast travel behavior and predict changes in behavior in response to change in the transportation system. First, survey methods restrict not only the question frame but the answer frame as well, anticipating the important issues and questions and the responses. However, these surveys methods are not well suited to exploratory areas of research where issues remain unidentified and the researched seek to answer the question "why?". Second, data collection methods using traditional travel diaries or telephone recruitment can under represent certain segments of the population, particularly the older persons with little education, minorities and the poor. Before the survey, focus group for example can be used to identify what socio-demographic variables to include in the survey, how best to structure the diary, even what incentives will be most effective in increasing the response rate. After the survey, focus, focus groups can be used to build explanations for the survey results to identify the "why" of the results as well as the implications. One Asia Pacific survey research result was made by tourism market investigation before. It indicated the travel in Asia Pacific market in the past, had often been undertaken in large groups through leisure package sold in bulk, or in large organized business groups, future travelers will be in smaller groups or alone, and for a much wider range of reasons. Significant new traveler segments, such as female business traveler. The small business traveler and the senior traveler, all of which have different aspirations and requirements from the travel experience.

Moreover, Asia tourism market will start to exist behaviors in the adoption of newer technologies, a giving the traveler new ways to manage the travel experience, creating new behaviors. This with provide new opportunities for travel providers. The use of mobile devices, smartphones, tablets etc. and social media are the obvious findings to become an integral part of the travel experience. Thus, quality method can attempt to predict Asia Pacific tourism market development in the future.

However, improving the predictive power of travel behavior models and to increase understanding travel behavior which lies in the use of panel data(repeated measures from the same individuals). Whereas, cross-sectional data only reveal inter-individual differences at one moment in time, panel data can reveal intra-individual changes over time. In effect, panel data are generally better suited to understand and predict (changes in) travel behavior. However, a substantial proportion was also observed to transition between very different activity/travel patterns over time, indicating that from one year to the next, many people renegotiated their activity/travel patterns.

Nowadays, past travelling experience time information can predict how traveler behavior and network performance will change in the future . For example, when steadily growing levels of vehicle ownership and vehicle miles traveled information has been identified as a potential strategy towards man aging travel demand, optimizing transportation networks and better utilizing available capacity. Toward, this goal to predict further tourist behavioral consumption. Many countries, government tourism development institutes has applied advanced traveler information systems (ATIS) which travel behavior models and high-fidelity network performance models made increasingly feasible through the rapid advances in computer power. Crucial components of this problem domain are the modeling of individual tourist drivers' response to travel information and the development accurate guidance of relevance to real would trip makers. So, this advanced traveler information systems (ATIS) can assist the tourist who like to rent travelling car tools to travel in any countries own free traveler information systems service conveniently. Also, this travel information system can be intended to assist travelers to make better travel choices. e.g. this system can improve the decision making of individual traveler rather than improvements of network performance overall. So, we need to understand how tourists make their travel plans. Also, understanding decision process that lead to booking of the trip is equally important, as it allows of a potential behavior.

- Can gather past online tourism sale information predict future traveling consumption of behaviour?

Nowadays, internet is popular, it seems that booking air ticket behavior of using internet is predicted to influence overall tourism air tickets payment method. Tourism industry has grown in the previous several decades. Despite its global impact, questions related to better understanding of tourists and whose habits. Using online travel air ticket booking benefits include booking electronic air tickets can be made from entering any electronic travel agents websites in the short time and electronic travel ticket payers do not need leave home, who can pay visa card to pre booking any electronic travel ticket from online channel conveniently.

How to analyze activity based travel demand ? Nowadays, human are concerning the traffic congestion and air quality deterioration, the supply oriented focus of transportation planning has expanded to include how to manage travel demand within the available transportation supply. Consequently, there has been an increasing interest in travel demand management strategies, such as congestion pricing that attempts to change aggregate travel demand. The prediction aggregate level, long term travel demand to understanding disaggregate level (i.e. individual levels) behavioral responses to short term demand policies, such as ride sharing incentives, congestion pricing and employer based demand management schemes, alternate work schedules, telecommuting limitation of travel agent traditionally work nature shall influence oriented trip based travel modelling passenger travel demand indirectly.

Finally, online travel purchase will be popular to influence the number of travel behavioural consumption nowadays. Any travel package products can be sold from websites to attract travellers to choose to prebook air ticket for any trips conveniently. In the past ten years, the internet has become the predominant carrier of all types of information and transactions. Regarding travel decisions, internet has also become an important sales channels for the travel industry, because it is associated with comparably lower distribution and sales costs, but also because ir adapts to hign supply and demand dynamics in this industry. Consequently, the travel and tourism industry tries to increase the internet sale specific share of sales volumes. So, internet sale channel has changed travel consumption behavioural pattern and characteristics and travel experience. For example, Switzerland has one of the highest population-to-computer ratio in Europe. It is also one of the most highly internet penetrated countries in terms of use of the WWW on a day-to-day basis, with more than 75 percent of the population older than 14 years using the WWW daily (ICT, 2005).

The reason of booking online tourism may include: convenience, fast transaction, finding traveling package choice easily, more airline seats available. So, online booking tourism will influence the traditional tourism agents visiting of sales and air tickets and travelling package numbers to be decreased. Finally, the online booking tourism market shares will be expanded to more than traditional tourism agents visits sale market in the future one day. So, the travel agents who still use the traditional tourism visiting sale channel which ought raise whose features to compare to differ to online tourism sale channel if these traditional touriam agents want to keep competitive ability in tourism industry for long term.

- Can gather past urban population of travel behaviour to predict future travel behavior?

Actively based patterns of urban population. It is a method of motivational framework means in which societal constraints and inherent individual motivations interact to shape activity participation patterns. It can be used to predict one city or urban the numbers of travel demand in the year. It has two elements: First, capability constraints refer to constraints are imposed by biological needs, such as eating and sleeping and/or resources, such as income, availability of cars etc. to undertake the urban or city's family activities in the year. Second, coupling constraints define where, when and the duration of planning activities that are to be pursued with other individuals. So, this method needs to gather information (data) to get the relationship between activities, travel and spending work time and space time to evaluate whether there are how many families who have real needs to spend time to go to travel in the year.

What is trip based versus activity based approaches? The fundamental difference between the trip-based and activity based approaches is that the former approach directly focuses on trips without explicit recognition of the motivation or reason for the trips and travel. The activity based approach , on the other hand, views travel as a demand derived from the need to pursue travel activities. So, it is better understand the individual or family behavior basis for individual or family travelling decision regarding participation in travelling activities in certain places or cities or countries at given times and hence the resulting travel needs. This behavioral basis includes all the factors that influence the why, how, when and where of performed activities and resulting individuals and household, the cultural/social norms of the community and the travel surrounding environment.

Another difference between the two approaches is in the way travel is represented. The trip based approach represents travel as a collection of trips. Each trip is considered as independent of other trips, without considering the inter-relationship in the choice attributes , such as time, destination and mode of different trips. As tours are chains of trips beginning and ending at a same location , say home or work. The tour based representation helps maintain the consistency across and capture the interdependency and consistency of the modeled choice attributed among the trips of the same tour.

In addition to the tour based representation of travel, the activity based approach focuses on sequences or patterns of activity participation and travel behavior, using the whole day or longer periods of time is the unit of analysis. Such as approach can address travel demand management issues through an examination of how people modify their activity participation, for example, will individuals substitute more out-of-home activities for in home activities in the evening of who arrived early form work due-to a work schedule change?

The major difference between trip based and the activity based approaches is in the way, the time dimension of activities and travel is considered. In the trip based approach, time is reduced to being simply a cost making a trip and a day's viewed as a combination, defined peak and off peak time periods. On the other hand, activity based approach views individuals' activity travel patterns are a result of their time use decisions with a continuous time domain. As individuals have 24 hours in a day or multiples of 24 hours for longer periods of time and decide how to use that travel among or allocate that time to activities and travel and with who, subject to their socio-demographic, transportation system and other and scheduling of trips. So, determining the impact of travel demand management policies on time use behavior is an important step to assessing the impact of such policies on individual travel behavior. The final major difference between this two approaches relates to the level of aggregation. In the trip based approach, most aspect of travel, e.g. number of trips etc. are analyzed at an aggregate level.

Consequently, trip based methods accommodate the effect of socio-demographic attributes of households and individuals in a very limited fashion, which limits the activity of the method to evaluate travel impacts of long term socio-demographic characteristics of the individuals who actually make the activity travel choices and the travel service characteristics of the surrounding environment. So, the activity based models are better equipped to forecast the longer term changes in travel demand in response composition and the travel environment of urban areas. Also, using activity based models, the impact of policies can be assessed by predicting individual level behavioral responses instead of employing trip based statistical averages that are aggregated over defined demographic segments.

- Can gather past senior age traveller behavior information predict future senior age traveller behavior?

In the past, Germany government had established tourism survey analysis to analyze survey data in order to arrive at reliable conclusions on future trends in travel behavior. To aim to find how demographic change will influence the tourism market and how the industry can adapt to those changes. The travel analysis provided data on tourism consumer behavior, including attitudes, motives and intentions. Since, 1970 year, it is based on a random sample, representative for the population in private households aged 14 years or older. Then, a continuous high scientific standard combined with a national and international users makes the travel analysis a useful tool and reliable source for tourism industry and policy decisions. It aimed to gather statistical data. e.g. on the age structure and on demographic trends, quantitative and qualitative analysis with time series data from the travel analysis. It shows e.g. not only the future volume , quite different from today's seniors, or how who will travel of family holidays will change, e.g. single parents of low, but grandparents of growing significance for tourism.

Demographic change is said to be one of the important drivers for new trends in consumer traveling change behavior in most European countries (e.g. Lind 2001). Because the growing number of senior citizens in the European Union and other industralised countries, such as the USA and Japan, looks to become one of the major marketing challenges for the tourism industry. United Nations statistics predict that the share of people being 60 age or older will grow dramatically in the coming future, and is expected to rise from 10 percent of the world population in 2000 year to more than 20 percent in 2050 year (United Nations Population Division, 2001). From its statistic, some data showed that travel propensity increased throughout life until the age of about 50 years of age and was then kept stable until very late in life 75 age. The most important results is that the travel propensity when getting older is not going down between 65 and 75 age of course, the overall development of this variable is influenced by a lot of other factors which are rsponsible for quite a variation over time. It is now possible to suggest that the general pattern of travel propensity is one of the key indicators for holiday life cycle travel behaviour, includes three stages. The growth stage tends to increase from early aduithood until 45 age old or when reaching some 80%. The next stage is stabilisation from the ages of around 50 age,until 75 age old, starting with a lower increase. Finally, the decrease stage is a slight decrease occurs once people reach the more advanced age of 75 age to 85 age old (Lohmann & Danielsson 2001).

So, it seems Germany government tourism prediction to future travellers' behaviour indicated these findings, such as on how future senior generations will travel, who had used survey data to examine the patterns of travel behaviour of a generation getting older and applied the findings to draw conclusions on the future. Also, it predicted that on the future of family trips, family semgmentation will be the travel behaviour patterns in the future. These findings together with the statistical data on demographic change allowed for a better understanding of the coming tends in family holidays. It's aim developed in consumer behaviour related to demographic change and predicted what will happen future of tourism one had to consider other influences and drivers as well, for example, trends on the supply side. e.g. low cost airlines or in travelling consumption behaviour in general whether how the past may provide a key to predict travel patterns of senior sitizens to the future.

Given the projected growth of the senior citizens market, designing specific marketing strategies to meet the prospective needs of elderly tourists will become increasingly important. It has been an implict assumption that it will be a close relationship between the travel behaviour of today's senior citizens and the those of future ones. The growing number of senior citizens in the world. e.g. China, Hong Kong, Japan, USA etc. countries. Global senior citizen tourism market will be based solely on demographic predictions about the future of the population's age structure. However, many of these seniors won't only live longer but will be fitter and more active until later in life. Many of the will also have plenty in life. Many of them will also have plenty of time and money to spend on travel. So, will these new seniors behave like today's senior citizens? Will they adopt the same travel behaviour as the previous generation or become a new market of oldies for the leisure and tourism indudtry? However, to determine the actual number of senior citizens who will be travelling and to sought to evaluate and specify certain difficult to predict the actual numbers of senior citizen to any country. However, they can be based on the implicit assumption that there is a close relationship between the travel behaviour of past, present and future seniors. But is this a valid assumption? As the reiseanalyse travel analysis survey, which was conducted in Germany every year, offered some interesting data possibiltieis. It was designed to monitor the holiday travel behaviour, opinions and attitudes of Germans and has been carried out since 1970 year, questions in the questionnaire. Data are based on face to face interviews, with a representative sample of more than 7,500 repondents, the interviews being carried out in January each year. All results refer to the average for the defined generated, which ranges generally over ten years. The group of people then at the age of 60 to 69 age is described. This corresponds to the same generation ten years ago, when they had an age of 50 to 59 age. When this methodological approach is not necessarily very sophisticated, it does have the important advantages of being cost effective.

- Can gather traveller past psychological change

to predict future travelling behavior?

On the psychological view point, I think individual traveler's character will have those kind of personal characteristics. First, simplicity searchers value above everything ease not transparency in their travel planning and holiday making, and are willing to avoid having to go through extensive research. Second, cultural purists use their travel as an opportunity to immerse themselves in an unfamiliar looking to break themselves entirely from their home lives and engage. Sincerely with a different way of living. Third, social capital seekers understand that to be well travelled is a personal quality, and their choices are shaped by their desire to take maximum of social reward from their travel. They will exploit the potential of digital media to enrich and inform their experiences, and structure their adventures always keeping in mind they are being watched by online audiences. Finally, reward hunters seek a return on the investment who make in their busy , high-achieving lives. Linked in part to the growing trend of wellness, including both physical and mental self improvement who seek truly extraordinary and often indulgent or luxurious' must have experiences.

Why needs to know the personal character of individual traveler's characteristics. Because if travel agents could feel which kinds of individual traveler's character, then who can predict which kind of travel package to design to them more easily. For example, how to determine future travel behaviour from past travel experience and perceptions of risk and safety? We need to concern that the influences of past international travel experience, types of risk associated with international travel and the overall degree of safety feeling during international travel on individual's travelling experiences likelihood of travelling to various geographic regions on their next international vacation trip or avoidance of those regions, due to perceived risk. Because individual traveler's experience of safety risk degree to the countries, it will influence who chooses to go to the countries/country to travel again.

Why travellers avoid certain destinations are as relevant decision making as why who choose to go to the country(countries) to travel. Perceptions of risk and safety and travel experiences are likely to influence travel decisions; efforts to predict future travel behaviour can benefit to individual tourist's decision making. As Weber & Bottorn (1989) defined risky decision is as "choices among alternatives that can be described by prodability distributions over possible outcomes" (p.114). Some psychologists judge subjective perceptions of physical reality, i.e. image of a particular tourist destination, whereas value judgement refers to the way individual rank destinations according to whose attributes. i.e. attractiveness, safety, risk etc. factors to form on overall image. So, if the individual traveler had unhappy and worried and unsafe experiences to go to where the place(country) to travel during whose vacation time before. Then, this negative travel experience will influence who is afraid to go to the place (country) to travel again. Risk of place, country, destination or region means the danger is relatively high to the place, ie. increasing in airplane accidents, crime or terrorist activity targeting citizens of potential traveler's nationality or the probability of occurrence is great , ie. recent occurrences involving travel regions/destinations under consideration or effective actions to control consequences exist. i.e. selecting safe regions and destinations, taking extra precautions when traveling to risky destinations. These risk factors will influence the individual traveler who chooses to cancel travel plan to go to the country again.

Another interesting research, how to predict behavioural intention of choosing a travel destination, which has focus of toursm research for years, but the complex decision making process leading to the choice of a travel destination has not been well researched. The planned behaviour model using its core constructs, attitude, subjective norm and perceived behavioural control, with the addition of the past behavioural variable on behavioural intention of choosing a travel destination.

Understanding why people travel and what factors influence their behavioural intention of choosing a travel destination is beneficial to tourism planning and marketing. Understanding travel motivation is the push and pull model. The idea of the push and pull model is the decomposition of an individual's choice of a travel destination into two forces. The first force is the push factor that pushes an indvidual away home and attempts to develop a general desire to go somewhere else, without specifying where that may be. The second force is the pull factor, that pulls on individual toward a destination, due to a region specific travel location or perceived attractiveness of a destination. The respective push and pull factors illustrate that people travel because who are pushed by their internal motives and pulled by external forces of a destination. Nevertheless, how push and pull factors guide people's attitude and how these attributes lead to behavioural intentions of choosing a travel destination have rarely been investigated. The decision making process leading to the choice of a travel destination is a very complex process. The planned behaviour model is as a research framework to predict the behavioural intention of choosing a travel destination. The model based on the three constructs of attitude, subjective norm, and perceived behavioural control (Fishbein & Ajzen, 1975).

In conclusion, the traveller's past travelling experience can influence travelers who decide to choose to travel the country, which include personal safety was perceived to the highest motivation factors among the important factors which include, scenic beauty, cultural interests, friendliness of local people, price of trip, services in hotels and restaurants, quality and variety of food and shopping facilities and services. The factors include both push and pull.

Push factors include knowledge, prestige, and enhancement of human relationship etc., whereas, the most significant pull factors include high technologic image, expenditure and accessibility etc. For example, Japanese travelers visiting Hong Kong. Push factors are such as exploration dream fulfillment and pull factors are such as benefits sought, attractions and good climate city. It will be the factor of future travel patterns and motivations of sub-cultural and ethic groups for Japanese choice to go to Hong Kong travelling.

- Can gather past travelling experience information predict future travelling behavior?

Can travel agencies and airlines organizations attempt to gather data concerns how many visitors number to every country in order to make more accurate evaluation concerns what factors cause why the country will have visitors increasing number or decreasing number till to nowadays from their past travelling behaviors' choices? It is one worthy and considerate question in tourism industry. If the country's airlines and travel agencies can gather every year travellers number data to evaluate what factors influence they choose to their country to travel, e.g. cheap air tickets, attractive seasonal weather environment, cheap and comfortable hotel living feeling etc. many different kinds of entertainment supplying factors to let them to choose to play in their journeys.

If these travelling business organizations can find which one factor is the most important to influence many visitors prefer to choose the country to travel. Then, the country can know whether what any travelling aspect strengths, it needs continue to keep or what any travelling aspect weaknesses, it needs to review in order to achieve the increase of visitors number every continue year in the future. They many follow lot of travellers' past similar or same travelling behavioral characteristics , those data to carrying predicting whether what factors they need to keep or review in order to attract future more visitors prefer to choose to go to itself country to travel successfully. I shall indicate some past travelling data gathering predicting methoss to explain why and how they can help any travelling business organizations to find the what the most important factors to influence whose country's consumer behaviors as below:

Firstly, we need to know what factors can influence local tourists' decision making on choosing a destination? Some visitors choose the country for destination, the reasons may include that the country itself social, cultural as well as the traveller personal and psychological factors , as well as the travel agencies' the number of tourists' destination attractions to the country, available amenities, travelling service package , price and variors types of tourism destinations arrangement etc. examples of the elements which can be considered in decision making.

For example, what is the purpose of tourism of the country? What is /are the factor(s) persuade(s) many travellers perfer to choose to the country in their past travelling experience? So, if the country could attempt to gather its diffeent tourism destination data from the past travellers' travelling experiences. Then, it can define future insights to tourists' behavior and analyze what factors will influence tourists' future destination choices in order to increase more attraction to those future possible popular travelling destinations in itself country.

Hence, researching past whether which destinations had been often visited by past travellers' experiences. Then, the country can follow these the country itself past travellers' liking popular travelling destinatons data to make more accurate future popular destinations prediction for its future travellers. Then, the country government can prepare to design the similar past travellers' liking travelling destinations buildings to be build more in itself countries in order to attract future many visitors' visiting needs when they choos to travel itself country. So, research past what buildings design can attract many travellers to like to visit, it can help the country to predict whether what buildings that the future travellers like to visit, or what kinds of hotel design that they choose to live in preferable.

Another consideration is that to understand what features of life course events are important in determining travel behavior changes to consider how the events themselves are influenced by travel preferences , to consider how different events interact to shape travel behavior or to shape view and understand travel behavior development over the life span, e.g. gathering the past travellers' behaviors may include how and why the residential relocation in the country, how any why travel behavior inter-relationship and the role of socialisation in travel behavior.

So, any country may gather its past social development data in order to predict how to motivate future foreign travellers choose to travel itself country more easily. It means that understanding how to develop the country itself social development or social structure in order to let many countries' different visitors feel it can own some social development strengths or characteristics , and they can attract the different countries' foreign travellers feel that they increase more interest to travel itself country in preference as well as it can also attract them to visit itself country to observe whether what the travelling country's actual social development is different to themselves countries. What are the actual social development to this travelling country owns? Instance, the country's social development may include that its social environment developments that prevail, where the travelling choice country's employment locations may be different to the travellers' themselves countries employment locations; what the travelling choice country's residential locations may be different to the travellers' themselves countries residential locations; what the travelling choice country's housing types, car ownership types , mode to work which are different to the travellers themselves countries in society.

In conclusion, if the country could fulfil itself lifestyle choices and short -term travelling activity and travel choices (travelling activity style, activity duration, destination, route , mode) to let many different foreign travellers to feel that the country has much social development or social culture or social structure is different to themselve countries own. Them , it can persuade or attract or increase their travelling desires to attempt to visit this country , due to they hope to find what the this country's actual social development is different to themselves countries' social development nowadays. Hence, if the airlines or travelling agencies organizations can attempt to gather data concerns how its past social and cultural development changed. Then, it may help them to predict that what social development and cultural development and social structure is the most important factor which had been improved to influence many past visitors choose to visit themselves country to travel in the past. Then , they may find what are the most inportant attractive social change factors to influence future visitors' purposes to themselve country in possible.

Bibliography

Backman, K., Backman, S., Uysal, M. And Sunshine, K. (1995). Event Tourism : An Examination Of Motivations And Activities. Festival Management And Event Tourism, 3(1), 15-24.

Fishbein, M., & Ajzen, Z. (1975). Belief, Attitude, Intention And Behaviour: An Introduction To Theory And Research, Boston: Addison Wesley.

Hsu, C.H.C., Cai , L.A., Li, M(2010). Expectation, Motivation And Attitude: A Tourist Behavioral Model. Journal Of Travel Research, 49(3), 282-296. http://dx.doi, org/10.1177/004728750 9349266.

ICT Information And Communication Technology Switzerland, 2005. ICT Fakten (ICT facts). Available from http://www.ictswitzerland.ch/de/ict%2fakten/factsfigures.asp(retrieved Dec.12, 2005) in German.

Lind, (2001): Befolkningen, Familjen, Livscykeln- Och Ekonomisk Tillvaxt. Institutet For Tillvaxtpo-litiska studier/ Vinnova/Nutek.

Lohmann, Martin (2001): The 31 st. Reiseanalyse-RA 2001. Tourism: vol. 49, no.1/2001;pp.65-67, Zagreb.

United Nations Population Division (2001). World Population Prospects: The 2000 year Revision, New York.

Weber E.U., & W, P.Bottom (1989). "Axiomatic Measures Of Perceived Risk: Some Tests And extensions." journal of behavioral decision making, 2 (2): 113-31.

FIVE

Environment Factor Influence Consumer Time Feeling

How and why time pressure can influence consumer behavior? To research time how influences consumer behavior, it has different theory to explain why and how the consumer is influenced to make the choice by different factors. For example, utility theory,it explains that consumers make choices based on the expected outcomes of their decisions. They are viewed as rational decision makers and they only consider self interest.

Utility theory views consumer is as a " rational economic man". However, the factors influence consumer behaviors may include these activities, such as need recognition, information search, evaluation of alternatives, the building of purchase intention , the act of purchasing choice, consumption and finally disposal. Hence, it seems that all the consumer's activities in whose purchase processes. They will influence their choice. For example, when the property purchase consumer , he plans to research different kinds of properties information concern price, location, housing areas, room numbers, building facilities and environment facilities. He will find some sample target properties information to make comparison in order to decide to buy which of property is the most suitable to satisfy his living need.

However, it is not only one activity for the property purchase buyer in his decision making process. It also include evaluation of alternatives activitiy when he ensures the accurate property information number in order to evaluate whether which one of all these property choices is the most suitable one. Hence, it explains that property information research and evaluation of alternatives both activities are needed to spend much time for this property buyer. If he does not plan to find one property to live in short time, it is possible that he can spedn one month, even more than one month or more than three months time to do the only property information gathering activity.

Hence, it seems that time factor is not the main factor to influence the property buyer to do property purchase decision immediately. Otherwise, if the property buyer plans to find one new property to live within one month. Then, time factor is possible one important factor to influence this property purchase chocie decision. For example, if he felt that he needs more time to spend to gather information concerns the large house area size and the properties have more than three bathrooms and/or bedrooms properties information. Then, he will be possible not to find any this kinds of all property information. So, it means that all these properties won't be his choice. It is because long time property information gathering activity factor influnce.

I assume that the property buyer is a economic man and he does not spend much time to do the property information gathering activity. So, this kind of property needs him to spend long time to gather properties inforation in order to make this kind of properties comparison. Moreover, because he expects to live one new property within one month. So, he only chooses the properties, they have less than three bedrooms and/or bathrooms to gather sample properties information in order to make property purchase decision within one month. Hence, the time variable factor can only influence the property purchaser when he/she needs to make decision to buy one new property to live in the short time. If some kinds of properties choices number has a lot and the property buyer feels to let that he/she must need to spend long time to find the suitable properties number to make evaluation alternatives comparison behavior.

Then, the time variable limiting pressure factor will be possible the main factor to influence the property buyer's choice in order to make the most suitable kind of property purchase decision. Hence, it is one case example of how time limiting pressure factor can influence consumer purchase choice decision, such as property purchases market case. The reason explains why the property buyer needs to spend time to do property information gathering. I assume that general property buyer behave rationally in the economic sense. They won't only believe property agent individual property photos advertisement , it concerns where the property location is and facility etc. information on property photos in order to evaluate whether the property price is reasonable to pay. Generally, property buyers need to attempt to gather property information and visit the different actual property locations to make choice. So, general property consumers would have to be aware of all the available different kinds of properties consumptin options from themselves properties information gathering and the properties agents' verbal properties introduction both be capable of correctly rating each property alternative and the available to select the optimum course of the final property purchase action.

Hence, in the property purchase and sold market, limiting time pressure factor will be important influential factor to decide whether the kinds of properties will be option to some property buyers when they feel need to find one suitable property to buy in short time. Otherwise, in some food consumption market , time limiting pressure factor will not be the main factor to influence consumer option. Such utility theory indicates consumers are as one rational economic man, whom do not expect to spend much time to do any options evaluation decision making.

However, in coffee market, buying a coffee comes almost automatically and does not need much information search. Hence, time limiting pressure factor won't one main factor to influence coff consumer to choose to buy the kind of coffee to drink. However, there are other factors to influence coffee consumers' kind of coffee drinking option from cultural, social, personal or psychological factors. So, coffee taste producer can follow these factors to estimate how coffee consumers might behave in the future when making any kinds of coffee making purchasing decisions.

Firstly, social factor can affect coff consumer behavior significantly. Every coffee consumer has someone around influencing his/her coffee buying decisions. The important social factors include reference groups, family, role and status , e.g. when the coffe buyer has high income job and his friends have good educational level and high income. Then, he will compare his reference group, such as his friends' coffee buying behavior choosing which kinds of coffee taste to drink in habits or lifestyles. If he chooses the kind of coffee taste to drink, its price is cheaper to compare his friends' drinking coffee tastes. Then, he may be influenced to follow his friends to drink the same kinds of coffee taste in order to keep their same social status and role between him and his friends.

Secondly, the coffee consumers will be influenced how to choose which kinds tastes of coffee to drink by personal factors, such as his age, life cycle state, occupation, economic situation , lifestyle and personality and self-concept. Age related factors are such as taste in food, e.g. the kinds of coffee taste. Although, coffee price is cheap, but if the coffee consumer's income is more and he/she can often spend to buy different kinds of taste coffees to drink. Then, his/her income level will have much purchasing power to influence his/her purchasing behavior. Hence the coffee consumer's frequency of consumption of different kinds of coffee taste drinking choice behavior will represent whether his/her income level is high or low in possible. For example, the consumer needs to go to automatic coffee shop to buy at least three cups or more different kinds of high class good taste coffee brands to drink per week. Although, these high class coffee brands' prices are higher than the low class of coffee brands. But the coffee consumer still only buys any one of these kinds of high class brands' coffee taste to drink. Hence, it seems that this coffee consumers ought have high income to let hims to buy at least three cups of high class brand of coffee taste to drink from automativ coffee ship per week.

So, income factor can influence the coffee consumer to choose either coffer purchase from supermarket or coffee drinking at automatic coffee shop. If the coffee consumer only chooses to buy coffee from supermarket, due to the bottles of different kinds of brand coffee can provide more different tastes of coffees choices from shelves to let him to buy to drink at home. So, it seems that the coffee consumer's income level is low in general. Otherwise, if the coffee consumer only chooses to go to automtic coffee shop to buy the high class brands of coffee tastes to drink at least thre times or more per week. It may mean that the coffee consumer has high income level to support him/her to often go to automatic coffee shop to buy different kinds of high class coffee tastes to drink frequently every week. Som high or low income level factor can influence every coffee consumer individual drinking coffee behavioral options.

Moreover, when the coffee consumer is younger coffee consumer will be possible to buy much coffee to drink. Because younger age people can accept to drink coffee habitually more than older age people. Also, it is possible that younger peopler feel often drinking coffee behavior will help them to bring more health feeling and /or raising nervous to learn , due to they need often to go to schools to study. Otherwise, older age people feel often drinking coffee behaviors won't help them to bring more health and they do not need to raise nervous to learn.

Finally, even, cultural difference factor will influence coffee consumers number fo any countries. For example, western countries'people like to drink any kinds of coffee tastes traditionally. Asia countries' people like to drink any different kinds of teas tastes traditionally. So, different kinds of teas tastes will be asia people's traditional drinking substitute to replace different kinds of coffee tastes more easily. Hence, culture difference will be one factor to influence asia coffee buyers number. So, it seems that time limiting pressure factor won't influence coffee consumers' coffee taste choices to different kinds of high class or low class brands, visiting coff shops or visiting supermarkets choices, frequent or not frequent coffee drinking behaviors.

- How and why time limiting pressure

influences consumer choice

Can consumer buying decisions be influenced by time limiting pressure. For these three situations, they will influence consumer hoe makes different buying decision, e.g. in the little time available, but the consumer needs to do more effort needed to choose to buy which kind of product among variety kinds of product choice or in a moderate amount of time available, or a considerable amount of time available. In this first situation, the consumer can not real attempt to find any weaknesses or unique characteristics of the products, because it has no enough time to allow whom to choose. So, his/her product evaluation won't be th most accurate to satisfy his/her needs because little time can only allow him/her to find some weaknesses of the products. Otherwise, in the final situation, because the consumer has a considerable amout of time to allow him/her to attempt to find the weaknesses and/or strengths characteristics of the products choice. So, he/she ought do the more reasonable or accurate evaluation of these products to choose the most effective economic beneficial product to buy. Thus, it seems that time limiting pressure factor can influence the consumer to make more rational or more reasonable economic beneficial consumption decision making to buy the product or consume the service.

Thus, a consumer buying decision will require these situations to do buying decisions, they may include either little time and conscious effort or a moderate amount of time and effort or a considerable amount time and effort. The products may include cheap products/services , e.g. fruit, DVD, university courses, computers, facial services, surgeries, sport shoes, reference books, soft drinks, magazines as well as expensive products/services, e.g. cars, houses, luxury goods, e.g. jewellery, female hand bags, holiday travelling entertainment. So, any expensive or cheap products or services, the consumer will need to spend either little or moderate or considerable amount time to do gathering information about the different kinds of products or services in order to find which brand of product or service can bring more economic benefit when he/she chooses to use the product or consume the service. He/she will compare his/her preference sample brands limiting number of products or services choices to decide to buy the brand of product or consume the brand service easily. However in the consumer's consuming decision making process, he/she will need to spend either little or moderate or a considerable amount of time to do the evaluation and choice consumption behavior. It means that time limiting pressure factor will influence the consumer how to make consumption choice consequently.

What are the impacts of reduced branding on consumer choice and time limiting pressure to influence consumer behavior? When one consumer needs to choose products to buy one in a time limiting pressure consumption environment, when branding on packaging is reduced, e.g. the brand of product has 10 different style of packages to let consumer choice, but it reduces to only 5 different style of packages to let consumer choice. How does it influence the consumer decision making when the consumer has little time to allow to choose these 5 different style of packages ? For example, when the consumer expects to spend only 10 minutes to choose any one style of package to buy drom this brand product. Currently, this brand of produxt has reduced different style of packages number from 10 to 5. Do you feel that the consumer will feel easy to do decision making to choose to buy the most attractive style of package product from this brand's 5 different style of packages choices? Is 10 minutes consumption choice time enough to let the consumer to make final purchase decision from these brand's 5 different style of packages choice? Will the time limiting pressure be reduced , due to this brand's 10 style packages are reduced to 5 style packages to let the consumer to choose within the 10 minutes expected limiting consumption choice time.

It is one interesting psychological consumption behavior to research whether the brand's reducing different style of packages number factor will influence the consumer to do the decision making in the short time in the time limiting pressure environment. For toothpaste, shapmo products example, if the brand of these products' style packages choice is reduced to 5 style packages from 10 style packages choice. When one consumer finds the brand of toothpaste or shampo has only 5 style packages on the shelves in supermarket. If the consumer has moderate or considerate amount time to let him/her to choose these both kinds product any one style of packages to buy. The 5 style packages to these both inds of products will be impossible to satisfy the consumer's choice need because he/she haas much time to stay in supermarket to choose. Otherwise, if the consumer has little time to allow to stay in the supermarket , e.g. ony 10 minutes. Then, he/she expects to spend only 10 minutes consumption choice time to do buying decision making within 10 minutes. These both kinds of the brand's products, its styl of packages choice number is reduced to 5, it is possible to satisfy the consumer's choice need to buy this brand of product either toothpaste or shampoo and both of thee brand of products to be chose to buy in the supermarket. So , the reducing style of package number to let consumer choice will be seem to let the conumer to do buying decision making in the limiting time pressure consumption environment.

In fact , package is such a visual to influence consumer decision making in the short time or personal limiting time choice process. If the product has more attractive package design, the it can bring more attention effort to influence the consumer to choose to buy the product in the short time information transfers to influence the consumer decision making to choose to buy more easily , when he/she is active in communication process. So, package, communicating with consumer in the selling place , has become an essential factor to influence the choice of consumer.

Scientific researches have proved that package decisions can attract consumer attention, transfer the desirable information abou tthe product, position , the product in consumer conscious, differentiate and identify of among similar kinds of products. In that way elements of package influence consumer decision making process and can determine the choice of consumer and the package itself can become more competitive advantage.

However it is not absolute that the brand of product has more package choices, it must have more customers to choose to buy its product. For example, there are two brands of shampoo in the supermarket shelf. One brand shampoo has 5 different style of packages and 5 different fruit productive elements to cause similar fresh fruit smells to attract consumers to buy. Another brand shampoo has 3 different style of packages and 3 different fresh fruit smells to attract consumers to buy in the same shelf location also. When one supermarket customer has little time to expect to stay in the supermarket, e.g. he expects only to stay the supermarket maximum to 15 minutes. he expects to buy one bottle shampoo and meats and fruits and vegatables within 15 minutes. Hence, he expects only to spend about 5 minutes to choose one brand of shampoo product as well as he demands to spend maximum 10 minutes to buy other foods within 15 minutes. When he stays in the shampr shelf location, he finds only two brands of shampoo products are displayed on the same shelf location. One brand of shampo has 5 different style packages to let him to choose, but he feels that these 5 diffeent style packages are not very attractive. Otherwise, the another brand of shampo has only 3 different style packages to let him to choose, but he feels that the 3 different style packages are very attractive. Due to he feels time causes pressure to choose these two brands of shampoo immediately. So, he does not want to spend more time more than 5 minutes to choose on brand of shampoo to buy. He will be influenced by the brand of different styles of packages more attraction to influence his buying decision making obviously. So, whether the shampoo brand's package is attractive or not, it will influence the consumer's buying decision making to choose either to buy the brand's shampo product in preference.

So, the more packages choice to the brand's product which may not mean that it has high opportunity to influence consumers' attention. Otherwise, the attractive package element if more important to compare right number of packages choices. Consumer package can influence these elements, e.g. colour, size, imageries, graphics, materials, smell, brand name, producer/country, information, special offers. Of the brand of products can have much attractive elements. Then, it can attract consumers to choose to buy the brand's attractive package products in short time decision making process, such as perception of needs, search for information , evaluation of alternatives, decision making, behavior after purchase. Such as supermarket case, I assume that any supermarket consumers do not expect to spend much time to choose which brand of product is the most suitable or earning more economic benefit to buy when they need to stay the shelf to need spend much time to select which brand of product to buy in the supermarket. Because in general, supermarket consumers ought plan to buy more than one kind of product or food, even more usually. So, limiting time pressure factor will influence their decision making. Similarly, as my explanation indicates why although, the product had attractive package elements and its has many packages number choices, but it does not mean that it can win the similar product which has not more attractive packages, even it has more packages choices number to let supermarket consumers to choose. So, an attractive package element factor will have more influential and potential to cause supermarket consumers to choose to buy it in the supermarket limiting time pressure consumption environment.

- How the time consumption pressure factor influences irrational consumption

decision making
When one consumer has a large number of options, he/she will feel time pressure to cause whose accurate and reasonable evaluation. Then, the personal time limiting pressure factor will bring these questions: How does the time limiting pressure influence the consumer evaluation? Will the consumer personal limiting time pressure bring advantages and / or disadvantages in whom consumption decision making? How to help the consumer to solve short time decision problem when he/she encounters extreme time pressure an dchoice overload?

I shall assume every consumer is general one economic man. He/she feels time is important, he /she does not want to spend much time to choose one brand of product to buy among a number of brands of products choices. I also assume that any consumers decision making satisfaction, which is based on search until they found a sufficiently good item, or run not of time. So, it seems that which the consumer needs to buy one kind of product, but the product has a lot number of different brands to let the consumer to choose. The consumer ought need to spend much time to make choice decision making. However, consumer is one economic man, he/she ought not to search all different brands to decide whether which brand of product can bring the much economic value or utility value to choose to buy. So, in general, consumers will only choose sample brands of products to decide to buy the satisfied brand of product. For example, when the consumer needs to buy one television. The television has 20 brands of similar televisions to let he to choose. He will not spend much time to search these similar 20 televisions information. He will only gather sample 10 to 15 or less different brands of televisions to compare what their strengths and weaknesses, unique characteristics. Then, he will make decision to choose to buy the best television from these sample televisions. Hence, in general, consumers will feel time pressure when they feel need to spend much time to choose a lot different brands of similar products. Because they feel time is not enough to let they can do other important matters when they need to spend much time to do search information behavior when they need to buy any products ususally. Hence, it is general consumers psychology that they will feel real choice under time pressure and choice overload, when they have too much a lot of similar brands of products to let them have opportunity to choose to make decision making to buy only one brand of product.

However, when a brand of product is familiar and given its simplicity and familiarity to general consumers' acknowledgement. It will have perference advantage to attract or influence consumers‘ attention or consideration. So, when the market has similar different brands of products are available to let consumers to choose. The largest choice set is not large enough to create overload to influence the brand's sale when consumers need to spend much time to choose these different brands similar products to buy. Because when the brand's any products are familiar and given its simplicity and familiarity to general consumers' knowledgement. Then, it can build utility confidence to influence general consumers , it will be preference sample brand of product to do buying making option. Hence, the brand's familiarity factor will influence general consumers‘ preference buying decision making option. So, any product manufacturers need to concern how to build its brand familiarity to let many consumers to acknowledge in order to raise its competitive effort. Raising brand's familiarity may be a good method to solve consumer individual choice under time pressure overload , because when the brand of product is preference sample

brand to any consumers. It's sale opportunity will also be raised. So, it brings the question: How can the brand of products can cause general consumers' preference choice. For food example, food brands were more likely to choose the implicitly preferred brand over the explicitly preferred one when choices were made under time pressure.
Imagining one customer enters a supermarket 10 minutes before closing time. He failed to write up a shopping list. So, when the staff is preparing to close store at the night, the consumer hurry trys not to for set too many of the ingredients for dinner . What brands of products , he opts for, as he can choose from a variety of similar foods, but time is short and the staff is looking at the consumer impatienty? It is possible that the consumer will probably quickly decide in favor of the foods he likes best, pay, and leave the evening.
Hence, supermarket consumer's first time feeling to the brand of food will influence whom choice. One target category and one attribute category share same response key: Pleasant vs unpleasant feeing, if the supermarket consumer has pleasant feeling when he sees the food photos and touchs the package of the brand of food to feel pleasant in the short supermarket closing time. Then, his pleasant feeling will be chooses to buy the brand of food to eat. Thus, the consumer individual pleasant or unpleasant feeling factor will influence whom consumption choice, such as this supermarket closing time pressure consumption.
In fact, many factors may influence whether consumer behavior is under more or less control. Hunger may influence control in the domain of eating behavior . So, such as the supermarket will close soon,it has store closing time pressure to influence the consumer needs hurry to make choice decision to buy food. If the consumer feels more hungry, he will not spend much time to find the right food to buy. He will be influenced by the different brand's food packages whether which brand of food package can bring a more pleasant to let him to feel, when he touchs and sees the brand of food package. He won't spend time to search whether the different kinds of brands of foods have how much different health elements because the supermarket will close store soon. So, he only depends his individual pleasant feeling to make final food purchase decision. If he feels all of the kinds of brands foods are unpleasant food packages when he sees and touchs them first time as well as he does not feel much hungry. Then, it is possible that he won't choose to any one food to eat. He will choose to go to restaurant to get dinner to replace buying food to cook to eat dinner at home at the night.
The another case is that time pressure concerns how on choice of information source impacts purchase decisions. When the consumer who buys one product , he needs to use the same number of information sources to search the product's information regardless of time pressure. Because he has more available time, he devotes more time , but only to selected the right sources to search information about the product. He will mostly use marketing dominant sources, e.g. magazine. he feels magazine can give more accurate information concerns to the product's good or bad quality real more reasonable and fair evaluation to let the consumer to acknowledge. so, when the consumer has much time to choose to buy which brand of product is the most best choice. He will buy magazine to find information. He believes magazine has more fair evaluation to different brands of product. It won't mislead consumers to make wrong decision making. Hence, in general, when consumers have much time to find information source to search which brand of product is more value to buy. They will attempt to buy consumer magazine to acknowledge whether

the different brands of product , which have unique characteristics, strengths or weaknesses in order to compare them to make more accurate evaluation to choose to buy which brand of the kind product. When they have no time pressure to influence their choice process time to be shortened or reduced. Otherwise, these consumers will depend on newspapers, television, radio advertisments information sources when they feel time pressure controls their consumption choice decision making process time to be shortened or reduced. Hence, time pressure will be possible to influence consumer individual information source channel choice.

● Time pressure consumption decision making process characteristics

How we can predict or know the consumer time pressure in whom decision making process? Will it bring advantages or disadvantages to influence the businessmens‘ benefits? I shall indicate some different consumption situations or environments to explain what will be impacted to sale number is increased or decreased to businesses when the consumer feel time pressure to avoid whom behavioral consumption to the product or the service.

Firstly, I shall explain that what effects of product popularity and time pressure on online shopping behaviors are . Electronic ecommerce is popular to any countries, in special, US, UK, China large areas countries, because when one customer feels need to spend one hour even more time to catch any transportation tool to arrive the shop to buy the kind of product. Then, due to far distance reason, he/she will choose to apply internet to buy the kind of product . If the seller has website to let the consumers to choose online shopping. However, it seems that online shopping behavior can reduce the consumer individual time pressure, when he/she feels need to catch any kinds of transportation tool to arrive the shop to buy the product. Moreover, when the consumer can turn on home computer to enter its website to choose the styles of the kind of products, which one is the most situable to choose. He/she can spend time to search the different styles kinds of product information to compare and evaluate which brand of product will b whose purchase choice easily at home.

Hence, in psychological view, he/she can feel that spending time to search information from internet behavior which is more valuable and it can bring more economic benefit to make final purchase decision more than the behavior of spending long time to catch any transportation tools to visit the shop. Moreover, it is possible to bring failure risk that he/she wastes time to catch any transportation tools to visit the shop if he/she can not find any one of suitable product(s) to choose to buy. Hence, it seems the online shopping can influence the consumer reduced time pressure and wastes time to do any shopping decision.

This is online shopping's attractive strengths to the consumers when they need to spend long time to catch any kinds of transportation tools to visit the shop or when the consumer feels hurry to do other important matters, he/she can not allow himself/herself to spend long time to do his/her visiting the shop behavior. Moreover, another online shopping's advantage is that product popularity can be perceived by examining the information presended on websites. For example, research on onlin reviews confirms the review quantity presented with products become positively influences to consumers' purchase intention and it can persuade the online visitor can make decision to buy the product when he/she has enter the seller's online website to find the most suitable product to choose to buy more easily. Hence, it seems that it is more easy to persuade the online visitor to make final purchase decision more than visiting the shop , when the online visitor can attempt to do the click mouse behavior to enter the seller's online shop, such as website. Then, he/she will be influenced to view the seller's different kinds of colourful and attractive product pictures from the seller's wesite.

Consequently, it has much opportunity to persuade the consumer to do the final purchase decision. if the seller's website is attractive to persuade him/her to visit its website to find any new products more than five times, even tem times or every weak several times , even day one time frequently visiting behavior from internet channel. Hence, due to internet is convenient tool to let consumers to find any product informatons from the seller's website at home or public library , computer, or mobile phone. Consumers must find any product informations any time in any places easily. So, online shopping can reduce any consumers' time pressure to visit any shops to expect to achieve final consumption decision aim in possible.

Thus, it seems that online shopping method can influence consumers to feel time saving and time presure reducing consumption both advantages more than visiting shops' shopping method when the consumer is living far away from the shop. When the consumer feels that he/she is experiencing situational time pressure, then, he/she will respond well to seek another time saving situational consumption environment. So , it explains when one consumer feels he/she has no much time to catch long time transportation tool to visit the shop on the day. When he/she has computer at home, he/she will attempt to type the shop name to research whether it has online shopping platform service from internet. Because he/she does not want to spend one hour, even more time to catch transportation tool to arrive the shop, when he/she can't walk to the shop in short time. Even, he/she may feel online shopping behavior won't influence his/her eating , sleeping, or recreational time to be reduced at home or any places , when he/she can behave the online shopping behavior at home or any where conveniently.

Consequently, promoting online shopping is as a time-saver is likely to be effective for these experiencing situational time pressure. Those with situational pressure would almost certainly welcome anything that would reduce their activity level and the demands on their time. In fact, there is really no adult learning method for store shopping because it is something everyone learns to do from early childhood. But for many adult consumers, they feel have interest to learn how to use internet and web to shopping. Some adult will feel interest and it is value to learn how to use internet channel to anticipate the complexity of shopping online. For example, Super Walmart cheap frocery store that carries many thousands of products and brands to let online shoppers won't feel confused when viewing its online merchant's home page with only a few menu items and links from its website. So, Super Walmart website can let online shoppers to feel difficult that they can save much time to enter any merchants' home page . They only need to view the Super Walmart's website ,then they can find any preference cheap grocercies to compare and evaluate which one(s) is (are) value to buy. So, Super Walmart's website can let global cheap grocery online shoppers feel it can help them to save time to find any merchant's products from internet conveniently. Consequently, online shopping will be one popular time saving consumption channel to reduce time pressure to some consumers nowadays.

Secondly, I shall explain that what determines purchase decisions for airline tickets when the traveller fees time stress. When a travelling planner has no enough time to prepare whose travelling journey, whether the time stress will influence he/she feels decision difficulties and frustration, when it will cause he/she needs to gather significant amounts of information to lead to make to choose which airline ticket is the most right choice? How and number of airline options and time pressure influence the airline ticket buyer's purchase decision?

However, there are both kinds of time pressures to influence the airline ticket buyer's airline choice decision, they focus on either real decision deadlines (physical time), such as the journey beginning day is any day of this week or tomorrow or subjective feeling of pressure with time (sense of urgency or psychological time), such as the traveller expects that he/she fears all airlines' all seats are full booked in this month. Moreover, he/she can plan to catch air plane to travel next month. So, he/she will attempt to gather any airlines' tickets prices, flight day and time and destination arrival and weather information in this month to avoid that it is too late to delay his/her next month travelling plan.

Hence, it seems that the effect of number of airlines choices and air tickets purchase deadlines (physical time limit) will influence how the traveller or air ticket buyer's purchase decision using secondary data to search of airline ticket. for example, if the traveller felt time is no enough to let him/her to go to travel agent to enquire any airlines' air tickets prices and seats and date and time air plan departure available time to concern the traveller's destination choice. Then, he/she will be probable to choose to buy electronic-ticket (e-ticket) from internet. If he/she has computer to link internet to gather any airlines' flying date and time and seat available information at home easily. Hence, it seems that one time pressure traveller will be probable to choose e-ticket purchase at home in preference. If the airline can provide online e-ticket purchase option to the time pressure traveller. Due to the pressure time traveller feels closer to departure, the negative impact of number of airline options is not as strong when he/she can view the airline's website to find the flight date, time and seat available information to purchase e-ticket to prebook the date and time to departure the traveller's country and to arrive his/her travelling destination information from the airline's website channel at home or anywhere any time conveniently. Hence, travel agency can bring a positive relationship between airline number of options and pre-booking airline that immediate possibility. When the time pressure traveller hopes the airline can build the good interactive relationship between number of options and decision time limit (number of days till planned travel effort on e-ticket purchase probabilities. So, if the airline website can let the traveller to predict when date and time is accurate available to arrive whom frequently destination choice country as well as the e-ticket's real price , it is not e-ticket preductive price and the real seats number available, it is not the estimated seats number available on the departure time and date to the travelling or arrival country destination. Then, all of these online information to the airline, which will raise the e-ticket pre-booking purchase chance to let the e-ticket buyer to make whose final e-ticket purchase choice decisin to win its e-ticket competitors easily.

Consequently, a real time e-ticket information can attract any time pressure e-ticket buyers to choose to buy its e-ticket (electronic airline ticket) more than visiting travel agent's paper airline ticket option when the travel feels hurry to buy airline ticket to travel in short time.

● Reducing time pressure consumption methods

How can sellers persuade consumers to choose to buy their products or consume their services in time pressure environment easily? It is a valuble research topic to concern how to know how consumer individual decision making to spend his/her available resources (time, money and efforts, or consumption relatd aspects) as well as how any why he/she chooses the preference brand to buy its any kind of products or consume its services, when he/she chooses to buy the brand of products or consume its services? Hence, marketers need to obtain an indepth knowledge of consumer buying behavior.

In any buying process, time factor will have about 10 % to 40 % to influence consumer decision. When the consumer feels hurry to consume, e.g. planning to go to travel, when he/she needs to choose to buy which airline's air ticket and what day and time is the right air ticket prebooking purchase decision right time choice; or enrolling which school to be choosed course to study decison, e.g. how long time is needed to be choose which school is the most suitable to provide the most suitable courses studying choce change; purchase warm clothes to wear in winter, when is the suitable time to choose to buy the cheaper warm clothers to prepare to wear in winter, e.g. Jan to Mar., April to June, July to Aug. month; when is the most suitable time to buy another new house to live, when the property consumer(buyer) has lived present house for long time, e.g. three years or more. All of these issues will include time factor to influence the consumer feels when he/she ought choose to buy the kind of product or consume the kind of service. However, the other factors will also include to influence his/her decision, e.g. family, friend relationship factor, advertising factor, social status factor, cultural difference factor, personal psychological need level or satisfactory level factor, young or old age factor, income level factor, economic environment factor, material enjoyable need factor etc. factors.

However, time pressure factor will be the consumer individual intrinsic (internal) psychological feeling factor, and it is the consumer individual intrinsic feeling to judge whether when he/she ought spend some money to buy the kind ofcnew product or the kind of consume service (what time is the most reasonable or the most suitable time) to make purchase choice decision. However, when the consumer feels hurry to make purchase decision. So, he/she will not hope to spend more time to gather more information to compare and evaluate which one is the right brand of product tochoose to buy or the right service to consume among different brands of products or services. Otherwise, if the consumer has more time or he/she can make the decision to buy any brand of product. Then, he/she ought spend more time to gather more information to compare and evaluate which one is the most suitable product choice to buy or which one is the right service choice to consume. So, time pressure factor will have some influence to any consumers to make decision about what time is the suitable time to buy the kind of product or consume the service. For example, heater product is usually when winter weather time, the heater products need number ought increase in winter weather time or season. But, it is possible that the heater products need number won't increase in winter season / weather possible, when one country , there are many householders or families , they have one heater number at least at home. Then, it is possible that these householders or families won't have consumption desires to buy one more heater product to use in winter at home, because they have had one heater to use at home in winter. So , when the country has have many customers number, they are using the kind of heater products at homes. Most people own at least one heater number factor will have possible to influence enough time available to cause they do not feel hurry to buy any heaters to use at homes, so, their do not feel time pressure to buy any heaters in short time. Because they do not plan to buy the kind of product to use at home in short time when they have one heater product at least to use at homes in present.

Hence, it brings this question: How to attract or persuade the customers, they are using the kind of product to let they feel time pressure to make decision to buy another new or same brand of product to replace to use? The product's better quality , long durable time useful, brand loyalty and past good purchase experience factors will influence him/her to feel time pressure to need to buy another new product in short time. So,when the consumer feel time pressure to make decision to purchase, he/she will choose when is the most right time to gather information, search, select, use and dispose of another new product to replace the old product in the short time.

Hence, the brand of product needs have good product motives, may be raised to the consumer's impluse, desires, considerations which make the buyer purchase the brand's new product to replace the present using product in order to achieve whose satisfactory needs to emotional product motives and rational product motives both. Moreover, persuading or encouraging the consumer feels he/she has real need to buy the kind of new product or replace the present old product (s), the brand of product marketer needs let the consumer feels these any one of nature of motive to raise his/her purchase decision desire in time pressure environment. The natures of motive may include: When the consumer feels desire for saving money, he/she will choose to buy it when the brand of product falls down, when he/she feels fear to be sickness, retirement, he/she will choose to buy insurance policy, when he/she feels pride, or high social status knowledgement, he/she will buy premium product , e.g. gold, expensive watch, car , when he/she feels fashion need, he/she will move house to live from rural to urban, or rural people imitate urban to learn to do their fashion living behavior, when he/she feels possession need, he/she will feel need to buy antiques for its future unique worth satisfactory feeling in possible, when he/she feels health need, he/she will choose to buy health foods, join memebership in health clubs, when he/she needs to enjoy comfortable feeling, he/she will feel need to buy micro-oven, washing machine to use at home, when he/she feels love and affection need, he/she will buy gift items to give to whose friends or families for presents in their birthday or lover day etc. special days to let they to feel happy. So, when the marketer can touch the consumer individual different nature of motives to satisfy his/her personal purchase feeling need and it can know how to influence them to feel that they have these any one of purchase motive needs in short time. Then, they will be persuaded to raise time pressure to make purchase decison to buy any kind of products in short time.

However, instead of attractive good product quality method can attempt consumers to make time pressure consumption behavior. The another method is brand loyalty building method, which can be attempted to encourage or persuade consumers to feel consumption desire need to make decision to buy the brand of any products in time pressure consumption environment. For example, when the consumers feel the brand is loyalty and it can build good image to his/her feeling , and this time pressure factor can inlfuence this brand of any products which has high discount price to attract the consumer individual attention , e.g. familiar brand high class cars, the good confident house agent's high class houses, and the expensive and infrequently buying items, come under this category. When their prices are fallen down to sell cheaper , e.g. twenty per cent discount or more than twenty percent discount sale price than the other similar competitive brands' any products' normal prices. Then, it is possible to let these expensive items' consumers have high involvement and high feeling need in time pressure consumption environment. Because they assume that this discount sale price will be short time sale price, e.g. after three months or next month etc. short time discount sale price in short time period. Then, these expensive items' prices will be raised to the normal sale price, even higher price. so, they have time pressure feeling to feel that it is right time to make consumption decision in order to avoid to lose these low price purchase benefit in this unpredictive cheap discount price purchase items. so, if the expensive item marketer can build long time good brand loyalty relationship to consumers. Then, it will have much influential effort to persuade consumers feel consumption desires need by its any extensive items in the unpredictive short term discount period, due to they do not want to loss this large discount purchase price chance. So, short time discounted sale price, it is another method to persuade consumers to choose to buy the brand's any products in short time pressure consumption environment.

The another persuading time pressure consumption method is that it can let consumers to think more habitual buying the kind of products. products like stationery, groceries, food etc. fall under this category. For example, when the consumer fees the brand of any products ,he/she has habitual purchase experience, of he/she feels that the brand's any products won't sell in market temporary, even he/she can not buy it to use again. Then, it is possible to infuence him/her to feel immediate purchase need to buy a lot of product or food number to keep to use or eat later in the time pressure environment, e.g. the food consumer buys the brand of any breads to eat in supermarkets habitually, but in this moth, he/she watchs TV advertisement to be acknowledge this brand of any breads won't be bought from any supermarkets as soon as possible. Hence, it is possible to influence him/her to plan to make choice to buy a lot of number of this brand of any breads in order to keep the enough of this brand of breads number to eat later. So, this brand of any breads sale loss in supermarkets that will cause the habitual food consumers of this brand of breads, whom make consumption choice to buy a lot number of this brands any breads in short time suddenly. Because they are eating this brand of any kinds of breads habitually. They feel much eating need to lot number of this brand of any breads in short period, because it can satisfy their habitual taste needs of this brand's any kinds of breads. So, brand loyalty and habitual consumption to the kind of product or food , ehich will result simply from the habit and it can influence the consumers feel consumption need to buy the brand's any kinds of products or foods when they feel that they may not buy it again or they can not earn discount advantage after the short time. So, any one of these sale strategies will have possible to raise the consumer individual consumption desire to the brand of products in the short time pressure consumption environment. Also it needs to spend much time to gather information in order to make purchase decision, because the brand had built confidence to consumers when they feel this brand's any products or foods are better to compare the similar brands' any products or foods habitually. So, time pressure consumption environment will persuade them to feel consumption desire to buy this brand's any products or foods in short time. When, they fer that they can not buy any more for this brand's any kinds of products or foods or discounting price in this final short purchase time.

In conclusion, these factors can influence consumer behaviors to be changed to feel time pressure need to do purchase decision making behavior from encough time gathering information available feeling behavior. They have these same views, e.g. habits and routines are very influential, particularly for behaviors repeated daily in a semi-automatic fashion. The consumer's past purchas experience to the brand's products, positive or negative emotion to the brand's products, and the brand's familization, recognition are strong influence , the information available , it is the consumer's mind and the relative important information given to let the consumer knows form different advertisement medias matters for decision making, greating between pieces of information and can be influenced by personal psychological timing limited pressure, the consumer's comparison to differences in price or other characteristics, many pursue value (or in bargain), and compare to alternatives or past knowledge, consumer personal greater value on the immediate future and heavily disocunt future costs or savings to the brand of product, feeling simple and easy decision making process to the product , it can lead the consumer to avoid to spend long time to make purchasing decision and the consumer will easy to choose to buy the product when he/she feels have a loss value if he/she does not decide to buy the product in the short time. SO, it seems that when the marketer can motivate the consumer's consumption desire to feel saving money, promote health, avoid waste time and less nervous workload to gather information for comparison and evaluation alternatives aim. It is seen favorably by the consumer personal time pressure purchase decision making and sense of justice influence factors.

However, sociologists have categorised the motives for consumption behaviors in the short time by the fundamental consumption decision making needs or wants which they satisfy, e.g. having a clear understanding what benefits, characteristics, economic value to the brand's any products , feeling consumption decision making process is a leisure activity. These drivers for consumption behaviorw will either bring positive or negative to influence the consumer personal emotion, either owning enough time available or time pressure environmental impacts can be seen to influence whether the consumer feels he/she needs how long time to be spent to make comparison and evaluate alternatives in order to make final purchase choice in whom decision making process. Hence, the consumer himself/herself time pressure consumption decision making feeling, it can bring positive purchase choice influence,when the marketer can build brand loyalty to let many consumers to feel in the market. Otherwise, if the marketer can not build brand loyalty to let many consumers to feel, but consumers feel time pressure to compare and evaluate its any products to other similar brands of products in the competitive market. Then, its products may be not the preference choices the many customers among the different brands of products choices. So, building long time brand loyalty relationship to satisfy consumers' needs, it will bring positive preference purchase choice to raise the sale effort to the brand of any products when consumers need to make purchase choice in time pressure consumption environment, e.g. seasonal discount sale period, products or foods shortage supply period, without any forever sale possibility in market. Hence , it seems that brand loyalty building factor will influence any brands of products /foods /service sale or provison number to be raised or reduced in possible. Also, it can explain why and how it has close cause and effect relationship between time pressure consumption environment and the brand loyalty building to the brand of products/foods/services to any marketers nowadays.

● What are the in-store and out-store time pressure
factors influence supermarket fast moving
consumer decision

It is one interesting question: How can the brand of product seller influence the supermarket/store fast-moving consumers' more visual attention when the supermarket/store visitor is hurry to make decision to choose to buy which brand of product in time pressure environment? Supermarket/store fast-moving consumers do not usually spend much time to say in any supermarket shelf locations to choose numerous similar alternative brands of products. However, I assume the fast-moving supermarket/store consumer's decision is dependent on the interaction between the supermarket different shelf location sale environment and the mind of the consumer. So, the eye tracking explores this rapid processing that lacks conscious access or control to any supermarket or store consumers. It brings this question: How product packing and placement (as in-store factors) and recognition, preferences, and choice task (as out-of-store factors) which will influence the supermarket / store consumer individual decision making process through visual attention. In split-second decision making, the ability to recognize and comprehend a brand of supermarket/store product can significantly impact preferences. Hence, how the supermarket/store consumer's eye truly sees what whom mind is prepared to influence how much consumption desire to choose to buy the brand's product in short tim decision making process when he/she stays in the shelf location, it has less than ten or more than ten different kinds of brands products or foods to let the visitor to choose in the supermarket or store.
Brand owners and product developers will feel responsibilities to overcome promotion or advertising or communicaton challenge in order to let consumers to know their products are launched on the market. However, it is not until the product reaches the supermarket shelf that has good quality to the effort is judged whether it has how much sale number every day in the supermarket. The judges are the consumers themselves how to make decision quickly through the personal time pressure environment with minor package information processing in the supermarket.

What does it take to be consider an option to influence the consumers' minds on visual attention in point-of-purchase decision making ? The supermarket's in-store activities and the consumer personal out-of-store activities will influence how his / her visual attention to the brand of products in the supermarket / store any shelf locations when he/she is walking to pass any shelf locations. So, it seems that any supermarkets or stores brands of products sale number , it has relation to every supermarket or store visitors' visual attention throughout the point to point (shelf to shelf) decision making process in the supermarkets / stores. So, how much does the supermarket's visitors' time spending to obtain attention to the brand of produc? it will have possible to influence the brand of any products' sale number in the supermarket/store. Hence, in this limited timeframe, the consumer enters a decision making process that is in itself influenced by in-store and out-of-store both factors.

I shall explain what is supermarket / store space quality factor, e.g. top level versus floor level to different shelf variable height, weigh , or shelf space location factor as well as the product price elasticity and price-quality relationship to the brand of products both factors to influence every consumer decision making in supermarket/ store. The in-store factor is more influential factor to compare out-of-store factor to influence consumers' decision in supermarket. For example, where the shampoo brand products are locating to be put on the shelf , it can influence the point to point behavior of shampoo product habitual buyers. If the buyer habitually chooses the shampoo brand products in the shelf location. Also, if all of the shampoo brand products are moved to another shelf locations to display its different kinds of shampoo products to cause the habitual buyer needs to spend much extra time to find where the another new shelf location is displaying the brand's shampoo products.

In this situation, information processing has a heightened decision making role as the buyer needs to spend much time to find where the brand's displayed shampoo products' shelf location to make non-habitual decision making between options. For habitual decisons, the consumer's visual attention is reduced to measuring visual search. However, when the brands of any shampoo products are moved to another new shelf location to display its different kinds of shampoo products. So, the act of another shelf new location search , it will influence the habitual shampoo buyer's visual attention to consider the brand of any shampoo products which are usually used to wash to his/her hair habitually. When he / she can find the other new brands of shampoo products are displayed on the old shelf displayed location of the brand of shampoo products. Hence, the traditional shelf displayed location to the brand of products, when the brand of products are moved to another new displayed shelf locations. This in-store factors that will influence traditional cosnumers through visual attention concerns to this brand of products more or less.

So, supermarket traditional shelf displayed variable location to the brand of products factor, which will have influence to the traditional consumers' visual attention to do either buying the brand's products or buying another brand's products to replace it, when the traditional consumer feels difficult that he/she needs to spend extra longer time to find whether where is the traditional useful product's displayed shelf location. Then, it will be possible to influence the traditional consumer's traditional purchase decision to the brand's product, and he/she will choose to buy another brand of product to replace when it can be displayed to the shelf location to attract the consumer's visual attention more.

It is one important in-store shelf displayed factor to influence the traditional fast-moving consumer individual purchase decision making behavioral change in any supermarkets or stores when they feel hurry to do personal time pressure consumption decision to make purchase final decision in the point to point counter purchase (the brand's of products are moved from the traditional shelf location visual attention moves to the strange shelf location visual attention) in supermarket time pressure consumption environment.

Hence, in supermarket time pressure consumption environment, in -store and out-of-sore both factors can influence fast-moving consumer individual purchase decision making. The in-store factors can influence product packaging, product placement components as well as the out-store factors can influence choice task, preference and brand recognition components. So, it is common to influence supermarket consumers choose do personal time pressure purchase consumption decision of visual attention purchase behaviors. The different brands' products are displayed to different shelf locations in order to cause shelf displaying products' different decision making effect.

However, instead of shelf displaying location factor, package will also influence consumers' decision making, due to the influence of minute differences in packaging design on visual attention. When, the supermarket consumer feels the brands are not familiar or unfamiliar. Then, he/she will spend more time to evaluate and verify the unfamiliar brands' products whether which one is value to buy in her/his decision making process. He/she will feel visual attention need in order to evaluate in set of brand alternatives to make conscious demand mind cognitive effort by involving working memory. So, if the product's package is attractive, even the consumer is unfamiliar the brand's any product choices which are displayed on the shelf location in the supermarket. The brand's attractive package factor can influence the consumer to raise whom visual attention. Then, the attractive package factor can increase much visual attention chance to many consumers when they are walking to pass through the unfamiliar brand's any products' shelf displaying location considerably. So, it explains when attractive package factor may solve the visual attention problem to fast-moving consumers when they are visiting one strange supermarket to find anywhere unfamiliar brand's products' shelf displaying locations. Because they are the non-traditional consumers to the unfamiliar brand's products, they won't be influenced to choose either buying or not buying the unfamiliar brand's products. When the unfamiliar brand's products are moved to another new shelf displayed location. So, if the unfamiliar brand has attractive package to let the non-traditional consumers feel visual attention when they are passing through the strange shelf displayed location. Then, it can raise purchase chance to the non-traditional consumers target number when they are staying in the strange supermarket.

In conclusion, the brand of products' shelf displaying location and package factors may bring much influence to any traditonal or non-traditonal consumer behaviors in supermarket or store time pressure consumption environment.

Airline fuel long time air pollution reduces frequent travellers' travelling times

If one airline's fuel often bring long time air pollution when it's airplanes fly on sky, it is possible to cause the environment protection travellers choose to catch other airlines' airplanes when they believe their fuel can not pollute air more than the airline. Even, if the airlines' airplances can not reduce air pollution when they often fly on sky. Then it will influences many frequent travellers reduce travelling number and they will change to choose short trip more than long trip, due to short trip airplane can reduce to spend much fuel to pollute air. I shall explain why and how airline fuel long time air pollution will influence the environment protection mind of travellers' travelling needs to be reduce as below:

In recent years, social, economic and environment pressures have pushed airlines to accept their social responsibility. Closely tied to this acceptance is a corporate policy that aims at raising social and environmental standards on a voluntary basis and that means beyond legal and contractual requirement. It means that corporate social responsibility is not just an optional

consideration to core airline business activities, such as airlines industry fuel consumption pollutes sky air to cause global warming problem. Rather, Ryanair airline needs to concern social responsibility because it's fuel emissions would cause negative influence to stakeholders. e.g. causing bad negative climate to influence farmers to grow rice and vegetables etc foods successfully, so global warming will make farmers stakeholder can not earn more income and food buyers stakeholder won't eat rice and vegetables etc. foods easily, even global warming will damage natural environment to cause strong wind or strong raining or water natural hazard to damage any countries' houses to make house owners stakeholder who lose their houses to live. Hence, in the long term, if Ryanair airline still continue consume too much fuels to use to fly to cause emissions to pollute air to any countries as well as other airlines do not achieve any actions to reduce to consume to use more fuels together efficiently. I believe that global warming will become very serious to influence human living and eating problem occurrence in our earth as soon as possibly. Hence, such as Ryanair airline is among of global airlines, which have responsibility to consider how to reduce fuel consumption to cause too much emissions to pollute air in our earth. Such as, I was Ryanair airline marketing manager , I ought need to let Ryanair airline to measure whether it ought only concern how to sell cheaper air fares and buy many airplanes and consume much fuels to fly to raise income or it ought concern it's fuel emissions to pollute environment to cause global warming to influence global human stakeholders encounter living and eating problem to face natural foods resource shortage to supply in the future.

The ecological concerns global warming problem is serious nowadays, it brings the possible long term harmful consequences of executive emissions to the atmosphere. The developed countries, such as Northern Europe and United States people needed often to play travel entertainment by airlines transportation choice. However, scientists proved airlines used fossil fuels to harm excessive emissions to natural environment which would cause global warming problem to cause devastation of low lying areas to influence natural environment danger, even the developing countries people life and their houses would also encountered to be hazarded in the long term. If I was the marketing manager of an airline, such as Ryanair, I must concern socially responsible needs to Ryanair airline. Although, Ryanair aircraft had become more efficient in use of fuel during 1990 years, but Ryanair airline's passengers were booming demand to cause to increase aeroplane numbers to supply to satisfy passengers' travel needs and to pursue raising profit aim every year.

In fact, Ryanair airline used fuels to give energy to push aeroplanes to fly and it also polluted sky air during it's aeroplanes often were flying to cause global warming. For example, Ryanair airline marketing strategy was low fare prices to attract to increase many passengers to choose to attract to increase many passengers to choose to sit it's aeroplanes and it designed a cheap weekend break by Mediterranean travel to increase the unknown and remote possibilities of global warming. Hence, Ryanair would increased many new airplanes to increase to use fossil fuels of excessive emissions to the atmosphere to cause the effects of aid rain, poor climate change , destructive winds, rising sea levels and devastation of low lying areas by global warming bad consequences. Hence, it seemed that Ryanair airline had responsibility to concern how to protect natural environment due to its airplanes numbers and passengers were increasing to cause to increase to use more fossil fuels to cause the possible long term harmful consequences of excessive emissions to the sky to bring global warming occurrence nowadays. As I was this Ryanair airline marketing manager, I shall recommend Ryanair airline needed to consider this global warming socially responsible issue due to its airplanes spent too much fossil fuels to cause harmful consequences of excessive emissions to the sky. It would bring threats to developing countries people life and houses by global warming, so it concerned only how to raise itself interest marketing behavior of performance, but it neglect the serious global warming to cause bad influence to any developing countries people life danger, it was possible that passengers would feel it was not a socially responsible airline company, so it could not build a good image to whom in this airline industry and its further passengers would choose its other competitors (socially responsible airline companies) to substitute its airline service provision.

● Why does Ryanaia airline's airplane fuel causes long time flying air pollution influences environment protection traveller's other airlines choices

I shall indicate Ryanair airline's fuel how influences serious air pollution to lead travellers‘ other airlines choices. I should suggest Ryanair airline needed to control fossil fuel numbers to reduce to harm excessive emissions to natural environment seriously and it could spend much expenditure to buy good quality of fossil fuels to active the reduction of too much emissions to damage natural environment aim and it could shorten the sky flying distance to fly to other countries' airports from its airport to aim to attempt to reduce to use much fuel to pollute sky air per day and it could cancel some long flight flying routes and increased short flight flying routes to reduce flight spending hours to attempt to reduce to use fossil fuels to provide every airplanes to fly to pollute sky air every day.

Although, these marketing strategies would be possible to reduce airline income, but it would also attract many further passengers to choose to sit to its airplanes to go to travel if it could build good image to prove it was a socially responsible airline to serve passengers to let them to like to choose to use its flying service to go to travel willingly, even it could lead other airlines to follow it to use its marketing strategic methods to reduce to spend too much fossil fuels to pollute sky air to raise global warming problem seriously together. Hence, if Ryanair airline could attempt to achieve to reduce the fossil fuel numbers to use to airplanes to fly , it was possible that the other airline companies should follow it to do the same behaviors to aim to do social responsible organizations to concern how to reduce the global warming problem to cause to harm to our natural environment seriously for long term in the future.

The case study refers to apparent hypocrisy of clients who may claim to be concerned about the environment, but nevertheless continue to fly what might bring about a narrowing of this gap between what consumers think and what they actually do?

In fact, some apparent hypocrisy of consumers who may claim to be concerned about the global warming harmful natural environment problem due to airline companies, e.g. Easy Jet,
Ryanair etc. western countries‘ airlines which allowed fossil fuels produced harmful consequences of excessive emissions to atmosphere, but nevertheless continue to fly. However, I might recommend these methods to bring about a narrowing of this gap between what consumers think and what they actually do.

I think to bring a narrowing of this gap between consumers were happy to carry on airplanes to fly and it would not influence them to concern about climate change problem at the same time.

There was certainly a possible that governments would intervene. Such as the UK government and European commission had floated the idea of taxing aviation fuel and brought aircraft emissions within scope of the European emission trading scheme. Thus, if these western countries governments raised to charge aviation fuel taxing, it would possible to threaten any western airlines to shorten any flight routes hours and flight flying distance to fly to destination of the countries' airports from these airline companies' every country's airport, so which would not need to use more fuels for its airplanes to use if it had shorten flight flying routes distance to arrive other countries' airports. Hence, the airlines did not want to pay higher aviation tax to government, so which would attempt to shorten some flight flying routes from long distance to be short distance when their airplanes needed to fly to some other countries' airport to aim to buy less fuel numbers or which would not buy more airplanes.

Due to they needed to pay high aviation tax expenditure to their countries governments every year. Thus, it was possible that high fuel tax expenditure would cause airlines to shorten flight routes time. The most important, when some airlines decided to buy less fuels. These airlines might bring about a narrowing of this gap between what consumers think and what they actually do and these airlines were possible to raise their competitive ability, due to which would possible to persuade the concerned environment protective passengers who would choose to buy these airlines air tickets to more than to buy the other airlines' air tickets. Due to some airlines could not reduce to buy more fuel numbers to provide their airplanes to fly and which would increase air pollution to sky seriously, those airlines' spending excessive long hours (time) of every flight flying routes to fly to different countries' airports which would use more fuel to fly to cause air pollution to harm natural environment seriously and which would let these clients to feel unhappy to choose to buy air tickets to sit their airplanes possibly. Hence, different governments raised aviation tax would cause many airlines to reduce to buy too much fuel numbers to use possibly. It seemed that airlines needed have a social responsible duty to concern they needed to buy more fuels if they increased airplanes numbers, then they would raise air pollution to cause global warming problem seriously. Hence, I think passengers would not buy air tickets to fly to travel by airplanes when who would have long days of holidays. Otherwise, who would choose to stay at home or who would choose to go to travel by cruises on water transportation on their holidays. However, in western developed economies, legislation to enforce environmentally sensitive methods of productive is increasing, so airlines might adopt environmentally sensitive flight service processes to gain a competitive advantages. The challenges of using fuels resources in more efficient and less polluting way has achieved research and development, e.g. wind power research, solar panels, heat pumps and carbon capture technology have presented opportunities for airlines to improve the efficiency of fuels and airline marketing to business and individual group passengers.

Legal actions to place control over the emission of air pollutants have been instituted in several ways, such as the form of a public nuisance low. This is when conditions cause discomfort, inconvenience, damage to property or injury from airlines fuels to cause air pollution. The governments have also intervened in the protection of the public to threaten the airlines' fuels emissions pollute air in the sky. As a result of much research, devices for pollution control have been developed, guidelines for air quality were established fuels tax increasing incentives were introduced to enforce ordinances for restricting the emission from airplanes' fuels. For example, governments can pass the clean air act, legislation to reduce air pollution in their countries. In conclusion, airlines can co-operate environmentally friendly management to prevent global warming, it is as a part of its corporate social responsibility and makes company wide efforts to do by saving energy and reducing aircraft fuel emissions. Hence, global airlines ought plan to achieve to reduce to consume excessive fuel emissions to reduce a narrowing of this gap between what consumers think and what they actually do concerned about the environment pollution was caused by airlines if which still wanted to make travelers who prefer to choose to go to travel by flying more than other water or ground transportation etc. methods.

How Easy Jet airline's fuel air pollution reducing measure and brings positive consumer's attitudes?

For another Easy Jet airline has created environment problems, e.g. harmful chemicals sift down from smoky trails of low-flying jets. The scream of Easy Jet airline engines is constantly heard by people who love near big city airports. It's aircrafts produce air pollution with consequent changes in climate.

It is a fact that many people prefer air travel rather than ground or water transportation, This has promoted a critical look at safety and quality control. Contributions to air pollution is a chief concern because of this revolutionary change in public transportation in the United States and around the world. The government must also establish standards for exhaust emissions. Thus, Easy Jet airline measure and monitor consumer's attitudes which needs to indicate to let them to believe that which suggests which airplane manufacturers are forced to develop low pollutant engines. Due to the problem of air pollution from its airplanes involve a complex set of interactions among technical, social and economic factors. Hence, it also needs to measure it's emission from Easy Jet aircrafts, particularly on landing and take offs, are a source of bitter complaints from nearby residents. In a few airports visibility has been dangerously restricted by particulate emissions and photo chemical smog. Easy Jet airline also needed to have energy savings activities to its operations, ranging from procedural and flight plan improvement to reduce flight distance and attitude and weight management and it also needed to create energy through maintenance to achieve to continue to reduce co2 emissions by introducing high efficiency aircraft and through other measures to monitor consumers' attitudes . In line with its aim to be an environmentally friendly airline that harmonizes the needs of natural , humans and airline businesses. It aims to be respected by society , live up to its social responsibilities and make a contribution to society. Although emissions from aircraft are not included among greenhouse gas reduction targets, but it also needed to make systematic efforts to improve energy efficiency and reduce emissions by creating a road map to actively participate . Furthermore, Easy Jet airline also needed continually to pursue a management style that concerns nature, people and fellow corporations, even under the most severe conditions as a major practice toward implementing its environmental policy. Easy jet airline achieves environment goals to measure and monitor consumer's attitudes, such as minimizes energy and resource consumption and introduces up to date and fuel efficient fleet and engines and develops and apply energy efficient operation technique, it establish strict internal environmental standards to set internal standards that are stricter than general environment laws applied worldwide and minimize pollutants through systematic management and observance of standards. It systematically analyses the airlines' environmental impact and make the outcome to carry out reductions and evaluates the environmental impact of its aviation operations, maintenance and service and improves environmentally friendly processes and it continually improves environmental systems through feedback .

In conclusion, Easy Jet airline can increase the recycling of waste to reduce fuel consumption of resources and it can make systematic efforts to reduce emissions by creating a roadmap and actively participating in global warming by saving energy and reducing aircraft emissions through engine washing to aim to consume fuels efficiency and reduce emission to pollute air.

What might be the avoiding environment protection travellers‘ reducing travelling numbers consequences for the marketing of a budget airline of Government policy measures which have the effect of doubling air fares in real terms?

If the country Government decided to raise higher flight fuel tax charge policy to budget airline. Due to the country Government hoped budget airline to reduce fuels consumption to provide to airplanes to use to reduce sky air pollution to cause global warning problem. In fact, budget airline needed to increase to use much fuels to provide to many flights to carry on passengers travel needs. Generally, budget airline would not like to choose to reduce to consume much fuels due to it's passenger numbers had been increasing. If budget airline decided to buy less fuels to reduce much fuels to consume for its flight needs. It would lose many passengers if it had not enough times of flights to provide airplanes to fly to different countries' airports to satisfy passengers‘ different flight route choices. However, the consequences for budget airline would also be passengers to choose to buy budget airline air tickets possibly if it decided to raise doubling air fares in real terms. Due to budget airline hoped to compensate its loss if it's country Government raised higher fuels tax to cause budget airline needed to pay high cost expenditure every year. Hence, budget airline needed to raise to spend two kinds of expenditure every year, such as purchasing more fuels expenditure and paying more fuels expenditure both. For long term, budget airline would choose to raise doubling or more air fairs in real terms in order to reduce to need to pay too much feel tax expenditure to compensate it's loss every year. In result, it's passengers would feel it's air tickets fares were not reasonable raised to compare it's other airline competitors, but it's flight services were not excellent to compare it's airline competitors specially. Hence, it's increasing air fares would cause many passengers to choose other airline competitors possibly.

How the budget airline implement avoiding long time fuel air pollution strategy to attract environment protection travellers' choice

Marketing manger might use cost benefit analysis to let budget airline to know how to invest in intangible asset, such as corporate social responsibility to give long term benefit to itself budget airline. I suggest this marketing manager needs to explain the reason why reducing fuel consumption is an investment in intangible asset to budget airline as below:

Airline transport has increasingly become a global technologically and dynamic growth industry. However, airline companies need to remain committed to satisfy the clients‘ growing demands in a sustainable manner when at the same time maintaining an optimal balance between economic progress, social development and environmental responsibility. The concept of corporate social responsibility is a challenge for who to face today's risky, competitive and complex airline business environment. There has been a need for airlines in the airline industry to develop an environment agenda and take measures to minimize the ever increasing environmental impacts created by their activities. The forms of corporate social responsibility in the airline sector includes working in partnership with local communities, socially sensitive investment as well as involvement in activities for conservation of the environment. The fact, airlines are spewing 20% more co2 into the environment then previously estimated and there is a tendency for amount to increase to 1.5 billion tons a year by 2025 year. So, airline industry must need to innovative, environmentally responsible industry that drives economic and social progress. It has risks (social, environmental, operational, threat, strategic and financial risks) that they have to deal with marketing managers airlines, such as budget airline marketing manager is responsible for the optional decision making about corporate risks in its daily business. Adrian, (P. 2012) indicated that the marketing manager of budget airline needs to indicate the benefits can be categorized into three namely to let budget airline to feel as below:

(a) Regarding the economic view, budget airline is essential for facilitating world business and tourism, it needs to create jobs and enables the expansion of trade across the global by opening
up new market opportunities. It also attracts businesses to locations all over the world, hence satisfying the mobility requirement of a growing portion of the world's population. It also aids in the movement of products and services quickly over long distance facilities economies and social participation by remote communities.

(b) From the social perspective, budget airline forms an unique global transport network that links people in different countries safely and efficiently. Air transport is increasingly accessible to a large number of people who can now afford to travel by air for pleasure and its business purpose.

(c) Lastly, in terms of the environmental perspective, there is a need for budget airline to minimize or contain the impact in its environment through the continuous improvement of its
fuel consumption, noise reduction and the introduction of new technologies. Budget airline marketing manager can enquire this question to whose company, such as how budget airline can quantify the benefits derived from such investments to do with how to quantify the benefits, so budget airline can be compared to the cost of investments. Through budget airline has be different over the years to value many intangibles, such as corporate social responsibilities. Budget airline marketing manager needs to make choices among several alternatives: it is important to adopt a tool that with allow choices to clearly weigh and distinguish between the options available. So, budget airline marketing manager needs to persuade whose company to believe to maximize the gain, which may be either economic or social and may be beneficial to an individual, a group or society at large, e.g. reducing fuel cost can maximize economic or social benefits for long term. The measurement of benefits from corporate social responsibility policy includes gains from additional income to an increased quality of life or a cleaner environment.

On the other hand, the costs are made up of the opportunities forgone, internal and external costs and externalities. For instance, increasing the flying route for budget airline, the noise and air pollution are the externality when the secondary effect could be an increase in the cost operations. In this case, the pollution creates the new cost (externality). The budge airline business cost is the increase in the cost of operating the additional route. The budget airline's fuel consumption causes air pollution will influence whose client stakeholders' powers of seeing and thinking, cultural setting, experience is from the past and motivation at the time of sensing to the airline image to be poor due to who will feel the budget airline is not a social responsible organization. It aims to earn profits from passengers, but it neglects to take care other stakeholders benefits due to its fuel consumption to pollute environment to cause global warming problem. It seems that budget airline needs to considerate to use more fuel consumption to cause global warming problem more than doubling air fares in real terms if Government decided to raise more fuel tax charging to it to reduce its income.

I suggest marketing manager of a budget airline to reduce to use more fuels to pollute air, so budget airline does not decide to increase double air fairs charges to clients due to Government raises fuel taxation expenditure. Because it will cause clients to cancel its air tickets if who feel its air fairs are not reasonable to raise prices to compare other airline competitors. The marketing manager of a budget airline might respond to promote this navigation system to persuade budget airline does not choose to double air fares if Government raised fuel taxing charge. Innovation of flight operation on the optimum routes using (RNAV) Area navigation, as conventional airways and routes between airports were built by connecting ground navigation aids to the destination, the budget airline often became rather inefficient. On the other hand, RNAV can build routes connected any points with almost straight line by confirming aircraft position by means of global positioning system etc in addition to radio navigation destination of fuel consumption and CO2 emission through shortened flight time and distance. Other reducing fuel consumption include reduction of aircraft weight, use of new type point for aircraft painting to reduce emission of polluted to air . Hence, budget airline will spend less fuels to avoid to pay high fuels taxation expenditure to its Government and it does not need to charge double air fairs in real terms to cause many passengers who will choose to find other airlines to buy cheaper air tickets or who will cancel their budget airline air tickets due to who feel budget airline charges unreasonable air fairs. So, if budget airline did not achieve as above any methods to attempt to reduce fuel consumption, I believe that it will lose many passengers due to it decide to charge doubling air fares in real terms to compensate its fuel tax increasing expenditure .

Consumer behavioral factors influence theory

To research consumer behavior, it has different theory to explain why and how the consumer is influenced to make the choice by different factors. For example, utility theory,it explains that consumers make choices based on the expected outcomes of their decisions. They are viewed as rational decision makers and they only consider self interest.

Utility theory views consumer is as a " rational economic man". However, the factors influence consumer behaviors may include these activities, such as need recognition, information search, evaluation of alternatives, the building of purchase intention , the act of purchasing choice, consumption and finally disposal. Hence, it seems that all the consumer's activities in whose purchase processes. They will influence their choice. For example, when the property purchase consumer , he plans to research different kinds of properties information concern price, location, housing areas, room numbers, building facilities and environment facilities. He will find some sample target properties information to make comparison in order to decide to buy which of property is the most suitable to satisfy his living need.

However, it is not only one activity for the property purchase buyer in his decision making process. It also include evaluation of alternatives activitiy when he ensures the accurate property information number in order to evaluate whether which one of all these property choices is the most suitable one. Hence, it explains that property information research and evaluation of alternatives both activities are needed to spend much time for this property buyer. If he does not plan to find one property to live in short time, it is possible that he can spedn one month, even more than one month or more than three months time to do the only property information gathering activity.

Hence, it seems that time factor is not the main factor to influence the property buyer to do property purchase decision immediately. Otherwise, if the property buyer plans to find one new property to live within one month. Then, time factor is possible one important factor to influence this property purchase chocie decision. For example, if he felt that he needs more time to spend to gather information concerns the large house area size and the properties have more than three bathrooms and/or bedrooms properties information. Then, he will be possible not to find any this kinds of all property information. So, it means that all these properties won't be his choice. It is because long time property information gathering activity factor influnce.

I assume that the property buyer is a economic man and he does not spend much time to do the property information gathering activity. So, this kind of property needs him to spend long time to gather properties inforation in order to make this kind of properties comparison. Moreover, because he expects to live one new property within one month. So, he only chooses the properties, they have less than three bedrooms and/or bathrooms to gather sample properties information in order to make property purchase decision within one month. Hence, the time variable factor can only influence the property purchaser when he/she needs to make decision to buy one new property to live in the short time. If some kinds of properties choices number has a lot and the property buyer feels to let that he/she must need to spend long time to find the suitable properties number to make evaluation alternatives comparison behavior.

Then, the time variable limiting pressure factor will be possible the main factor to influence the property buyer's choice in order to make the most suitable kind of property purchase decision. Hence, it is one case example of how time limiting pressure factor can influence consumer purchase choice decision, such as property purchases market case. The reason explains why the property buyer needs to spend time to do property information gathering. I assume that general property buyer behave rationally in the economic sense. They won't only believe property agent individual property photos advertisement , it concerns where the property location is and facility etc. information on property photos in order to evaluate whether the property price is reasonable to pay. Generally, property buyers need to attempt to gather property information and visit the different actual property locations to make choice. So, general property consumers would have to be aware of all the available different kinds of properties consumptin options from themselves properties information gathering and the properties agents' verbal properties introduction both be capable of correctly rating each property alternative and the available to select the optimum course of the final property purchase action.

Hence, in the property purchase and sold market, limiting time pressure factor will be important influential factor to decide whether the kinds of properties will be option to some property buyers when they feel need to find one suitable property to buy in short time. Otherwise, in some food consumption market , time limiting pressure factor will not be the main factor to influence consumer option. Such utility theory indicates consumers are as one rational economic man, whom do not expect to spend much time to do any options evaluation decision making.

However, in coffee market, buying a coffee comes almost automatically and does not need much information search. Hence, time limiting pressure factor won't one main factor to influence coff consumer to choose to buy the kind of coffee to drink. However, there are other factors to influence coffee consumers' kind of coffee drinking option from cultural, social, personal or psychological factors. So, coffee taste producer can follow these factors to estimate how coffee consumers might behave in the future when making any kinds of coffee making purchasing decisions.

Firstly, social factor can affect coff consumer behavior significantly. Every coffee consumer has someone around influencing his/her coffee buying decisions. The important social factors include reference groups, family, role and status , e.g. when the coffe buyer has high income job and his friends have good educational level and high income. Then, he will compare his reference group, such as his friends' coffee buying behavior choosing which kinds of coffee taste to drink in habits or lifestyles. If he chooses the kind of coffee taste to drink, its price is cheaper to compare his friends' drinking coffee tastes. Then, he may be influenced to follow his friends to drink the same kinds of coffee taste in order to keep their same social status and role between him and his friends.

Secondly, the coffee consumers will be influenced how to choose which kinds tastes of coffee to drink by personal factors, such as his age, life cycle state, occupation, economic situation , lifestyle and personality and self-concept. Age related factors are such as taste in food, e.g. the kinds of coffee taste. Although, coffee price is cheap, but if the coffee consumer's income is more and he/she can often spend to buy different kinds of taste coffees to drink. Then, his/her income level will have much purchasing power to influence his/her purchasing behavior. Hence the coffee consumer's frequency of consumption of different kinds of coffee taste drinking choice behavior will represent whether his/her income level is high or low in possible. For example, the consumer needs to go to automatic coffee shop to buy at least three cups or more different kinds of high class good taste coffee brands to drink per week. Although, these high class coffee brands' prices are higher than the low class of coffee brands. But the coffee consumer still only buys any one of these kinds of high class brands' coffee taste to drink. Hence, it seems that this coffee consumers ought have high income to let hims to buy at least three cups of high class brand of coffee taste to drink from automativ coffee ship per week.

So, income factor can influence the coffee consumer to choose either coffer purchase from supermarket or coffee drinking at automatic coffee shop. If the coffee consumer only chooses to buy coffee from supermarket, due to the bottles of different kinds of brand coffee can provide more different tastes of coffees choices from shelves to let him to buy to drink at home. So, it seems that the coffee consumer's income level is low in general. Otherwise, if the coffee consumer only chooses to go to automtic coffee shop to buy the high class brands of coffee tastes to drink at least thre times or more per week. It may mean that the coffee consumer has high income level to support him/her to often go to automatic coffee shop to buy different kinds of high class coffee tastes to drink frequently every week. Som high or low income level factor can influence every coffee consumer individual drinking coffee behavioral options.

Moreover, when the coffee consumer is younger coffee consumer will be possible to buy much coffee to drink. Because younger age people can accept to drink coffee habitually more than older age people. Also, it is possible that younger peopler feel often drinking coffee behavior will help them to bring more health feeling and /or raising nervous to learn , due to they need often to go to schools to study. Otherwise, older age people feel often drinking coffee behaviors won't help them to bring more health and they do not need to raise nervous to learn.

Finally, even, cultural difference factor will influence coffee consumers number fo any countries. For example, western countries'people like to drink any kinds of coffee tastes traditionally. Asia countries' people like to drink any different kinds of teas tastes traditionally. So, different kinds of teas tastes will be asia people's traditional drinking substitute to replace different kinds of coffee tastes more easily. Hence, culture difference will be one factor to influence asia coffee buyers number. So, it seems that time limiting pressure factor won't influence coffee consumers' coffee taste choices to different kinds of high class or low class brands, visiting coff shops or visiting supermarkets choices, frequent or not frequent coffee drinking behaviors.

How and why time limiting pressure
influences consumer choice

Can consumer buying decisions be influenced by time limiting pressure. For these three situations, they will influence consumer hoe makes different buying decision, e.g. in the little time available, but the consumer needs to do more effort needed to choose to buy which kind of product among variety kinds of product choice or in a moderate amount of time available, or a considerable amount of time available. In this first situation, the consumer can not real attempt to find any weaknesses or unique characteristics of the products, because it has no enough time to allow whom to choose. So, his/her product evaluation won't be th most accurate to satisfy his/her needs because little time can only allow him/her to find some weaknesses of the products. Otherwise, in the final situation, because the consumer has a considerable amout of time to allow him/her to attempt to find the weaknesses and/or strengths characteristics of the products choice. So, he/she ought do the more reasonable or accurate evaluation of these products to choose the most effective economic beneficial product to buy. Thus, it seems that time limiting pressure factor can influence the consumer to make more rational or more reasonable economic beneficial consumption decision making to buy the product or consume the service.

Thus, a consumer buying decision will require these situations to do buying decisions, they may include either little time and conscious effort or a moderate amount of time and effort or a considerable amount time and effort. The products may include cheap products/services , e.g. fruit, DVD, university courses, computers, facial services, surgeries, sport shoes, reference books, soft drinks, magazines as well as expensive products/services, e.g. cars, houses, luxury goods, e.g. jewellery, female hand bags, holiday travelling entertainment. So, any expensive or cheap products or services, the consumer will need to spend either little or moderate or considerable amount time to do gathering information about the different kinds of products or services in order to find which brand of product or service can bring more economic benefit when he/she chooses to use the product or consume the service. He/she will compare his/her preference sample brands limiting number of products or services choices to decide to buy the brand of product or consume the brand service easily. However in the consumer's consuming decision making process, he/she will need to spend either little or moderate or a considerable amount of time to do the evaluation and choice consumption behavior. It means that time limiting pressure factor will influence the consumer how to make consumption choice consequently.

What are the impacts of reduced branding on consumer choice and time limiting pressure to influence consumer behavior? When one consumer needs to choose products to buy one in a time limiting pressure consumption environment, when branding on packaging is reduced, e.g. the brand of product has 10 different style of packages to let consumer choice, but it reduces to only 5 different style of packages to let consumer choice. How does it influence the consumer decision making when the consumer has little time to allow to choose these 5 different style of packages ? For example, when the consumer expects to spend only 10 minutes to choose any one style of package to buy drom this brand product. Currently, this brand of produxt has reduced different style of packages number from 10 to 5. Do you feel that the consumer will feel easy to do decision making to choose to buy the most attractive style of package product from this brand's 5 different style of packages choices? Is 10 minutes consumption choice time enough to let the consumer to make final purchase decision from these brand's 5 different style of packages choice? Will the time limiting pressure be reduced , due to this brand's 10 style packages are reduced to 5 style packages to let the consumer to choose within the 10 minutes expected limiting consumption choice time.

It is one interesting psychological consumption behavior to research whether the brand's reducing different style of packages number factor will influence the consumer to do the decision making in the short time in the time limiting pressure environment. For toothpaste, shapmo products example, if the brand of these products' style packages choice is reduced to 5 style packages from 10 style packages choice. When one consumer finds the brand of toothpaste or shampo has only 5 style packages on the shelves in supermarket. If the consumer has moderate or considerate amount time to let him/her to choose these both kinds product any one style of packages to buy. The 5 style packages to these both inds of products will be impossible to satisfy the consumer's choice need because he/she haas much time to stay in supermarket to choose. Otherwise, if the consumer has little time to allow to stay in the supermarket , e.g. ony 10 minutes. Then, he/she expects to spend only 10 minutes consumption choice time to do buying decision making within 10 minutes. These both kinds of the brand's products, its styl of packages choice number is reduced to 5, it is possible to satisfy the consumer's choice need to buy this brand of product either toothpaste or shampoo and both of thee brand of products to be chose to buy in the supermarket. So , the reducing style of package number to let consumer choice will be seem to let the conumer to do buying decision making in the limiting time pressure consumption environment.

In fact , package is such a visual to influence consumer decision making in the short time or personal limiting time choice process. If the product has more attractive package design, the it can bring more attention effort to influence the consumer to choose to buy the product in the short time information transfers to influence the consumer decision making to choose to buy more easily , when he/she is active in communication process. So, package, communicating with consumer in the selling place , has become an essential factor to influence the choice of consumer.

Scientific researches have proved that package decisions can attract consumer attention, transfer the desirable information abou tthe product, position , the product in consumer conscious, differentiate and identify of among similar kinds of products. In that way elements of package influence consumer decision making process and can determine the choice of consumer and the package itself can become more competitive advantage.

However it is not absolute that the brand of product has more package choices, it must have more customers to choose to buy its product. For example, there are two brands of shampoo in the supermarket shelf. One brand shampoo has 5 different style of packages and 5 different fruit productive elements to cause similar fresh fruit smells to attract consumers to buy. Another brand shampoo has 3 different style of packages and 3 different fresh fruit smells to attract consumers to buy in the same shelf location also. When one supermarket customer has little time to expect to stay in the supermarket, e.g. he expects only to stay the supermarket maximum to 15 minutes. he expects to buy one bottle shampoo and meats and fruits and vegatables within 15 minutes. Hence, he expects only to spend about 5 minutes to choose one brand of shampoo product as well as he demands to spend maximum 10 minutes to buy other foods within 15 minutes. When he stays in the shampr shelf location, he finds only two brands of shampoo products are displayed on the same shelf location. One brand of shampo has 5 different style packages to let him to choose, but he feels that these 5 diffeent style packages are not very attractive. Otherwise, the another brand of shampo has only 3 different style packages to let him to choose, but he feels that the 3 different style packages are very attractive. Due to he feels time causes pressure to choose these two brands of shampoo immediately. So, he does not want to spend more time more than 5 minutes to choose on brand of shampoo to buy. He will be influenced by the brand of different styles of packages more attraction to influence his buying decision making obviously. So, whether the shampoo brand's package is attractive or not, it will influence the consumer's buying decision making to choose either to buy the brand's shampo product in preference.

So, the more packages choice to the brand's product which may not mean that it has high opportunity to influence consumers‘ attention. Otherwise, the attractive package element if more important to compare right number of packages choices. Consumer package can influence these elements, e.g. colour, size, imageries, graphics, materials, smell, brand name, producer/country, information, special offers. Of the brand of products can have much attractive elements. Then, it can attract consumers to choose to buy the brand's attractive package products in short time decision making process, such as perception of needs, search for information , evaluation of alternatives, decision making, behavior after purchase. Such as supermarket case, I assume that any supermarket consumers do not expect to spend much time to choose which brand of product is the most suitable or earning more economic benefit to buy when they need to stay the shelf to need spend much time to select which brand of product to buy in the supermarket. Because in general, supermarket consumers ought plan to buy more than one kind of product or food, even more usually. So, limiting time pressure factor will influence their decision making. Similarly, as my explanation indicates why although, the product had attractive package elements and its has many packages number choices, but it does not mean that it can win the similar product which has not more attractive packages, even it has more packages choices number to let supermarket consumers to choose. So, an attractive package element factor will have more influential and potential to cause supermarket consumers to choose to buy it in the supermarket limiting time pressure consumption environment.

- How the time consumption pressure factor influences irrational consumption decision making

When one consumer has a large number of options, he/she will feel time pressure to cause whose accurate and reasonable evaluation. Then, the personal time limiting pressure factor will bring these questions: How does the time limiting pressure influence the consumer evaluation? Will the consumer personal limiting time pressure bring advantages and / or disadvantages in whom consumption decision making? How to help the consumer to solve short time decision problem when he/she encounters extreme time pressure an dchoice overload?

I shall assume every consumer is general one economic man. He/she feels time is important, he /she does not want to spend much time to choose one brand of product to buy among a number of brands of products choices. I also assume that any consumers decision making satisfaction, which is based on search until they found a sufficiently good item, or run not of time. So, it seems that which the consumer needs to buy one kind of product, but the product has a lot number of different brands to let the consumer to choose. The consumer ought need to spend much time to make choice decision making. However, consumer is one economic man, he/she ought not to search all different brands to decide whether which brand of product can bring the much economic value or utility value to choose to buy. So, in general, consumers will only choose sample brands of products to decide to buy the satisfied brand of product. For example, when the consumer needs to buy one television. The television has 20 brands of similar televisions to let he to choose. He will not spend much time to search these similar 20 televisions information. He will only gather sample 10 to 15 or less different brands of televisions to compare what their strengths and weaknesses, unique characteristics. Then, he will make decision to choose to buy the best television from these sample televisions. Hence, in general, consumers will feel time pressure when they feel need to spend much time to choose a lot different brands of similar products. Because they feel time is not enough to let they can do other important matters when they need to spend much time to do search information behavior when they need to buy any products ususally. Hence, it is general consumers psychology that they will feel real choice under time pressure and choice overload, when they have too much a lot of similar brands of products to let them have opportunity to choose to make decision making to buy only one brand of product.

However, when a brand of product is familiar and given its simplicity and familiarity to general consumers' acknowledgement. It will have perference advantage to attract or influence consumers‘ attention or consideration. So, when the market has similar different brands of products are available to let consumers to choose. The largest choice set is not large enough to create overload to influence the brand's sale when consumers need to spend much time to choose these different brands similar products to buy. Because when the brand's any products are familiar and given its simplicity and familiarity to general consumers' knowledgement. Then, it can build utility confidence to influence general consumers , it will be preference sample brand of product to do buying making option. Hence, the brand's familiarity factor will influence general consumers' preference buying decision making option. So, any product manufacturers need to concern how to build its brand familiarity to let many consumers to acknowledge in order to raise its competitive effort. Raising brand's familiarity may be a good method to solve consumer individual choice under time pressure overload , because when the brand of product is preference sample brand to any consumers. It's sale opportunity will also be raised. So, it brings the question: How can the brand of products can cause general consumers' preference choice. For food example, food brands were more likely to choose the implicitly preferred brand over the explicitly preferred one when choices were made under time pressure.

Imagining one customer enters a supermarket 10 minutes before closing time. He failed to write up a shopping list. So, when the staff is preparing to close store at the night, the consumer hurry trys not to for set too many of the ingredients for dinner . What brands of products , he opts for, as he can choose from a variety of similar foods, but time is short and the staff is looking at the consumer impatienty? It is possible that the consumer will probably quickly decide in favor of the foods he likes best, pay, and leave the evening.

Hence, supermarket consumer's first time feeling to the brand of food will influence whom choice. One target category and one attribute category share same response key: Pleasant vs unpleasant feeing, if the supermarket consumer has pleasant feeling when he sees the food photos and touchs the package of the brand of food to feel pleasant in the short supermarket closing time. Then, his pleasant feeling will be chooses to buy the brand of food to eat. Thus, the consumer individual pleasant or unpleasant feeling factor will influence whom consumption choice, such as this supermarket closing time pressure consumption.

In fact, many factors may influence whether consumer behavior is under more or less control. Hunger may influence control in the domain of eating behavior . So, such as the supermarket will close soon,it has store closing time pressure to influence the consumer needs hurry to make choice decision to buy food. If the consumer feels more hungry, he will not spend much time to find the right food to buy. He will be influenced by the different brand's food packages whether which brand of food package can bring a more pleasant to let him to feel, when he touchs and sees the brand of food package. He won't spend time to search whether the different kinds of brands of foods have how much different health elements because the supermarket will close store soon. So, he only depends his individual pleasant feeling to make final food purchase decision. If he feels all of the kinds of brands foods are unpleasant food packages when he sees and touchs them first time as well as he does not feel much hungry. Then, it is possible that he won't choose to any one food to eat. He will choose to go to restaurant to get dinner to replace buying food to cook to eat dinner at home at the night.

The another case is that time pressure concerns how on choice of information source impacts purchase decisions. When the consumer who buys one product , he needs to use the same number of information sources to search the product's information regardless of time pressure. Because he has more available time, he devotes more time , but only to selected the right sources to search information about the product. He will mostly use marketing dominant sources, e.g. magazine. he feels magazine can give more accurate information concerns to the product's good or bad quality real more reasonable and fair evaluation to let the consumer to acknowledge. so, when the consumer has much time to choose to buy which brand of product is the most best choice. He will buy magazine to find information. He believes magazine has more fair evaluation to different brands of product. It won't mislead consumers to make wrong decision making. Hence, in general, when consumers have much time to find information source to search which brand of product is more value to buy. They will attempt to buy consumer magazine to acknowledge whether the different brands of product , which have unique characteristics, strengths or weaknesses in order to compare them to make more accurate evaluation to choose to buy which brand of the kind product. When they have no time pressure to influence their choice process time to be shortened or reduced. Otherwise, these consumers will depend on newspapers, television, radio advertisments information sources when they feel time pressure controls their consumption choice decision making process time to be shortened or reduced. Hence, time pressure will be possible to influence consumer individual information source channel choice.

Time pressure consumption decision
making process characteristics

How we can predict or know the consumer time pressure in whom decision making process? Will it bring advantages or disadvantages to influence the businessmens' benefits? I shall indicate some different consumption situations or environments to explain what will be impacted to sale number is increased or decreased to businesses when the consumer feel time pressure to avoid whom behavioral consumption to the product or the service.

Firstly, I shall explain that what effects of product popularity and time pressure on online shopping behaviors are . Electronic ecommerce is popular to any countries, in special, US, UK, China large areas countries, because when one customer feels need to spend one hour even more time to catch any transportation tool to arrive the shop to buy the kind of product. Then, due to far distance reason, he/she will choose to apply internet to buy the kind of product . If the seller has website to let the consumers to choose online shopping. However, it seems that online shopping behavior can reduce the consumer individual time pressure, when he/she feels need to catch any kinds of transportation tool to arrive the shop to buy the product. Moreover, when the consumer can turn on home computer to enter its website to choose the styles of the kind of products, which one is the most situable to choose. He/she can spend time to search the different styles kinds of product information to compare and evaluate which brand of product will b whose purchase choice easily at home.

Hence, in psychological view, he/she can feel that spending time to search information from internet behavior which is more valuable and it can bring more economic benefit to make final purchase decision more than the behavior of spending long time to catch any transportation tools to visit the shop. Moreover, it is possible to bring failure risk that he/she wastes time to catch any transportation tools to visit the shop if he/she can not find any one of suitable product(s) to choose to buy. Hence, it seems the online shopping can influence the consumer reduced time pressure and wastes time to do any shopping decision.

This is online shopping's attractive strengths to the consumers when they need to spend long time to catch any kinds of transportation tools to visit the shop or when the consumer feels hurry to do other important matters, he/ she can not allow himself/herself to spend long time to do his/her visiting the shop behavior. Moreover, another online shopping's advantage is that product popularity can be perceived by examining the information presended on websites. For example, research on onlin reviews confirms the review quantity presented with products become positively influences to consumers' purchase intention and it can persuade the online visitor can make decision to buy the product when he/she has enter the seller's online website to find the most suitable product to choose to buy more easily. Hence, it seems that it is more easy to persuade the online visitor to make final purchase decision more than visiting the shop , when the online visitor can attempt to do the click mouse behavior to enter the seller's online shop, such as website. Then, he/she will be influenced to view the seller's different kinds of colourful and attractive product pictures from the seller's wesite.

Consequently, it has much opportunity to persuade the consumer to do the final purchase decision. if the seller's website is attractive to persuade him/her to visit its website to find any new products more than five times, even tem times or every weak several times , even day one time frequently visiting behavior from internet channel. Hence, due to internet is convenient tool to let consumers to find any product informatons from the seller's website at home or public library , computer, or mobile phone. Consumers must find any product informations any time in any places easily. So, online shopping can reduce any consumers' time pressure to visit any shops to expect to achieve final consumption decision aim in possible.

Thus, it seems that online shopping method can influence consumers to feel time saving and time presure reducing consumption both advantages more than visiting shops' shopping method when the consumer is living far away from the shop. When the consumer feels that he/she is experiencing situational time pressure, then, he/she will respond well to seek another time saving situational consumption environment. So , it explains when one consumer feels he/ she has no much time to catch long time transportation tool to visit the shop on the day. When he/she has computer at home, he/she will attempt to type the shop name to research whether it has online shopping platform service from internet. Because he/she does not want to spend one hour, even more time to catch transportation tool to arrive the shop, when he/she can't walk to the shop in short time. Even, he/she may feel online shopping behavior won't influence his/her eating , sleeping, or recreational time to be reduced at home or any places , when he/she can behave the online shopping behavior at home or any where conveniently.

Consequently, promoting online shopping is as a time-saver is likely to be effective for these experiencing situational time pressure. Those with situational pressure would almost certainly welcome anything that would reduce their activity level and the demands on their time. In fact, there is really no adult learning method for store shopping because it is something everyone learns to do from early childhood. But for many adult consumers, they feel have interest to learn how to use internet and web to shopping. Some adult will feel interest and it is value to learn how to use internet channel to anticipate the complexity of shopping online. For example, Super Walmart cheap frocery store that carries many thousands of products and brands to let online shoppers won't feel confused when viewing its online merchant's home page with only a few menu items and links from its website. So, Super Walmart website can let online shoppers to feel difficult that they can save much time to enter any merchants' home page . They only need to view the Super Walmart's website ,then they can find any preference cheap grocercies to compare and evaluate which one(s) is (are) value to buy. So, Super Walmart's website can let global cheap grocery online shoppers feel it can help them to save time to find any merchant's products from internet conveniently. Consequently, online shopping will be one popular time saving consumption channel to reduce time pressure to some consumers nowadays.

Secondly, I shall explain that what determines purchase decisions for airline tickets when the traveller fees time stress. When a travelling planner has no enough time to prepare whose travelling journey, whether the time stress will influence he/she feels decision difficulties and frustration, when it will cause he/she needs to gather significant amounts of information to lead to make to choose which airline ticket is the most right choice? How and number of airline options and time pressure influence the airline ticket buyer's purchase decision?

However, there are both kinds of time pressures to influence the airline ticket buyer's airline choice decision, they focus on either real decision deadlines (physical time), such as the journey beginning day is any day of this week or tomorrow or subjective feeling of pressure with time (sense of urgency or psychological time), such as the traveller expects that he/she fears all airlines' all seats are full booked in this month. Moreover, he/she can plan to catch air plane to travel next month. So, he/she will attempt to gather any airlines' tickets prices, flight day and time and destination arrival and weather information in this month to avoid that it is too late to delay his/her next month travelling plan.

Hence, it seems that the effect of number of airlines choices and air tickets purchase deadlines (physical time limit) will influence how the traveller or air ticket buyer's purchase decision using secondary data to search of airline ticket. for example, if the traveller felt time is no enough to let him/her to go to travel agent to enquire any airlines' air tickets prices and seats and date and time air plan departure available time to concern the traveller's destination choice. Then, he/she will be probable to choose to buy electronic-ticket (e-ticket) from internet. If he/she has computer to link internet to gather any airlines' flying date and time and seat available information at home easily. Hence, it seems that one time pressure traveller will be probable to choose e-ticket purchase at home in preference. If the airline can provide online e-ticket purchase option to the time pressure traveller. Due to the pressure time traveller feels closer to departure, the negative impact of number of airline options is not as strong when he/she can view the airline's website to find the flight date, time and seat available information to purchase e-ticket to prebook the date and time to departure the traveller's country and to arrive his/her travelling destination information from the airline's website channel at home or anywhere any time conveniently. Hence, travel agency can bring a positive relationship between airline number of options and pre-booking airline that immediate possibility. When the time pressure traveller hopes the airline can build the good interactive relationship between number of options and decision time limit (number of days till planned travel effort on e-ticket purchase probabilities. So, if the airline website can let the traveller to predict when date and time is accurate available to arrive whom frequently destination choice country as well as the e-ticket's real price , it is not e-ticket preductive price and the real seats number available, it is not the estimated seats number available on the departure time and date to the travelling or arrival country destination. Then, all of these online information to the airline, which will raise the e-ticket pre-booking purchase chance to let the e-ticket buyer to make whose final e-ticket purchase choice decisin to win its e-ticket competitors easily.

Consequently, a real time e-ticket information can attract any time pressure e-ticket buyers to choose to buy its e-ticket (electronic airline ticket) more than visiting travel agent's paper airline ticket option when the travel feels hurry to buy airline ticket to travel in short time.

Reducing time pressure consumption
methods

How can sellers persuade consumers to choose to buy their products or consume their services in time pressure environment easily? It is a valuble research topic to concern how to know how consumer individual decision making to spend his/her available resources (time, money and efforts, or consumption relatd aspects) as well as how any why he/she chooses the preference brand to buy its any kind of products or consume its services, when he/she chooses to buy the brand of products or consume its services? Hence, marketers need to obtain an indepth knowledge of consumer buying behavior.

In any buying process, time factor will have about 10 % to 40 % to influence consumer decision. When the consumer feels hurry to consume, e.g. planning to go to travel, when he/she needs to choose to buy which airline's air ticket and what day and time is the right air ticket prebooking purchase decision right time choice; or enrolling which school to be choosed course to study decison, e.g. how long time is needed to be choose which school is the most suitable to provide the most suitable courses studying choce change; purchase warm clothes to wear in winter, when is the suitable time to choose to buy the cheaper warm clothers to prepare to wear in winter, e.g. Jan to Mar., April to June, July to Aug. month; when is the most suitable time to buy another new house to live, when the property consumer(buyer) has lived present house for long time, e.g. three years or more. All of these issues will include time factor to influence the consumer feels when he/she ought choose to buy the kind of product or consume the kind of service. However, the other factors will also include to influence his/her decision, e.g. family, friend relationship factor, advertising factor, social status factor, cultural difference factor, personal psychological need level or satisfactory level factor, young or old age factor, income level factor, economic environment factor, material enjoyable need factor etc. factors.

However, time pressure factor will be the consumer individual intrinsic (internal) psychological feeling factor, and it is the consumer individual intrinsic feeling to judge whether when he/she ought spend some money to buy the kind ofcnew product or the kind of consume service (what time is the most reasonable or the most suitable time) to make purchase choice decision. However, when the consumer feels hurry to make purchase decision. So, he/she will not hope to spend more time to gather more information to compare and evaluate which one is the right brand of product tochoose to buy or the right service to consume among different brands of products or services. Otherwise, if the consumer has more time or he/she can make the decision to buy any brand of product. Then, he/she ought spend more time to gather more information to compare and evaluate which one is the most suitable product choice to buy or which one is the right service choice to consume. So, time pressure factor will have some influence to any consumers to make decision about what time is the suitable time to buy the kind of product or consume the service. For example, heater product is usually when winter weather time, the heater products need number ought increase in winter weather time or season. But, it is possible that the heater products need number won't increase in winter season / weather possible, when one country , there are many householders or families , they have one heater number at least at home. Then, it is possible that these householders or families won't have consumption desires to buy one more heater product to use in winter at home, because they have had one heater to use at home in winter. So , when the country has have many customers number, they are using the kind of heater products at homes. Most people own at least one heater number factor will have possible to influence enough time available to cause they do not feel hurry to buy any heaters to use at homes, so, their do not feel time pressure to buy any heaters in short time. Because they do not plan to buy the kind of product to use at home in short time when they have one heater product at least to use at homes in present.

Hence, it brings this question: How to attract or persuade the customers, they are using the kind of product to let they feel time pressure to make decision to buy another new or same brand of product to replace to use? The product's better quality , long durable time useful, brand loyalty and past good purchase experience factors will influence him/her to feel time pressure to need to buy another new product in short time. So,when the consumer feel time pressure to make decision to purchase, he/she will choose when is the most right time to gather information, search, select, use and dispose of another new product to replace the old product in the short time.

Hence, the brand of product needs have good product motives, may be raised to the consumer's impluse, desires, considerations which make the buyer purchase the brand's new product to replace the present using product in order to achieve whose satisfactory needs to emotional product motives and rational product motives both. Moreover, persuading or encouraging the consumer feels he/she has real need to buy the kind of new product or replace the present old product (s), the brand of product marketer needs let the consumer feels these any one of nature of motive to raise his/her purchase decision desire in time pressure environment. The natures of motive may include: When the consumer feels desire for saving money, he/she will choose to buy it when the brand of product falls down, when he/she feels fear to be sickness, retirement, he/she will choose to buy insurance policy, when he/she feels pride, or high social status knowledgement, he/she will buy premium product , e.g. gold, expensive watch, car , when he/she feels fashion need, he/she will move house to live from rural to urban, or rural people imitate urban to learn to do their fashion living behavior, when he/she feels possession need, he/she will feel need to buy antiques for its future unique worth satisfactory feeling in possible, when he/she feels health need, he/she will choose to buy health foods, join memebership in health clubs, when he/she needs to enjoy comfortable feeling, he/she will feel need to buy micro-oven, washing machine to use at home, when he/she feels love and affection need, he/she will buy gift items to give to whose friends or families for presents in their birthday or lover day etc. special days to let they to feel happy. So, when the marketer can touch the consumer individual different nature of motives to satisfy his/her personal purchase feeling need and it can know how to influence them to feel that they have these any one of purchase motive needs in short time. Then, they will be persuaded to raise time pressure to make purchase decison to buy any kind of products in short time.

However, instead of attractive good product quality method can attempt consumers to make time pressure consumption behavior. The another method is brand loyalty building method, which can be attempted to encourage or persuade consumers to feel consumption desire need to make decision to buy the brand of any products in time pressure consumption environment. For example, when the consumers feel the brand is loyalty and it can build good image to his/her feeling , and this time pressure factor can inlfuence this brand of any products which has high discount price to attract the consumer individual attention , e.g. familiar brand high class cars, the good confident house agent's high class houses, and the expensive and infrequently buying items, come under this category. When their prices are fallen down to sell cheaper , e.g. twenty per cent discount or more than twenty percent discount sale price than the other similar competitive brands' any products' normal prices. Then, it is possible to let these expensive items' consumers have high involvement and high feeling need in time pressure consumption environment. Because they assume that this discount sale price will be short time sale price, e.g. after three months or next month etc. short time discount sale price in short time period. Then, these expensive items' prices will be raised to the normal sale price, even higher price. so, they have time pressure feeling to feel that it is right time to make consumption decision in order to avoid to lose these low price purchase benefit in this unpredictive cheap discount price purchase items. so, if the expensive item marketer can build long time good brand loyalty relationship to consumers. Then, it will have much influential effort to persuade consumers feel consumption desires need by its any extensive items in the unpredictive short term discount period, due to they do not want to loss this large discount purchase price chance. So, short time discounted sale price, it is another method to persuade consumers to choose to buy the brand's any products in short time pressure consumption environment.

The another persuading time pressure consumption method is that it can let consumers to think more habitual buying the kind of products. products like stationery, groceries, food etc. fall under this category. For example, when the consumer fees the brand of any products ,he/she has habitual purchase experience, of he/she feels that the brand's any products won't sell in market temporary, even he/she can not buy it to use again. Then, it is possible to infuence him/her to feel immediate purchase need to buy a lot of product or food number to keep to use or eat later in the time pressure environment, e.g. the food consumer buys the brand of any breads to eat in supermarkets habitually, but in this moth, he/she watchs TV advertisement to be acknowledge this brand of any breads won't be bought from any supermarkets as soon as possible. Hence, it is possible to influence him/her to plan to make choice to buy a lot of number of this brand of any breads in order to keep the enough of this brand of breads number to eat later. So, this brand of any breads sale loss in supermarkets that will cause the habitual food consumers of this brand of breads, whom make consumption choice to buy a lot number of this brands any breads in short time suddenly. Because they are eating this brand of any kinds of breads habitually. They feel much eating need to lot number of this brand of any breads in short period, because it can satisfy their habitual taste needs of this brand's any kinds of breads. So, brand loyalty and habitual consumption to the kind of product or food , ehich will result simply from the habit and it can influence the consumers feel consumption need to buy the brand's any kinds of products or foods when they feel that they may not buy it again or they can not earn discount advantage after the short time. So, any one of these sale strategies will have possible to raise the consumer individual consumption desire to the brand of products in the short time pressure consumption environment. Also it needs to spend much time to gather information in order to make purchase decision, because the brand had built confidence to consumers when they feel this brand's any products or foods are better to compare the similar brands' any products or foods habitually. So, time pressure consumption environment will persuade them to feel consumption desire to buy this brand's any products or foods in short time. When, they fer that they can not buy any more for this brand's any kinds of products or foods or discounting price in this final short purchase time.

In conclusion, these factors can influence consumer behaviors to be changed to feel time pressure need to do purchase decision making behavior from encough time gathering information available feeling behavior. They have these same views, e.g. habits and routines are very influential, particularly for behaviors repeated daily in a semi-automatic fashion. The consumer's past purchas experience to the brand's products, positive or negative emotion to the brand's products, and the brand's familization, recognition are strong influence , the information available , it is the consumer's mind and the relative important information given to let the consumer knows form different advertisement medias matters for decision making, greating between pieces of information and can be influenced by personal psychological timing limited pressure, the consumer's comparison to differences in price or other characteristics, many pursue value (or in bargain), and compare to alternatives or past knowledge, consumer personal greater value on the immediate future and heavily disocunt future costs or savings to the brand of product, feeling simple and easy decision making process to the product , it can lead the consumer to avoid to spend long time to make purchasing decision and the consumer will easy to choose to buy the product when he/she feels have a loss value if he/she does not decide to buy the product in the short time. SO, it seems that when the marketer can motivate the consumer's consumption desire to feel saving money, promote health, avoid waste time and less nervous workload to gather information for comparison and evaluation alternatives aim. It is seen favorably by the consumer personal time pressure purchase decision making and sense of justice influence factors.

However, sociologists have categorised the motives for consumption behaviors in the short time by the fundamental consumption decision making needs or wants which they satisfy, e.g. having a clear understanding what benefits, characteristics, economic value to the brand's any products , feeling consumption decision making process is a leisure activity. These drivers for consumption behaviorw will either bring positive or negative to influence the consumer personal emotion, either owning enough time available or time pressure environmental impacts can be seen to influence whether the consumer feels he/she needs how long time to be spent to make comparison and evaluate alternatives in order to make final purchase choice in whom decision making process. Hence, the consumer himself/herself time pressure consumption decision making feeling, it can bring positive purchase choice influence,when the marketer can build brand loyalty to let many consumers to feel in the market. Otherwise, if the marketer can not build brand loyalty to let many consumers to feel, but consumers feel time pressure to compare and evaluate its any products to other similar brands of products in the competitive market. Then, its products may be not the preference choices the many customers among the different brands of products choices. So, building long time brand loyalty relationship to satisfy consumers' needs, it will bring positive preference purchase choice to raise the sale effort to the brand of any products when consumers need to make purchase choice in time pressure consumption environment, e.g. seasonal discount sale period, products or foods shortage supply period, without any forever sale possibility in market. Hence , it seems that brand loyalty building factor will influence any brands of products /foods /service sale or provison number to be raised or reduced in possible. Also, it can explain why and how it has close cause and effect relationship between time pressure consumption environment and the brand loyalty building to the brand of products/foods/services to any marketers nowadays.

What are the in-store and out-store
factors influence supermarket
fast moving consumer decision

It is one interesting question: How can the brand of product seller influence the supermarket/store fast-moving consumers' more visual attention when the supermarket/store visitor is hurry to make decision to choose to buy which brand of product in time pressure environment? Supermarket/store fast-moving consumers do not usually spend much time to say in any supermarket shelf locations to choose numerous similar alternative brands of products. However, I assume the fast-moving supermarket/store consumer's decision is dependent on the interaction between the supermarket different shelf location sale environment and the mind of the consumer. So, the eye tracking explores this rapid processing that lacks conscious access or control to any supermarket or store consumers. It brings this question: How product packing and placement (as in-store factors) and recognition, preferences, and choice task (as out-of-store factors) which will influence the supermarket / store consumer individual decision making process through visual attention. In split-second decision making, the ability to recognize and comprehend a brand of supermarket/store product can significantly impact preferences. Hence, how the supermarket/store consumer's eye truly sees what whom mind is prepared to influence how much consumption desire to choose to buy the brand's product in short tim decision making process when he/she stays in the shelf location, it has less than ten or more than ten different kinds of brands products or foods to let the visitor to choose in the supermarket or store.
Brand owners and product developers will feel responsibilities to overcome promotion or advertising or communicaton challenge in order to let consumers to know their products are launched on the market. However, it is not until the product reaches the supermarket shelf that has good quality to the effort is judged whether it has how much sale number every day in the supermarket. The judges are the consumers themselves how to make decision quickly through the personal time pressure environment with minor package information processing in the supermarket.
What does it take to be consider an option to influence the consumers' minds on visual attention in point-of-purchase decision making ? The supermarket's in-store activities and the consumer personal out-of-store activities

will influence how his / her visual attention to the brand of products in the supermarket / store any shelf locations when he/she is walking to pass any shelf locations. So, it seems that any supermarkets or stores brands of products sale number , it has relation to every supermarket or store visitors' visual attention throughout the point to point (shelf to shelf) decision making process in the supermarkets / stores. So, how much does the supermarket's visitors' time spending to obtain attention to the brand of produc? it will have possible to influence the brand of any products' sale number in the supermarket/store. Hence, in this limited timeframe, the consumer enters a decision making process that is in itself influenced by in-store and out-of-store both factors.

I shall explain what is supermarket / store space quality factor, e.g. top level versus floor level to different shelf variable height, weigh , or shelf space location factor as well as the product price elasticity and price-quality relationship to the brand of products both factors to influence every consumer decision making in supermarket/ store. The in-store factor is more influential factor to compare out-of-store factor to influence consumers' decision in supermarket. For example, where the shampoo brand products are locating to be put on the shelf , it can influence the point to point behavior of shampoo product habitual buyers. If the buyer habitually chooses the shampoo brand products in the shelf location. Also, if all of the shampoo brand products are moved to another shelf locations to display its different kinds of shampoo products to cause the habitual buyer needs to spend much extra time to find where the another new shelf location is displaying the brand's shampoo products.

In this situation, information processing has a heightened decision making role as the buyer needs to spend much time to find where the brand's displayed shampoo products' shelf location to make non-habitual decision making between options. For habitual decisons, the consumer's visual attention is reduced to measuring visual search. However, when the brands of any shampoo products are moved to another new shelf location to display its different kinds of shampoo products. So, the act of another shelf new location search , it will influence the habitual shampoo buyer's visual attention to consider the brand of any shampoo products which are usually used to wash to his/her hair habitually. When he / she can find the other new brands of shampoo products are displayed on the old shelf displayed location of the brand of shampoo products. Hence, the traditional shelf displayed location to the brand of products, when the brand of products are moved to another new displayed shelf locations. This in-store factors that will influence traditional cosnumers through visual attention concerns to this brand of products more or less.

So, supermarket traditional shelf displayed variable location to the brand of products factor, which will have influence to the traditional consumers' visual attention to do either buying the brand's products or buying another brand's products to replace it, when the traditional consumer feels difficult that he/she needs to spend extra longer time to find whether where is the traditional useful product's displayed shelf location. Then, it will be possible to influence the traditional consumer's traditional purchase decision to the brand's product, and he/she will choose to buy another brand of product to replace when it can be displayed to the shelf location to attract the consumer's visual attention more.

It is one important in-store shelf displayed factor to influence the traditional fast-moving consumer individual purchase decision making behavioral change in any supermarkets or stores when they feel hurry to do personal time pressure consumption decision to make purchase final decision in the point to point counter purchase (the brand's of products are moved from the traditional shelf location visual attention moves to the strange shelf location visual attention) in supermarket time pressure consumption environment.

Hence, in supermarket time pressure consumption environment, in -store and out-of-sore both factors can influence fast-moving consumer individual purchase decision making. The in-store factors can influence product packaging, product placement components as well as the out-store factors can influence choice task, preference and brand recognition components. So, it is common to influence supermarket consumers choose do personal time pressure purchase consumption decision of visual attention purchase behaviors. The different brands' products are displayed to different shelf locations in order to cause shelf displaying products' different decision making effect.

However, instead of shelf displaying location factor, package will also influence consumers' decision making, due to the influence of minute differences in packaging design on visual attention. When, the supermarket consumer feels the brands are not familiar or unfamiliar. Then, he/she will spend more time to evaluate and verify the unfamiliar brands' products whether which one is value to buy in her/his decision making process. He/she will feel visual attention need in order to evaluate in set of brand alternatives to make conscious demand mind cognitive effort by involving working memory. So, if the product's package is attractive, even the consumer is unfamiliar the brand's any product choices which are displayed on the shelf location in the supermarket. The brand's attractive package factor can influence the consumer to raise whom visual attention. Then, the attractive package factor can increase much visual attention chance to many consumers when they are walking to pass through the unfamiliar brand's any products' shelf displaying location considerably. So, it explains when attractive package factor may solve the visual attention problem to fast-moving consumers when they are visiting one strange supermarket to find anywhere unfamiliar brand's products' shelf displaying locations. Because they are the non-traditional consumers to the unfamiliar brand's products, they won't be influenced to choose either buying or not buying the unfamiliar brand's products. When the unfamiliar brand's products are moved to another new shelf displayed location. So, if the unfamiliar brand has attractive package to let the non-traditional consumers feel visual attention when they are passing through the strange shelf displayed location. Then, it can raise purchase chance to the non-traditional consumers target number when they are staying in the strange supermarket.

In conclusion, the brand of products' shelf displaying location and package factors may bring much influence to any traditonal or non-traditonal consumer behaviors in supermarket or store time pressure consumption environment.

What consumption is most influenced in preference choice by time pressure

What kinds of services or products are most influenced to consumer behavioral change by time pressure? Can time pressure factor influence more preference to other factors, such as age, culture, income level, habitual shopping, family or friend relationship etc. factors to influence consumer behavioral choice to these kinds of services or products in consumption market? I shall indicate some kinds of services or products consumption models to explain how time pressure can influence consumers to choose to consume its services or buy its products.

Firstly, for theme park entertainment industry example, has it time pressure to cause any theme park visitors, e.g. Walt Disney entertainment theme park to influence them to feel time pressure to enjoy their emotions to play any entertainment machine facilities and it brings negative emotion to choose the entertainment theme park entertainment consumption activities.

For Walt Disney entetainment theme park example, every visitor needs to pay a fixed ticket fee to enter Disney theme park. So, however, he/she chooses to play how many number of entertainment activities facilities, e.g. only one entertainment playing facility, or more than one entertainment playing facilities. The Disney visitor needs to pay the same ticket fee to enter Disney. So, it will cause th visitors feel unfair , they do not choose to play any entertainment facilities or play only less number of entertainment facilities. Because they need to pay the same ticket price to same to the visitors, who choose to play many entertainment facilities number in Disney. So, it brings this question: Does the Disney visitor feel time pressure when he/she chooses to play many number of entertainment facilities , but he/she will not enjoy to carry on other activities in Disney, e.g. shopping, visiting cinema to watch movies, walking around the whole Disney anywhere to view scene activities. Because US Disney entertainment theme park is very large . It has not only entertainment facilities to attract visitors to play. It has many places are value to visitors to visit or enjoy the other free charge entertainment activities , such as visiting Disney gardens, visiting ocean park, visiting Disney cinema to watch free movies, view scene or seeing free charge ocean animal performance shows , going to Disney shopping centres to shopping, visiting Disney library to read books, visiting Disney ocean park to view different kinds of beautiful fishes non-entertainment machine facility playing activities. All of these activities are value to any Disney visitors to choose to play or visit, instead of entertainment machine facilities activities. So, if one visitor hopes only to spend one day in US Walt Disney entertainment theme park. He/she will feel hurry to choose to play any machine entertainment facilities, or he/she won't choose any machine entertainment facilities to play in Disney because he/she also hopes to play other non-machine entertainment facilities activities, e.g. visiting garden, visiting ocean park, visiting library, visiting cinema to watch free movies, visiting garden to play free charge boats water entertainment activities, watching ocean animal show performance etc. different kinds of entertainment activities, even walking around anywhere fun and excite places in Disney theme park. Hence, the Disney visitor will feel time pressure to choose either playing any kinds of entertainment machine facilities or visiting different places in the whole one day in Disney.

Hence, time pressure factor may influence any one of Disney visitors how to choose any entertainment activities to spedn time in Disney. It will bring this question: Because the Disney ticket price is fixed fee, can the Disney visitor will feel unfair to cause negative emotion, if the Disney visitor feels time pressure to choose to play any kinds of machine entertainment activities or doing other non-machine entertainment activities in the Disney visitor's limited timeframe, during he/she stays in Disney? So, it seems that time pressure psychological factor will may influence some Disney visitors to feel unhappy, negative emotion, when they feel their entertainment activities choices are wrong or doing wring entertainment decision making in his/her limited timeframe. Consequently, time pressure factor will influence some feeling time pressure Disney visitors won't choose to enter Disney again. Hence, time pressure factor can have much influence to theme park visitors' behavioral change, instead of whether the entertainment theme park's machine entertainment facilities are attractive or enjoyable playing or how many entertainment facilities are supplied to let visitors to play in the entertainment theme park. So, entertainment theme park service providerd need to consider whether their ticket prices are reasonable to let visitors feel, if they do not want to reduce theme park visitors number seriously.

The another example is restaurant food service industry. Can time pressure influence food consumers to choose the restaurant to eat? Instead of food taste, price, seats available providing, restaurant location, public transportation facilities available etc. factors, which can influence the food consumer individual choice to the restaurant.

Is time pressure another one main factor to influence food consumers choice to the restaurant? In what suitation, food consumers will feel time pressure to influence whose preference restaurant choice? I assume that the restaurant 's price is reasonable, public transportation facility is convenient to catch to go to the restaurant, food taste is acceptable to the food consumer. Although all above these factors are accepted to the food consumer . But when the food consumer feels hurry to hope to find one restaurant to eat and he/she hopes to spend less time to sit down to eat in the restaurant , e.g. less than one hour. Then, the food consumer will compare all the restaurants are near to whose working place or school , if he/she is one student or one working person. Because he/she needs to eat lunch to go to school or go to office to work. So, the restaurant's food taste, price is not the main factor to influence him/her to choose to eat. Otherwise, whether the restaurant needs him/her to spend how long queue time to wait, or/and the restaurant needs how long cooking time to let him/her to eat, the restaurant needs him/her to walk how long time to arrive the restaurant. All of these factors concern " efficient cooking time, queue waiting time serice performance" issues to the restaurant, which are the main evaluation requirements to influence the feeling time pressure food consumer to make decision whether he/she either still ought follow the better food taste, cheap food price factors to be preference decision or he/she ought follow short time queue time waiting or without queue time waiting, fast cooking waiting time factors to be preference restaurant consumption decision.

Hence, it seems that a feeling time pressure food consumer, he/she ought choose the restaurant to eat in preference when it does not need him/her to wait long queue time and wait long cooking time. Otherwise, when the food consumer does not feel hurry to eat, he/she outhgt choose the restaurant, it can provide good taste food, cheap price in preference to eat.

Hence, time pressure personal feeling will influence students or working people food consumers' preference restaurant choice when the restaurant can provide short time queue waiting or without queue waiting and fast cooking time service preference to satisfy their needs.

However , in some situation, time pressure can influence consumers to choose the service, even its price is expensive than other services. For example, public transportation tool choices service. When one passenger has need to find one kind public transportation tool to catch from the place to another destination, but the destination is far away from his/her location. He/she hopes to catch the kind of public transportation tool to arrive the destination about one hour. Although, his/her location has cheap public transportation tools to choose, e.g. bus, train, tram, ferry, underground train. But, he/she feels that all of these public transpotation tools need to spend longer time to compare taxi to arrive the destination. Although, these public transportation tools can be possible to arrive the destination withing one houe and they must charge cheaper fee to compare taxi. But, however the passenge hopes to arrive the destination in the shortest time. The most important influential factor is that the passenger feels personal time pressure to need to arrive the destination fastly and taxi public transportation tool is believed the fast transportation tool to arrive any destination to compare other general public transportation tools , when it has no traffic jam external environment factor influence. So, time pressure factor will influence passenger to choose taxi transportation tool in preference. Also, it seems that when the place often has many time pressure passengers are living. Then, the place's taxi business will be possible better than other locations. Hence, it implies that time pressure factor will bring need or demand number to be increased to some services.

Time pressure also influences how consumers choose to buy the kind of product, when he/she feels that the kind of product will be old fashin or it is not popular to use in society. For example, computer product, the traditional desktop large heavy weight computers will be possible to be replaced to use at home or office or any building places. Due to the laptop small light weight computers , it can be brought to anywhere by the users easily, even it can be brought to catch public transportation tool to use, it can be brought to restaurant, library, shopping centre etc. different public places to use conveniently. Due to some working people feel hurry to use computer to do their tasks, e.g. typing one document in short time. If they are not working in office and they have no computer on hand. They will worry about that they can not finish their tasks to give their bosses in limited time on the working day.

Hence, laptop computer will be one good chocie of task tool for busy working people when they need to often to use computer to finish urgent tasks in any time. Hence, it seems that the feeling time pressure working people will choose laptop computer in preference more than desktop traditional computer working tool. Due to the feeling time pressure workers, they feel that they can not finish their daily tasks in office. So, they will feel to need to use laptop computer task tool to help them to do office tasks . When they are catching transportation tool to go home or office time or lunch time , or holiday time. So, laptop computer product is more popular to time pressure working people target consumers.

Laptop computer products can also increase the feeling time pressure student consumers' needs. Because when one students feel home time is not enough to use computer to do their homeworkers at homes. When some students finish all lessons in schools and they need to catch public transportation tools to go home, in this catching public transportation time, they will be possible to hope to use one laptop computer to do their homeworks. So, one student who often feels time pressure to do whose homeworks, he will feel need to buy one laptop to carry it to anywhere, e.g. library, garden, school etc. different places. Then, he/she can do whom housework at any places in any time conveniently. Hence, it seems that their laptop computer products will be time pressure consumers' preference task tool.

In conclusion, the different factors influence consumer behaviors. Time pressure factor may be one main factor to influence consumers to choose to buy the kind of product or consume the kind of service in preference. So, when th consumer feels time presure to influence him/her to do preference choice to consume the kind of service of buy the kind of product. It is possible to occur to influence he/she does irrational economic choice decision. Hence, time pressure factor can being positive or negative both consumption emotion to some kinds of services or products . Hence, the increasing or decreasing number of consumers to some kinds of products or services, it has absolute relationship between of them. So, any product sellers or service providers can not neglect the importance of how time pressure factor influences consumer behavior in our nowadays society.

Time pressure impacts consumer
behavioral effect

I shall indicate cases to explain that how time pressure environment factor impacts consumer behavior as well as what effects will be brought by time pressure consumer behavioral cause. Instead of above discussions concern how customer personal time pressure psychological factor influence, whether hoe time pressure environment factor will also influence consumer behavior. What are the difference between time pressure environment factor and time pressure consumer personal psychological factor? I shall explain as below:

Firstly, the impact of life satisfaction is caused by time pressure on consumers responses. Can effective advertising can impact of life satisfaction when the consumer feels need to buy the kind of product in any time pressure environment? Can effective advertising bring direct impact on sales when the consumer feels need to buy the kind of product in time pressure environment? Effective advertising may being advantages, includes customers feel easy to accept of price increases, favorable publicity, and reshaping market segmentation.

However, when the customer feels need life satisfaction in time pressure lif environment. The time pressure life environment ought impact on the consumer responses on advertising. Hence, when the consumer needs to live in the time pressure life environment. The over-commercialization of advertising ought impact the consumer chooses to buy the brand of product, when the seller has attractive advertising to bring purchase incentives to influence consumption desire to the time pressure environment influential consumer. For example, when the summer season will change to winter season, the ice cream consumers begins to feel weather will change to cold weather. Because many people feel more colf in the beginning. This is seasonable time pressure environment feeling, it may influence many ice-cream likers feel ice-cream may be possible shortage in hot weather or summer season, due to many ice-creams will be bought in summer weather to cause supermarkets in possible. So, if the brand ice-cream can make attractive advertisement to persuade ice-incream number will be reduced in the coming winter season beginning. So, it may influence many ice-cream likers choose to buy this brand's ice-cream in preference in summer. Because they feel fear none of any this brand's ice-creams can be sold in supermarkets in summer. Because they feel this brand's ice-cream , it's problem to let they can buy any different kinds of ice-cream taste to eat from any supermarkets in summer season. Hence, it explains why effective or attractive advertising may increase sale number, when consumers feel the brand's product number will be shortage or reduced from the seasonal time pressure external environment factor influence.

Secondly, I shall discuss what is the relationship between the effects of product popularity and time pressure on consumer responses? When a brand is popular to let many customers to familiarize in society. Does it increase time pressure to influence consumers choose in preference? Time pressure remaining to product popularity concerns how much sale number is raised to persuade consumers to choose to buy a preference for ecommerce online shopping. It seems to be one time pressure online sale environment. The effects of the ecommerce online shopping environment has relationship beteen pressure and product popularity on perceived risk and purchase intention.

In ecommerce online sale environment time pressure is operationized at the time remaining for consumers to sign up the online seller' website and property popularity is operationlized to the number of products already sold at the moment when consumers visit the web page. Hence, when on online consumer has intention to buy any products from internet. He/she will attempt to type the product name, then he/she will find some webpages which can provide the different brands of product photos, their prices informations to let the consumer to compare whether which brand of product price is more reasonable, better quality , good product image from the web pages' advertisement information to let him/her to evaluate. Hence, any product web page will influence how every online custmer feeling is good or bad to the web page's any brands of products. If the consumer feel the web page has many high product popularity indicators, it may bring a high consumption desire to let the online cusomer to evaluate the web page all prodocts in order to compare which brand of product is the best to choose to buy in time webpage view pressure consumption environment. Otherwise, if the consumer feels the web page has high product popularity indicator , it may bring a less consumption desire to let the online consumer to evaluate any of the webpage products to choose to buy. So, online webpage advertising information will be one time pressure online ecommerce consumption environment.

I assume that online shopping consumers won't like to stay to view on any webpage long time. It is possible that they choose to click more web pages to hope to find more different familiar and unfamiliar both brands of products informations in order to make more accurate comparison and evaluation from more different kinds of brands of products in order to make the most accurate online shopping decision. Hence, any brands of products online webpage information will be one time pressure limited sale environment to consumers feel that they need to make the most accurate online purchase decision in short time. Moreover, it seems that if the brand of products which can be showed on the popular product webpage, the it will have much sale chance to let online purchasers familiarize in order to increase sale opportunity more easily.

Finally, I shall explain what is the meaning of external time pressure consumption environment is the long time queue waiting consumption environment. I shall explain how to achieve one simplistic queueing system to solve long time queue waiting problem to bring consumers' negative emotion influence to choose to consume the service or buy the product in preference.

For entertainment service example, e.g. queueing at the cinema counter to buy one ticket to watch the movie , or queueing at the music hall to buy one ticket to listen the music performance show activities. The audiences' ticket purchase aims to sit down in the cinema or music hall to enjoy to listen and see pretty music performance or watch the attractive movie comfortable within one to two hours entertainment time. If the movie or music performance show is attractive, the cinema or music hall will have many audiences accept to spend long time to queue to buy the ticket. However, if the cinema ot music hall needs audience consumers to queue long time to buy the ticket, e.g. one houe , even more than one houe queueing time to wait to buy the ticket to watch the movie or listen the music performance show. Then, the long time queue waiting problem will be possible to cause a lot audiences number to be reduced, because they feel that they need to spend much time pressure to queue to by the ticket to listen the music performance show or watch the movie.

However, of these unacceptable too long queue time audiences can have another/ other cinema(s), music hall(s) to buy the same price , even more low price of movie ticket or music performance show ticket in short time. Then, they must leave the present cinema queue and go to the another cinema or music hall to buy ticket to watch the same movie or listen the same music performance show. So, long time queue is one external time pressure environment to influence consumer's preference choice to the service provider, when they feel it has another service provider does not need them or these audiences need to spend same long time queue time to wait to buy the ticket in order to enjoy the service, e.g. listening music performance show, watching movie.

Hence, in a high time pressure queue situation where decision makers, e.g. audiences have less time than needed (or perceived needed). It is very likely that they feel the queue waiting time stress of copying with themselves queue waiting time maximum limitation. So, if the movie ticket purchase audience feels that he/she will need to spend more than half hour to queue and half hour is himself/herself the maximum acceptable queue time level. So, his/her queue long time pressur negative emotion feeling will influence him/her to leave the cinema to choose another cinema. He/ she feels that ir does not need him/her to queue more than half hour in order to buy the ticket to watch the same movie in the another cinema, he/she can feel more comfortable to watch the movie. So, long time queue will influence some audiences choose aother service provider to replace it in possible short time, when they feel waiting in a queue is irritating, frustrating and hence costly.

What is a simplistic queueing system and how it can solve above queue problem. For a grocery store queueing counter case example, for one Apply brand computer shop example, the day's most busy queue time , there are about between fifty and hundred Apply brand potential computer buyers numbers every hour in the day. They need to queue to enquire the salespeople concern to any useful opinions to let them to know in order to make purchase decisions. But, the Apple brand computer shop lacks enough salespeople to answer their enquiries concern any computer purchase challenges. Every computer enquiry potential purchaser needs to spend at least half hour , even more time to queue to wait the salesperson to answer his/her enquiry in the counter queueing line. Hence, the feeling long time queue enquiry waiting consumers will feel time pressure to queue. Then, they will choose to leave the Apple brand computer shop's counter queue line. Consequently, the Apple brand computer will lose many potential computer buyers on the busy day.

The most simple solution is that it can increase the salespeople number in the most busy enquiry time every day.

Hence, when every computer potential enquiry customer can contact every salesperson to listen whom opinion concerns his/her any computer enquiry issues in order to let he/she feels that they every one can provide excellent sale service computer issues enquiry explanation performance to satisfy his/her enquiry need to let himself/herself to feel in the short enquiry time. Due to they do not need to spend long queue time to wait every salesperson's feedback or opinion to solve their enquiries in the computer shop. Because they do not feel presure to spend long time to queue to wait the computer shops's every salesperson's opinion. So, they will raise satisfactory feeling to thie Apple computer shop's every salesperson individual sale enquiry service performance.

Consequently, the day's computer sale number will be possible to raise after the salespeople can spend much time to solve their enquiries effectively and efficiently.

- The reasons cause consumers feel

time pressure

What factors can cause consumers feel time pressure to but the product in the personal time limited dominated consumption environment? It is one interesting question: Why does the consumer feel time pressure to make short time purchase decision making? I shall indicate some cases to explain this possibility as below:

First, I shall indicate household purchaser time pressure consumption behavior. Consumer house buyer behavior, some house buyer will feel personal time pressure to choose the different houses to make house purchase decision in short time. For example, if the house developer has a 30% discount house price to sell only in the short three months. So, after this three months, all house purchaser will need to pay the original house price. If the house developer's houses prices are between US doller one million to two million every house. For one million house price after 30% discount , the house buyer only needs to pay seventy million. For two million house price after 30 % discount, the house buyer only needs to pay one hundred and fourty million. So, expensive product's financing factor will influence the buyer's consumption time pressure, such as the house discount price case, due to the house developer's houses prices are very expensive. However, if any house buyers can make decisin to buy its houses in three months. Then, they can pay les 30% of the houses prices. Such as the original price one million house, the house buyer can pay less thirty million amount or the original price two million houses prices. The house buyer can pay less sixty million amount. So, the large discount financing amount may be attractive purchase method to influence many house buyers feel time pressure to decide whether they ought choose to buy the property developer's houses in these three months. It is one short term cheap house financing price to let many house buyers feel time pressure to make house purchase decision from this house developer in these three months . Hence, short term high discount price to expensive product financing factor will influence consumers feel it is right time to make pressure consumption decision.

Hence, such as this three months house discount price case, when the property buyer gain this property developer's knowledge of three months house discount price message. This sudden three months house discount price message will be one attractive knowledge of factor to impact the potential property buyers' house purchase desires to be raised in three months time pressure house purchase consumption environment. So, it is one feeling sudden time pressure consumption desire good example for this three monts large discount attractive houes price to influence house buyers to make house purchase decision from the house developer in these three months. Consequently, house developer will have possible to raise the large house sale number , if this 30 % house discount price can let many property buyers feel it is one worth purchase price in these three months. So, they will consider that they can not pay less 30% discount price to buy this house developer's any houses after three months. So they need to make house purchase decision in these three months short term time pressure house consumption market for this property developer.

So, this time pressure financing advantage will only bring benefit to this property developer, this time pressure financing advantage won't bring benefit to other property developers, because all property buyers feel need to make property purchase decision in these three months suddenly, due to this property developer can provide a special 30 discount price to any property final decision making to choose to buy its houses in these three months temporary short time. It seems that three months short time can cause final house purchase choice time pressure to any potential property buyers. They expect to gain high discount price to buy any expensive houses. So, these expenaive house potential buyers will feel need to make final expensive house purchase decision to choose to buy this property developer's expensive houses in these final three months perios. So, time pressure can occur in any short period, when the seller can provide any special sale promotion to persuade consumers to feel need to make sudden time pressure that purchase decision is they hope to earn special sale promotion consumption in the short limited sale perios for the seller.

Hence, consumer personal time pressure feeling, it can be predictive to any time occurrence pychological consumption, feeling, such as the property developer's sudden high per cent discount price to expensive house less dinancing burden factor to influence the expensive house buyers feel that whether they ought do choice house purchase decision in these short term three months , because the house developer's unpredictive and sudden attractive expensive houses reducing prices strategy. So, this property developer's short term three months high house discount price time pressure consumption strategy may persuade or attract , even encourage many potential expensive house buyers choose to spend lesser amount to buy this property developer's discount houses, either is paid by house mortgage bank loan lending payment method or installment payment method or on-time all payment method. So, the different house payment choice buyers will be influenced to make immediate property purchase decision in these three months time pressure period from this property developer's expensive discounted house number influence.

However, in this house market time pressure consumption environment, the property developer's expensive house supply number may also have influential effort to excite the expensive house buyers' house purchase consumption desires, for example, if the other expensive house property developers' between US one million and US two million of every property price's these houses in the country's property marker totel suppy number is one thousand property unit number. The potential property buyers , they plan to buy these amounts of expensive houses , the property needers estimate three thousand buyers number at least. Hence, it seems that these expensive house buyers' demand id more than three times to expensive property supply number.

Moreover, the other property developer's expensive property developers ' expensive house prices have no any discount in this three months periods, and some property developers' expensive house prices tend to increase 1 to 10 per cent in these three months period. Hence if the property developer can supply at least three thousand property units number between US one million and US two million sale price and all of these expensive houses are reduced 30 per cetnt discount to sell in these three months .

Consequently, it is possible to persuade all estimated three thousand expensive house potential buyers choose to buy this property developer's houses in these three months in possible. So, it explain that why this property developer's expensive discounted house supply number will influence these property buyers' preference choice. If this property developer has only one thousand expensive houses to be supplied by discounted 30% sale price. Then, it will cause shortage of expensive houses to satisfy these three thousand expensive house buyer estimated number in the country in three month discount sale promotion period.

Consequently, this property developer will lose two thousand these prices of expensive house potential buyers number in all these three months discounted sala period . I assume that all these three thousand expensive house property buyers will be influenced to make choice to buy its all dicounted expensive houses in these three month time pressure discounted sale period. So, it needs to do data gather concerns how many of thee expensive house potential house buyers number in its country in order to avoid discounted expensive houses supply number to cause shortage supply challenges and bring these expensive house potential buyers lose number in these three months period.

In conclusion, it explains why that supply number will influence this property developer's sale number in these three months sale period. Consequently, time pressure sale strategy ans supply number has close relationship to influence the seller's sale number in the time pressure sale period.

Secondly, I shall discuss how does environment time pressure factor influences consumer behavior? Does time pressure influence consumer donating behavior? I assume that external environment time pressure factor can influence consumer changes whom original purchase decision making. What circumstance's time can influence consumer individual to feel time pressure to consume. For example, when the consumer expects have one hour to choose whether which brand of product to buy among the different kinds of products. The circumstance is changed suddenly. It influences the consumers feel that they has only 10 minutes to make the final purchse decision.

Why does the consumer feel enough brand of product? What external circumstance factors influence he/she feels only 10 minutes time to make the final purchase decision suddenly? For travel fair time limited external environment influential pressure travelling consumption case example, the international travel fair can indicate that time limited pressure has positive significant influence on traveller perceived value and purchase intention in short time. In addition, perceived value is served as a mediating factor between the relationship of time limited pressure and feeling travelling entertainment purchase intention to the travel fair visitors. It has a beneficial reference for planning a travelling show or fair marketing strategy.

One attractive travelling fair/show can promote the country's different attractive travelling destinations to let the travellinf show's visitors to know. It can particularly influence the visitors' long time travelling planning , it can be shorten be short time travelling planning, e.g. after one year's travelling planning can be influenced to make immediate focused on choosing the country's travelling decision if he/she feels the country has more attractive travelling destinations, he/she prefers to go to travel in short time, e.g. within 6 months . So, when the travelling exhibition fair/show can provide the country's beautiful scene photos to let the visitors to view. Then, it will bring effective time pressure feeling to let some travelling visitos feel travelling needs immediately in the travelling exhibition show/fair . This travelling exhibition show/fair can bring the time limited pressure benefit. It is as an external environment factor that can influence the travelling visitors' travelling desires to be raised , when they can view many benefitical scene photos of the country' different undiscovered travelling destination . Then, it can increase their travelling desires to the country in possible.

I shall explain why travelling exhibition show/fair can play an important role in travelling consumer perceived quality and travelling country destination choice decision making to influence travelling visitors feel time limited pressure. However, perceived value has been show to be a value has been shown to be a value of perceived quality and perceived sacrifice to cause travelling visitors feel more interesting to choose to travel the country when they can view the attractive beautiful scence photos in the travelling exhibition show/fair.

A successful travelling exhibition show/fair can bring time limited process increases , the travelling visitors pay more attention to key travelling destination features and positive travelling information from the scene photos and travelling destinations introduction. So , the country's attractive travelling destinations scene photos and clear travelling introduction to different destinations information will be important message to let the different countries' travelling visitors to know when they spend a limited time to enter the travelling exhibition show/fair to view the different scene photos . If the travelling visitor feel very satisfied to the country's travelling exhibition show/fair. Then, this travelling exhibition excite whom travelling interest to choose to go to the country to travell in short time, when the travelling visitors are influenced to feel the country has many beautiful destinations where they feel have travelling interest in the limited time pressure travelling exhibition show/fair environment. If the travelling exhibition show/fair needs they to pay enter fee and it has only two hours or less time to premit to stay in the travelling exhibition show/fair.

Hence, if the time pressure limited travelling exhibition show/fair can let the travelling visitors feel attractive and enjoyable view feeling when they look every the country's any scene beautiful photos and indication how to the different travelling destinations and explains why the country's travelling places are value travelling destinations to let the exhibition visitors to know, when they do not know or discover these any one of value travelling places in the country before. Then, this limited time staying travelling exhibition show/fair will bring positive time pressure to influence some travelling visitors feel interesting to visit the country's inknown or undiscovery travelling destinations in short time. So, all attractive travelling exhibition shows/fairs are one external environment time limited positive pressure factor to excite some travelling visitors' travelling desires in short time in possible.

Instead of travelling exhibition show/fair can bring external environment positive limited time positive pressure to excite travelling visitors' travelling consumption desires, the another external environment positive limited time positive pressure case is that mobile coupons of limited mobile phone sale number or discount mobile phone call payment plan in short time case. How and why mobile coupons can excite any mobile consumption and/ or mobile phone call user choice to the mobile phone sale company or mobile phone call service provider.

An effective mobile plane useful limited time beneficial purchase strategy can encourage some mobile phone consumers to choose to use the brand mobile useful phone call service plan immedicately. if the mobile phone call service plan is attractive to the mobile phone call consumer . For example, dynamic discounts strategies are used by marketers to send scaraity message which lead to higher consumers' mobile phone purchase intention. An utility increasing discount straregy provides mobile phone call users with an increasing discount over time (e.g. 30% discount for in-store consumption for 30 minutes, after which the discount increases to 40 % , an utility discount strategy provides the same discounts for mobile phone call users over a specific promotional period (e.g. 40% discount from 9AM to 5 PM) phone call using time. An utility decreasing discount strategy offers mobile phone call users with a decreasing discount over time (e.g. 40% discount for in -store consumption for 10 minutes, after which the discount decreases to 30%).

However, these three different discount strategies for bargaining have different impacts on outcomes. However, they have same influences to lead mobile phone call users feel time pressure to do choose whether this mobile phone call using plan is suitable. If the mobile phone call user feels this mobile phone call using plan is suitable to use, then this mobil coupon promotion strategy can influence mobile phone user feels limited time pressure to persuade him/ her to choose to use its mobile phone call service under different time limitation, quantity limitation and discount strategies on the mobile phone user's mobile phone call plan using intention.

Furthermore, I hypothesize that the brand of mobile phone quantity, limited scarcity message that gives a perception that the brand of any kinds of mobile phones are limited for purchase, it will have a positive impact on mobilt phone consumers‘ perceived value of mobile products, leading to a greater tendancy to make mobile phone purchase decision immediately. Hence, mobile coupon is one type of price-incentive promotion. In various price incentives, discount strategy is a mode of price negotiation between the mobile product conumer and the merchant, such as the mobile phone seller , mobile phone call user and mobile phone call service provider.

However, mobile coupons offer discount under a time constraint to induce perceived scarcity. Scarce commodities are more attractive than those with plenty inventory due to the speciality and uniqueness of the former perceived by the consumer. However, scarcity has both forms. They incluce quantity scaracity can let consumers feel need to buy the product in short time. Otherwise, due to stock shortage or low inventory to influence they can not brought the kind of product. Time scarcity means products are for sale only for a designated

May time dominate consumption
final purchase decision making

Whether can time limited pressure dominate consumer individual to make more rational purchase decision? Can the consumer make more rational decision , when he/she has enough time to make final purchase decision? I shall explain why and how the consumer can make more rational decision when he/she has enough time as well as I shall explain that without time pressure environment. It may dominate consumers to make more rational or more accurate decision making.

I assume that it is the final time limited pressure day to nee the consumer to spend more nervous do time final purchase decision among the different kinds of similar products choices, e.g. air conditions . If the consumer decides that the day is the final purchase decisin to choose to buy one air conditin among these different brands of similar air conditions in the super store. So, if on the that day, he/she can not make any final decisin to choose which brand of air condition to buy on that final consumption day in the super store when the super store visitor sees the final air condition consumption day advertisement in this year in this super store . Then, he/she won't buy any air condition again if he/she can not buy on that day in this super store.

The another time dominates immediate purchase behavior is that I assume that one common air condition can not be bought in short time later if all air condition consumers can not make decision to buy any air condition in this super store. So, his/her personal time limited pressure can dominate whose final or condition purchase decision in this super store on that day. If the store has many different brands of air conditions to lead him/her to spend long time to compare which is th best worth to buy in this super store. Then, it will let him/her to feel difficult to make the air condition final purchase decision in the store on that day. Otherwise, if the super store has less different brands of air conditions to need him/her to spend less time to compare which is the best worth to buy in the store. Then, he/she may make the final air conditin purchase decision making more easily on that day.

So, the final air condition purchase day of the super store, the super store's air condition final day's time can dominate the air condition buyer to make air condition purchase decision immediately. Due to he/she feels that all of these day brands air conditions can not bought from this super store after that day. So, he/she needs to make the air condition purchase decision making in this super store on that final air condition purchase day in this year. Because it is the final air condition purchase day in this super store of all sir conditions products. If he/she can not make the choice to buy any one brand of air condition in this store. Then, it is possible that he/she will lose this store's final cheap price air condition purchase benefits. However, if this super store has too many brands of air conditions need him/her to choose. It will cause him/her to spend more time to choose. Consequently, it will cause he/she feels difficult to compare which brand of air condition is the best and he / she does not choose to buy any one in this super store.

Hence, this super store ought have less number different brands of air conditions to let every air condition consumer to choose in order to let they can make final air condition purcahse decision on this air condition cheap price purchase final day. So, less different number brands of air conditions will dominate the consumers to spend less time to make purchase decision immediately and easily on that final sale day in this super store. Hence, it seems that the super store's final air conditions sold day time will dominate many air condition visitors to make purchase decision when they visit this super store in summer season on that day in this super store. Because all this super store's air condition consumers do not expect that they can not buy the best quality of air conditin in this super store final sold day , due to air condition stocks number shorten challenge is not supplied enough on that final cheap purchase day in this super store. Consequently, that time pressure will increase to influence them to make the final air condition purchase decision in the final sold day' s short time, before this super store closing time on that day. Their time pressure feeling comes from the super store 's air condition number shortage supply in possibility. It will dominate them to make the final air condition purchase decision in this super store in short time.

The anothe time dominates immediate purchase behavior case is that I assume that one common picture painter(actor), he finds one architect to help him to build one house. The architect only needs to folloe his house picture to build one house. The common picture painter tells him that he will give him building expenditure and building profit after he helps him to build the house profit after he helps him to build the house successfully. After six months, the architect made one decision, he did not demand the famous picture painter paid him for the building service fee. But, he needed him give the house picture to him to replace the building service fee. Because the picture painter feels that he didn't need to pay the building service fee to him to buy the architect's building service in these six months building time. Hence, he accepted his offer to give his common house picture to the architect for his reward.

I assume that this six months time dominate the architect to make the final building service fee decision either acceptance the common picture painter customer's building service fee or acceptance his common house picture replaces the building service fee. However, the architect believes that this common house picture can have higher selling price to compare his building service fee income. Consequently, I assume that his evaluation is right, this house picture selling price is more than three times to compare his past six months's building service income. So, it proved that his choice is right, because he could earn more than three times of his building service income after he decided to accept the common picture painter's this house picture to attempt to sell it in the picture auction market. It seems that this six months long house building time can dominate these both buyer and seller's purchase and selling behaviors, such as this picture painter and this architect. When the architect has this six months enough time to let the picture painter to change his building service offer decision from building service fee payment to his common house picture offer exchange. This architect can achieve his intention to let him to accept his free house picture sold product exchange offer more easily. Otherwise, if the architect can not need six months to build this house, he only needs three months or less time to build this house, then it is possible that the picture painter won't accept his this house picture offer to replace his building service fee easily. If he considers that whether his this house picture's selling price has possible to sell higher price to compare this building service fee for this house picture. He will choose to sell this house picture himself. Hence, due to the picture painter can not sell this house picture in this past six months. So, in this six months period, the house painter can not sell this house picture in picture auction market. This six months period can dominate his low market worth selling feeling to this house picture as well as it can influence him to make this house picture exchange decision to replace his house service fee.

The picture painter will ask himself, ought the house picture painter need to wait how long time to sell this picture in auction market, because he does not know whether the architect needs how long time to build this house? So, this house building time can dominate the picture painter's acceptance of the architect's this free house picture product exchange offer, which is easier acceptance or difficult acceptance . In this six month' house building period between the architect service provider and the picture painter house buyer. Hence,the house building time can dominate the house building provider and the picture painter's house building buyer both's house picture free exchange purchase change behavioral choice between of them influentially.

The another time dominates consumption behavior case is that time rich or time poor factor, e.g. one fast food famous restaurant , its success is not only due to its fast food good taste factor, its restaurant location whether is close to the time poor people's offices, it is one main factor. Because this fast food famous restaurant only choose to build its restaurants to close to offices in any large cities in different countries. Hence, the franchisees need to pay expensive franchise loyalty income to buy its franchise in order to it can supply fast foods to the franchisees to sell, but they also need to pay expensive rent to this fast food franchiser, due to their fast food restaurant locations has been chose to locate in the main cities in different countries from the fast food famous restaurant's location decision. Hence, whether long or short time fast restaurant rent period to the franchisees , which can dominate the fast food restaurants's royalty and rent income. For example, if one fast food franchisee only sign one year contract to buy the fast food franchisor's loyalty to help it to sell its fast foods only one year, because it does not ensure how many fast food consumers will choose to buy these fast foods to eat, due to its price is decided by the fast food franchisor. If the cities have other fast food restaurants to let them to choose, they may find other fast food restaurants to replace it to eat fast foods very easily. If this fast good restaurant is not the most famous and it operates only short time. So, it can not earn more fast food franchisees' confidence to accept to pay long time rent to operate its fast food restaurants in cities and pay long time royalty fee to it. Otherwise, if the fast food restaurant had operated its restaurant for a long time period to raise its fast food loyalty's to let many different countries' fast food eaters to familiarize or acknowledg its fast food brand in popular. So, long fast food opersation time can confirm that it has many fast food eaters, they prefer to choose to eat its fast foods. It can increase the franchisees' confidence to choose to rent its fast food restaurants and pay royalty to it in preference. Hence, the fast food franchisor's restaurant operation time whether it is long or short time, this franchisor's fast food restaurant operating time pressure factor will dominate the fast food franchisees' choices to decide to pay how long rent sand franchise royalty income to rent its restaurant to do the franchisee's fast food business in the cities locations in different countries. So, it seems that the fast food franchisor's business operation time can dominate the frahchisees' choice.

In special , in fast food industry, time rich and time poor consumers behavior will dominate their fast food choices. Time rich people feel they have enough or too much time when time poor people feel time is a major constraint in their daily life. The explansion of the fast food business, and the increase eatting of fast food are indicators of this trend. At the same time, shorter working hours increased wealth and less pressure on domestic rountines have opened up new segments of leisure consumption. But, " free time" in certain areas has not for many people, lead to an increases feeling of time richness.

So, it explains that why many fast food consumers who feel not enough time to work daily. They are time poor working people usually. So, instead of fast food taste factor influences consumer number. The people who feel time rich or poor, e.g. employmet rich or poor lunch time to the employee, it will dominate the employee chooses to go to fast food restaurant in preference. So, the fast food restaurant can supply rich time to let them to eat lunch in short time, if the employee has less time to eat lunch or more tasks need hime to do on that day afternoon. Hence, feeling time rich or poor to the people factor, which will dominate some consumers' choices to some kinds of businesses, such as fast food industry, or for public transportation tool choice case example, one time poor passenger feels need to go to the destination in short time. The time poor passenger will prefer to choose taxi in preference, then it is possible train or underground train, next it is tram, fainally, it is bus or ferry public transportion tool choices. Otherwise, for one time rich passenger, he has more time to go to the destinaton. The time rich passenger will prefer to choose the cheap public transportation tool , such as bus, ferry, underground train, ferry, train. The final choice is taxi. So, passenger's time pressure will influence whose public transportation tool choice.

● Time pressure dominiates consumer psychological factor

What are the factors of time pressure dominate consumer purchcase psychological behaviors? How any why do this time pressure psychological factors dominate consumer behaviors? It is possible that time pressure can dominate consumer mind and behavior either choose to buy the product/consume the service or not buy the product/ consume the service. Every consumer's final purchase decision, he/she is influenced how to make by himself/herself personal psychological limited time pressure . It means that he/she will have one time maximum standard to demand himself/herself to make the final purchase decision in whose individual psychological time standard (the consumer's individual psychological limited consumption time). So, it seems that ever consumer's final decision how he/she chooses to buy the product or consume the service, his/her consumption behavior will be dominated by whose psychological time limited consumption pressure.

So, time pressure issue seems evolutionary psychology, it looks at how consumer behavior has beed affected by psychological adjustments during time pressure evoluation. It seeks to identify which consumer psychological traits are evolved through adaptations, e.g. time pressure consumption adaptations to choose the final purchase decision in the final time limited consumption pressure environment, e.g. the consumer expects this day is the final day to choose to buy what kinds of the product. If he/she can't make final purchase decisin on the day, he/she will choose to buy the kind of product later, even he/she does not choose to buy the kind of product in the first or again, that is the products of natural selection, or the supermaket visitor case, he expects to choose which kind of food to eat within final 15 minutes, if he/she can't make the final decision to buy what kind of food to eat within final 15 minutes in this supermarket , or the restaurant eatting consumer case, he is queueing to wait to enter the restaurant to eat. He/ she expects the final queue waiting time is 15 minutes maximum. If after this 15 minutes, he/she can not be permited to enter this restaurant, then he/she will choose to leave this restaurant and he/she will find another restaurant to replace it. So, it seems that any consumer will have himself/herself consumption limited stardard time to decide whether he/she ought choose to buy any products or consume any services in any consumption environment.

Hence, the cause of consumption time pressure dominates consumer behavior, it is based on these hypothesis: Every consumer has demand characteristic and time pressure can dominate how he/she make final decision to buy or not buy any product or consume any service as well as any consumer needs have time pressure consumption demand because he/she does not expect to epend more time to choose what kinds of products to buy or what kinds of services to consume. He/she expects to make purchase or consumption final decision in short time.

IN fact, consumers will be encoded to influence how they make final purchase decision. There are three main ways in which product information can be encoded. They include: Visual (product picture) ; for example, the conumer stores the memory by visualizing it as on product image. Aconstic (sound); here the consumer stores the information as a sound , this explains why some consumers sometimes get the brand name(words) that sound the same mixed up when they try to remember them. Semantic (meaning); here the object is stored in terms of what it means rather than as an image or sound, e.g. when the brand of toys can let many children feel fun to play. Then, when many parents feel familiar to the toy brand, they must remember this toy brand company is selling any kinds of toys to let children to play. So, famous brand can let consumers familiarize what products that it is selling. Such as the toy brand company can let parents feel its toys are fun to let their children to play. All these sensory information can dominate consumers make final choice purchase behavior to buy its product or consume its service in preference in any time limited pressure environment, if the brand can give positive information memory to let many customers to remember.

So, it seems that consumers are dominated to choose which kinds of products to buy or which kinds of services to consume by positive or negative emotion, time pressure in any consumption environment immediately. It is one time pressure consumption environment theory factor, it can influence consumer behavior is changed in any consumption environment time. Consequently, it explains that why time pressure can dominate consumer behaviors in possible. Also, any product seller or service provider needs to consider how to manage consumption time process to be longer to cause its consumers doe not choose to buy its product or consume its service consequently.

Methods avoid consumers
feel time pressure

In business society, it seems that any consumers will feel time pressure to cause their purchase decision making process changes in any consumption suitations, when they feel time pressure either by themselves or third parties influence, e.g. not buying any thing, not consuming any service, irrational making consumption final decision etc. consumption behaviors. How to reduce their time pressure to avoid they do above consumption behaviors. I shall indicate some consumption suitations to explain how to avoid their reducing consumption , due to time pressure factor influences as below:

Firstly, I shall indicate supermarket consumption environment example. In general, supermarket visitors will expect to spend less time to visit any supermarkets to make choice to biy any foods. They will stay short time when they expect to buy less foods, even, they will stay more short time when they expect to buy more less foods in any supermarkets. So, any supermarkets will need to calculate their clients' limited time pressure how to influence their foods consumption number. If the supermarket visitor expects to spend maximum 20 minutes to buy any foods in the supermarket. Then, he may choose some different kinds of foods to buy, e.g. icecream, fruit, bread, jam, fish etc.

different kinds of foods, Otherwise, if the another supermarket visot expects to spend maximum 10 minutes to buy any foods in the supermarket. Then, he may choose less different kinds of foods to compare the first one, e.g. fish, jam, icecream only or bread, fruit , jam only. So, the second one supermarket visitor will buy less different kinds of foods, because he expects to spend 10 minutes maximum , his shopping spending time is less 10 minutes to compare the first one supermarket visitor. Because different supermarket visitor personal time pressure will limit him/her to choose more or less different kinds of foods to buy. However, time pressure will not influence every kind of foods number because every kind of food purchase number will not be influenced to buy more or less , due to the supermarket visitor personal time pressure variable factor influences his/her foods purchase number. Otherwise, the different kinds of food choice will be influenced to choose to either buy or not buy , due to every supermarket visitor personal time pressure is different.

Hence, supermarkets can focus on how to avoid any kinds of food purchase choice loses , due to supermarket consumer personal time pressure influences. In fact, in supermarket every shelf, it usually has many different brands of every kind of foods to let supermarket visitors to choose to buy. For example,the kind of jam food number has many brands are placed on shelf to let them to choose, e.g. there are more than 10 different brands of jam food are placed on one shelf. It will bring one choice problem. IF one supermarket visitor expects to choose one brand of jam within 5 minute, then he finds the shelf has more than 10 different brands of jam are placed on the shelf. Then he will feel time pressure to cause difficulty to choose the best brand of jam to buy from these 10 brands of jam. It will bring the negative emotion if he feels that all of these 10 brands of jam taste and price has no more difference. Consequently, these 10 brands of jam choice will cause he can not make the final jam purchase decision within this 5 minutes individual time limited. Anyway, if there are only 5 brands of jam are placed on this shelf, then the 5 minutes time limited consumer will has less brands of jam choices, it will influence him to do more easy choice to buy one kind of brand jam food from the shelf. It is one limited time pressure of psychological choice factor to influence any consumers feel to do any brand of food choice more easy in short time. Hence, I recommend supermarket shelf ought place every kind of food brand maximum to 5 brands , it is the best food brand number to every supermarket's shelves to let any consumers to choose different kinds of foods to make the easy food choice way in supermarket food market.

So, in super store market, it is similar to supermaket market. Super stores' main products are cloths, shoes, bags, stationarys, electronic products, e.g. fans, air conditions, televisons, radios, warmers, washing machines, dry machines, computers etc. However, super store visitors will like to spend more time to stay in any super stores, due to they feel to need more time to make purchase decision in order to make the most right choice to buy these any products. They usually expect to stay half hour , even one hour or more time in super stores. Their time pressures are depended on whether what kinds of products that they expect to buy in the super store. For example, if the super store visitor expects to buy one laptop computer. He will expect to make purchase choice decision within half hour, even more time. Otherwise, if the super store visitor expects to buy stationery, e.g. pen and rubber and pencil, he will expect to make purchase choice decision within 10 minutes. So, when the super store visitor expects to buy the product is more expensive, then his time pressure time will be longer than the super store visior expects to buy the product is cheap, such as stationery and laptop two kinds of products.

However , due to super store 's expensive and cheap product consumers whose time pressures are different. So, brands choice number will have much different between them. For laptop example, due to superstore visitors can accept to spend longer time to make laptop purchase choice. So, one shelf can place 5 to 10 different brands of laptops , another shelf can place 5 to 10 different brands of laptops to let them to choose. Otherwise, for stationery example, due to superstore visitors can not accept to spend longer time to make stationery purchase choice. so, one shelf can place less than 5 brands of pens, the another shelf can place less than 5 brands of pencils or another shelf can place less than 5 brands of rubbers , another shelf can place less than 5 brands of rulers to let them to make purchase choice in short time.

Secondly, for restaurant eaters example, when one restaurant has many eaters choose to enter this restaurant to eat its food, then it only chooses to let some eaters to enquire ticket number to queue to wait. Of course, some eaters will not like to wait too long time, so they will leave the queue to choose another restaurant to replace it in possible. For example, in afternoon eating time, these are two busy eaters, the student feels hurry to go to school or the working person feels hurry to go to office after lunch, although the restaurant service staff had given him one ticket to let them to queue to wait. However, their expected queue waiting time is within 15 maximum, but there are many eaters are queuing and their ticket numbers are small numbers. So, they feel that they must not enter this restaurant within 15 minutes themselves limited queue time. Consequently, their late entering this restaurant after 15 minutes issue will influence that they will choose another restaurant in possible. So, the restaurant long time queue will cause some eaters choose another restaurant in busy time. I recommend that the restaurant can limit every eater's eatting time, e.g. it calculate every eater's restaurant entering time and it limits every must leave the restaurant within half hour in busy eatting time. It can post notice to let them to know in the front door, e.g. Every eater needs to leave our restaurant within half hour, otherwise, you will need to bring your food to leave please. So, every eater know that they need to eat all food within half hour, otherwise, they need to bring their food to leave this restaurant. Then, this restaurant can increase more seats to let many queue waiting eaters , they do not queue to spend long time to wait to enter this restaurant. Consequently, many queue waiting eaters will choose to enter this restaurant, due to their queue waiting times are not exceed their time pressure limited time.

The final case is cinema queue . In general, any cinemas will have many audiences need to wait to buy tickets to watch movies. However, if the cinema has many audiences , they need to spend one hour, or two hours , even more than two hours to queue to wait to buy the ticket to watch any movies in the cinema. If some audiences' expected queue waiting times are within one hour. So, if these audiences' expected queue waiting timesa are more than one hour. Then, they will choose to leave this cinema and choose other cinemas to replace it in possible. How to avoid these time pressure audiences losing number increases in cinema busy time? I recommend that this cinema ought increase ticket purchase counter service staffs number , e.g. opening more three to five ticket purchase counters number in order to let these one hour time queue time waiting audiences can purchase ticket to watch their movies within one hour. So, opening urgent ticket purcahse service counters number issue is depended on whether there are how many audiences are waiting to buy ticket in the cinema in the time. However, it is only one best way to avoid the cinema audiences number loses in cinema busy time.

Time press how influences video playing game consumer purchase behavior

I shall explain that why it has relationship between the video game student consumer individual learning time and the working people individual working time both can influence video game playing consumer individual video game choice behavior. I shall assume that the different kinds of video game content difficult or easy win competition and entertainment spending on playing time factor will have more influence how the student or working person individual choice of what kind of video game purchase. Otherwisem evey video game price and brand and video game entertainment design content will have less inflience to every video game consumer individual purchase choice.

Why do the every video game's learning playing time and the playing time is spent to satisfy the feeling of winning game both factors will be the main factors to influence the feeling busy learning student or feeling rest working personal target video game playing consumer individual kind of which video game software purchase choice? Why do feeling busy learning students or feeling rest working people will be prefer to choose to buy the kinds of need spending little time to learn to play to achieve the easy winning of the video game content aim in short time?

Nowadays, the different brands of video game products have different prices, various entertainment design contents and the easy or difficult win content feeling to be promoted to sell to satisfy the students or working people video game players' entertainment needs. However, time pressure will be one important factor to influence students of working peoples' video games choices. I shall explain that the time pressure factor how will influence the feeling busy learning or feeling rest working video game players or video game content software consumers to choose to buy the kinds of video games softwares which can let them to feel to spend little playing and learning time and they can feel easy to win the the video game competition in short time preference in this electronic enterainment video game industry.

Nowadays, video game target customers, they are young students and adult working people in common. When , the student does not need to go to school and he/she stays at home, he /she will like to play video game after he/she finishs to learn just a moment usually or the adult working person finishs jobs on the day, after he/she ate dinner, he/she will also like to play video game at home. So , video game can be one kind of entertainment product to let they feel enjoy to play when they re staying at homes.

Video game can be one kind of entetainment culture or entertainment behavior at home to them in popular. A player's ability to perform within a game entertainment is important, and players tend to knowledgeable about their achievements and failures within any game world. So, when one student hopes toget pass grade in school examination. He will choose to spend little time to attempt to win the video game content competition in short time because it can let him to feel that may increase his confidence to pass the grade in the school examination later in possible when he ensures that he had won the video game content competition. He believes that he can be trained to raise whose judgement and mind and analysis abilitiy in his playing visdo game proceed. Instead of playing video game can increase student learning confidence, it can also increase the working people's confidence, when the working person hopes to be promoted or increased salary later from his supervisor's appreciation. He will attempt to spend little time to win the kind of video game content competition in short time. He will have more condifent to achieve to raise his working performance to let his supervisor appreciation if he can learn how to win the kind of video game competition in short time.

It seems that whether the player needs to spend how much time to learn how to win any kind of video content game competitin , this " spending learning time of winning any video content game competition in time pressure playing environment feeling factor will influence the student or working person 's video game content purchase choice. If the video game design is more complex or difficult to let the player to feel to learn to win the game competition as well as it also needs them to spend more long time to learn to play and win the kind of video content game competition. Then, it has possible to influence the hard learning students or hard working people video game consumers, they do not choose to buy any kinds of need spending long learning and playing time to win the kinds of video content game competitive software products. So, it seems that the spend how much playing and learning time to win the video game content competition factor will bring time pressure to let the hard working people or hard learning student video game consumers choose to buy the video content game software products are easy to learn to play in preference because they expect to pass grade or appreciate easy, if they feel that they can learn how to win the video game content competition in short time as well as they do not spend much playing time to win the kind of video game content competition and they will reduce their learning time at homes.

I shall explain why price won't be the main factor to influence video game players' purchase choices in preference. Some video game software sellers feel reduced sale price can attract many video game buyers' choice in preference. It is one wrong mind, due to video game software price is not too much high, it is one kind popular cheap entertainment software product. So , the kinds of similar entertainment content design video game products , their sale price difference between the kind of most expensive , the highest price video game software and the kind of the cheapest , the lowest price video game software won't be difference very much. Their price difference level may be US 410 to US$50 or even less than US$50 level. So,, one video fame entertainment player won't feel that the kind of similar content design of video game software's higher price which will influence he chooses to buy another cheaper similar of kind video game content design software product to replace to the prior higher price one. Because their price difference are not too much or video game software entertainment product is not on kind of expensive product to let them to feel. So, it seems what video game software price won't influence the video game players' prior one of preference choice, it is not easy to be replaced from later cheaper one, when the video game player feels like to play the kind of high price of video game content software before.

Can the video game content influence player individual purchase motivation in preference? In fact, there are many different kinds of video game contents to let players to choose. This free-to -play busines model that has rapidly speed to achieve games services to general . So, some students or working people players can free download some kinds of video game softwares to play from online channel. It will be attractive to the no paid video game players. Hence, free download video game content will influence the paid video game players' purchase decisions for in -game content are not only affected by people's existing general attitudes, consumption values, and movitations , but also by the design decisions and the needs built into the game by the developers. Because the paid video game players won't like to buy the similar content video games, which can be free download to play from online or internet channel. They will feel infair or not worth or loss if they choose to pay to buy the similar video game content entertainment software, after they discovered that they may be free download this kind of similar video game content to play from internet.

It will bring this question: Why will time pressure influence video game player chooses to download free video game to play in preference? When one student feels that he has no enough time to study, he won't choose to fo to any video game shops to do video game software comparative behavior to compare which one's price is lower, game playing content is more attractive, brand is familar in order to make final purchase decision in preference. If he discovered that there has one kind of video game content, which can be free download to play from internet or online channel . So, when the student feels that he needs have much time to study on the day. Hw will choose to attempt to find some kind of video game contents from computer tool which has the attractive entertainment content , it can let he to feel enjoy to play and it is free download from mobile or computer. Then, he won't choose to spend unpredictive time to visit any video game shops to make purchase decision on that day. So, time pressure will be one factor to influence some video game software consumers to feel whether they ought either visit any video game shops to make purchase choice or download some free video game contents at homes for the feeling no enought learning time student players. Even time pressure will also influence adult working people video game players, when the working person feels tries after his full day busy working on that day. Then, he will want to stay at home to rest . Although, he expects to visit any video game shops to choose which video game software product(s) to buy on that day, but when he discovered taht there are some video game contents which ar attractive to influence him to do free download behavior from internet at home. Also, he feels very tried and he will choose to stay at home on that day. If he can find some free video game contents are attractve to influence he chooses to do free download video game contents behavior and replace visiting video game stores behavior on that day. So, free download video game content entertainment activity will be one attractive promotin video game software method to assist the video game sellers' new video game products to let many feeling time pressure learning or working video game players to know from internet channel.

Consequently, online free entertainment video game content download playing choice will influence many video game shops will lose many feeling time pressure video game players number every day in possible. Also, it means that the lazy students or disliking learning students or no job people or (less working hours) part time working people, they will be the main target video game customers, due to they accept to spend much time to visit their video game shops to choose any kinds of video game softwares to buy in preference.

- How can video game advertisement method influence feeling time pressure and feeling without time pressure video game software consumer purchase purchase?

In fact, video game sellers can choose new media chnnel to advestise their new video game software products, e.g. computer online advertisemen channel, instead of video game pictures in shops, magazine, newspapers, television, radio ,cinema, public transportation tools poster traditional advertisement channels. However, computer online advertisement channel can attract many feeling learning time pressure of students consumers and feeling lack of enough rest time working people consumers to let them to choose to view their video game software advertisements from online websites at homes conveniently.

It is easy to understand , due to these feeling lack of enough learning time student video game players and feeling lack enough rest time working people video game players, they go back home after they finished learning in schools or they finished jobs in workplaces on that video game purchase planning day. After they eat their dinners, they may turn on computers to search information from internet. Suddenly, they discover some attractive video game contents photos or images are advertised from the video game seller's website or public yahoo websie , even they can choose to buy any one of these video game softwares from online shopping channel. Then, they will feel convenient to buy any one of these video game softwares from internet channel. SO, online video game advertisement will be the feeling time pressure video game players' first time contact channel at homes or the fastest advertisement contact channel to compare visiting video game store post advertisement, television , radio , magazine contact advertisement channels, when they are staying at homes.

Due to internet is popular to be used to search any information for consumers. So, the traditional magazine, newspapers, television, radio and visiting video game stores advertisement channels won't be more attractive to the feeling time pressure video game consumers . They will chooce to find any information from internet at homes in preference , when they have at least one computer to use at home, they can click website to search any information from internet easily.

The most important factor is that they can feel to spend little time to search information from internet to compare spending more time to find anywhere places whether they has magazines or book stores to sell video game magazine and newspapers publishers, radios and television won't inform them when they have video game advertisements to let they know whether what new video game softwares will promote to sell as soon as possible when they buy newspapers or turn on radios or televisions at home.

Otherwise, internet will be easy to let the feeling presure video game software consumers to know when whose liking new video content game software(s) will be promoted to sell from internet advertisement easily. Also, the feeling time presure video software consumers can choose to buy their liking video game software (s) from online shopping channel in possible if the video game seller can provide one website to let him/her to pay visa to buy and then it can deliver the video game software(s) to his/her home immediately or tomorrow or later time when the buyer's home located in overseas or far away from the video game seller's warehouse and their softwares are needed to be delivered by air plane transportation.

So, the feeling time pressure video game players won't need to leave their homes to spend more time to visit any video game stores to make final video game purchase decision any time. Hence, online advertisement and shopping channel will be one good sale promotion method to any feeling time pressure video game players nowadays. It will influence the traditional visiting video game stores' video game consumers' purchase behaviors to change to online purchase behaviors at homes conveniently, because they avoid to waste much time to visit video game stores as well as avoid to waste much time to choose any video game products in different video game stores, when they are staying in different video game stores. Visiting video game purchase behavior will need they spend whole day time to make final purchase choice, even it is possible that they can not make any video game softwares purchase decision after they visit many video game stores on that day.

Otherwise , online game advertisment channel can let them to feel to spend little time to search any new video game contents from every web page as well as every web page can show the new video game content images or photos or pictures to let every online users to see clearly when he/she sits down to turn on computer to search any kinds of video game content information to view at home in short time.

In conclusion, online video game advertisement and online shopping channel can attract many feeling time pressure video game players' consideration when they need to search any kinds of new or old video game contents information and it also changes their purchase decision to online shopping from traditonal visiting video game store shopping behavior. Video game industry's advertisement method , sale method is the kind of video game playing content's easy or difficult feeling degree , spending how much playing time to win the competiton in the game entertainment environment factors will influence the feeling time pressure video game players' final purchase decision making choice behavior to any video game software publishers nowadays.

SIX

EMOTION FACTOR HOW INFLUENCES CONSUMER BEHAVIOR

Behavioral economy method predicts consumer behavior characteristics

Behavioral economy is consisted from psychology and standard economic model. Standard economic model is the way most economists think about consumer welfare and consumer choice in microeconomic environment. I shall apply behavioral economic model to explain underground train and Disney entertainment theme park and University and unground train transportation and environmental protection businessmen etc. enterprises which rationality in the standard economic model relies heavily on the assumption that consumers are rational. In this case of consumer individual behavior consumption process, I assume that consumers are fully aware of all the options who have, who can always and consistently to rank their options in accordance will whose preferences and always choose the option who like best.

Thus, these assumptions of the standard economy model of consumer include such as: consumers have known preferences and consumers choose the best option available. The advantages of the standard model, from there three assumptions, such as a logically consistent theory of consumer behavior can be biult, that theory can be used to make predictions about consumer behavior and those predictions can be compared with reality. These models often correspond to actual consumer behavior. But behavioral economy model can give evidence from psychology to show that consumer often are irrational and also who are predictably irrational. Clearly, psychology has shown that the rationality assumptions of standard economics are wrong. For example, if irrational consumers were irrational in randomways, who would cancel each other out, leaving the overall outcome determined by the behavior of rational consumers. In that case, economic theories that ignored irrational between would work just fine. But psychology has shown that consumers are irratonal in similar and predictable ways, therefore, irratonality doesn't cancel out and can't be ignored. Moreover, the fact that consumers are predictably irrational means that whose predictably irrational behavior can be relatively easily inserted into economic theories to make economic predictions more accurate. In fact, consumers often are unable to make use of what who know about their available options and their preferences to figure out the best available option, and even when who know what is best for them, evidence shows tht who often make bad choices anyway. Unfortunately for economic view point, there's plenty of reliable evidence of predictably unselfish behavior to consumers. It is true, that the free market competitiion will encourage consumers to make the best option.

In summary, standard economic theories assume that consumers are rational and self interested. However, behavioral economic theories assumes that psychology shows who are not rational usually. I shall indicate how consumer's psychological decision to choose their behavioral consumption in actual life environment for underground train and Disney entertainment theme park and University and unground train transportation and environmental protection businessmen etc. enterprises. Some consumption of these enterprises evidences also show that consumer individual irrationality , these enterprises have predictable features in these enterprises consumption suitation. I shall use these enterprises to explain why behavioral economy can make economic predictions more accurate by using these enterprises' consumption evidences on their predictabl irrational behavior to these enterprises. Although, these global enterprises' market competition is serious, consumers may be expected to learn to reduce irrational behavior over time, these processes may not work well and may take. You can read these underground train and Disney entertainment theme park and University and unground train transportation and environmental protection businessmen etc. enterprises to make judgement why behavioral economic model is more accurate to predict consumer behavior to compare standard economic model.

In behavioral economy view point, if the manufacturer expect to advertise whose products to achieve the maximum sale numbers. So, the manufacturer must expect to pay the most reasonable advertisement cost to achieve the maximum sale numbers. How can marketing of advertisement information influence consumer has positive attitude to influence many consumers choose to buy the manufactuer's consumption behavior? Consumer attention to advertisement or any marketing communication depends on four levels of consumer involvement: pre-attention, focal attention, comprehension and elaboration. Each calls for different level of message processing. Pre-attention demands only limited message processing, the consumer only identifies the product. Focal attention involves basic information as product name on use. In comprehension level, the message is analyzed, through elaboration, the content of the message is integrated with other information that helps to build attitude towards the product. It is suggested that marketers make advertisement with can induce elaboration. In general, steps in consumption decision making process include: first step, consumer feels need recognition. Second step, who will search any information concerns to the product. Third step, who will evaluate of alternatives. Fourth step, who will make purchase decision. Finally, who will do post purchase behavior to judge whether the product's price is reasonable or unreasonable to decide whether to consume the product again in the future. Thus, advertisement can be one factor to influence consumer choice in behavioral economy view point.

Behavioral economics studies all human environment behavior: all types of consumer spending and saving behaviors, entreprepreneurship and all work related behavior including job choice and investments in human capital, all types of business behavior ranging from decisions on prices, output, investment, finance and preferences and reactions to economic policies and programs by consumers as well as businessmen. In addition, the analysis could be focused on the micro or the macro level. So, insights from behavioral economics would naturally be incorporated into the discriplines of economics as well as psychology. Thus, behavioral economy focuses on the rationality of the process of decision making when economics was mainly focused with the rationality of the outcomes.

Economics is used equailibrium conditions to define the apprpriate outcomes, but psychology's main focus is on how consumers learn and adapt to a constantly changing environment. Economic theory indicates cnsumers learn from whose mistakes, so that their behavior will change to the rational and optimum outcomes in equibilrium . However, consumption was not a passive, variable completely is determined by the rational calculation of economic factors. So, it explains that how behavioral economy theory can be applied to predict consumer behavior.

In general, human economic activities include production, distribution, consumption and resource maintenance. Economic actors can be individuals, small groups (such as a family, or a group of roommales) or large organizations, such as a government or a multi-national corporation. Economics is about how these actors behave and interact as who engage in economic activities. In conclusion, I agree that every consumer's realistic behavior is in economic theories that deal with judgemetn under uncertainty.

Psychological method predicts consumer behavior characteristics

Consumer behavior is comparatively a new field of study. It led every manufacturer's attention from product to consumer and specially focused on consumer behavior. The evaluation of marketing concept from selling concept to consumer oriented marketing has resulted in buyer behavior becoming an independent discipline. The growth of consumerism and consumer legislation emphasizes the importance that is given to the consumer. Thus, consumer behavior is a study of how individuals make decision to spend their available resources (time, money and efforts) or consumption related aspects (what who buy? when why buy? how who buy? etc.) Hence, marketers need to obtain an depth knowledge to know to use what psychological method(s) is(are) the suitable to predict consumers buying behavior to raise customer numbers easily . Finally, this knowledge acted as a tool to the marketers to forecast the future buying behavior of customers to reduce any new products of investment risk before who decide to manufacture to sell to the market.

Consumer behavior is the study of individuals or organizations and the processes consumers use to research, select , use and dispose of products or services, experience or ideas to satisfy needs and its impact on the consumers and society. The term " customer" is specific in terms of brand , company or shop. It refers to person who customarily or regularly purchases particular brands or purchases from particular company's products or purchases from particular shops. Whereas, the " consumer" is a person who generally engages in the activities, search, select, use and dispose of products, services , experiences or ideas. Thus, consumption behavior concerns to predict how the consumer activities to be done to influence who chooses to buy the product or consume service among of all competitive and similar products or services provision to the market. However, consumer purchase decision and nature of motive which have close relationship. For example, in the psychological view point, when the consumer desires for saving money, who will decide to purchase when the price falls down; when the consumer feels fear, who will feel purchasing insurance policy need; when the consumer feels health need, who will choose to buy health foods to eat or/and to join to be membership in health clubs; when the consumer has possession need, who will decide to buy antiques for appreciating whose future values for saving. Thus, businessmen ought need to predict what the nature of motive will be whose target customer group, then who can persuade whose target customer group to choose to buy whose products or consume whose service more easily.

How to explain consumer behavior? Consumer behavior is said to be an applied discipline as some decisions are significantly affected by their behavior or expected action. The two significantly perspective that are micro and societal perspectives. The micro perspectives involve understanding consumer for the purpose of helping a firm or organization to achieve its objectives. Whereas, the societal or macro perspective applies knowledge of consumers to aggregate-level faced by mass or society as a whole. The behavior of consumer has significant influence on the quality of the standard of living.

Consumers can divide either organization buyer or individual buyer. First, organizational buyers are more geographically concentrated than consumer markets, who are fewer in number , but who are bulk buyers compared to individual buyers, whose markets are either vertical or horizontal. (vertical structures who cater only one or two industries, whereas, in horizontal structure , the buyer base is too broad. Organizational demand is derived from consumer demand. The nature of demand is influential and inelastic. Organizational buying lot of formalities have proposals , quotations, procedures are to be followed unlike consumer buying, e.g. decision process is much complex with high financial risk, technical aspects, multiple influencing factors etc. Also, it requires more extensive negotiation over larger time period than consumer buyer. Second, in psychological view point, individual consumer whose personal and/or product and/or situational factors can influence consumer decision making? self-concept, needs, and values are the three psychological factors that influence individual consumer how who chooses to buy one product or consume one service. For example, the more number of consumers share a certain self image, certain value and needs. They tend to use products and services the reflect whose life style. They get highly involved in purchasing products like designer wear, imported cars, health care products etc. On the product factor aspect, e.g. the consumer involvement grows as the level of perceived risk in the purchase of a product on or service increase. It is likely that consumers will feel more involved in the purchase of their house than in the purchase of tooth paste. It is a much riskier purchase. Beside, product differentiation can also affect consumer have to choose from increases. This may be due to the fact that consumers feel variety which means greater risk. On the situational factor aspect, the product is brought or used can generate emotional involvement. For example, buying a pair of socks for yourself is far less involved than buying a gift for a close friend. Social pressure can significantly increase involvement. One is likely to be more self conscious about the products and brand one looks at when shopping with friends than when shopping alone. So, individual consumer shopping decision will be influenced by whos friends, when whose friends give ideas to influence whose buying choice decision easily.

Models of consumer involvement have two level: First, low involvement products are those, which are at low risk, perhaps by important of being inexpensive and repeatedly used by consumers. Marketers may try to sell the product without changing the attitudes of consumers. For example, writing pen with the " uninterrupted flow" and tooth paste with " mouth wash" positioning attracts new consumers. Some buying decisions are taken will let of thinking or great feelings. Some are made through force of habit and others are made consciously, that attributes consumer choice to information (learn) , attitude (feel) and behavior (do) issues. Second, high involvement products are purchases in first requires more information, both because of the importance of the product to the consumer and thinking issues related to the purchases. Major purchases , such as cars, houses and other expensive and infrequently buying items. The purchases decisions in high involvement product involve less of information than feeling. Typical purchases tied to self-esteem, jewelry, apparel, cosmetics and accessories. The strategy model is feel-learn-do. To encourage purchases much approach customers with emotion and appeal. Otherwise, the purchase in low involvement product is primarily by the need to satisfy personal tastes, many of which are influenced by self-image products like newspaper, soft drinks, liquor etc. Marketers can promote these low involvement products through reference groups and other social factors . Because low involvement product involves less in thinking and more of habitual buying. Products like stationery, groceries , food etc. The role of information is to differentiate any point of difference from competitors. Brand loyalty may result simply from the habit. It suggests marketers induce trial through various sales promotion techniques.

Chapter One

What is the relationship between behavioral economics and psychology

At the core of behavioral economics is used psychology of economics analysis to improve economics on its own terms generating theoretical insights, making better prediction of field consumption of behavioral phenomena, and suggesting better policy to any company or government decision makers. It rejects economic theories based on utility maximization, equilibrium and efficiency. It is useful because it provides economists with a theoretical framework that can be applied to almost any form of economic (and even non-economic) behavior to predict behavioral consumption more easily to businessmen. So, behavioral economy is different to general economy concept, it applies psychological methods to attempt to predict consumption behavior.

Simpifying much assumption that are not central to the economic theory to apply to psychological behavior. Other assumption simply acknowledge human limits on computational power and self-interest. These assumptions can be considered procedurally rational because human needs to solve problems that are often so complex that who can't be solved exactly by even modern computer technology. So, if businessmen apply psychological method to predict behavioral consumption to earn the more benefits or profit, it is more reasonable to compare to apply computer methods to predict consumption behavior.

Theories in behavioral economics should be judged by reality, generality and tractability concepts to apply why we (consumers) do our behavior (consumption of choices) from psychological analysis. We share the positivist view that the ultimate test of a theory is the accuracy of its predictions. But we also believe that better predictions are likely to result from theories with more realistic assumptions. In psychology, such as connectionist models that capture some of the essential features of neural functioning, which are based on utility maximization, yet are reaching the point where they are able to predict many judgemental and behavioral phenomena. Contrary to the positivistic view, however, businessmen ought believe that predictions of consumers' feelings (e.g., of subjective well-being) should be an important goal to earn more profit more easily.

Most of the ideas in behavioral economics are not new. When-economics first became identified as a distinct field of study, psychology didn't exist as a discipline to apply to economy subject. For example, "invisible hand" and "the wealth of Nations" which belong to theory to moral sentiments, which laid out psychological principles of individual behavior that are arguably as profound as whose economic observations. Another example, such as a simple model of social utility means that one (consumer) or person's utility was affected by another person's , such as whose family or friends' influence why to choose to buy this product or use this service in consumption market.

Nowadays, economists hoped their discipline could be like a natural science to apply psychological methods to predict behavioral consumption to assist businessmen to earn more economic benefit or to reduce cost or profit to win whose competitors. But psychology was not very scientific. However, later economists are very much appealed to psychological insights to attempt to assist businessmen how to predict consumers how who will prefer to choose to consume to buy this product or use this service.

Throughout the second half of the century, many criticisms of the positivistic perspective took place in both economics and psychology. The economists of the time had less disagreement with psychology than they realized. They assume without foundation that behavior always aims at the goal of maximum pleasure and minimum pain; but behavior is not goal-oriented. Also the economists of the time believed false conclusions are drawn from false psychological assumptions to predict consumer individual behavioral consumption wrongly.

The importance of psychological measures and bounds on rationality. These commentators attracted attention, but did not alter the fundamental direction of economics. One development was the rapid acceptance by economists of the expected utility and discounted utility models which are making decision under uncertainty and choice, respectively. Whereas the assumptions and implications of utility analysis are rather flexible, and the expected utility and discounted utility models have numerous precise and testable implications. So, it seems economy and psychology can have close relationship to be connect to be applied to predict consumer individual consumption of behavior to assist any enterprises can earn more profit or more economic benefit more easily in global competitive consumption market nowadays.

In behavioral economy view, economists began to accept counter examples that could be not be permanently ignored, developments in psychology identified promising directions for new theory to be applied how to assist businessmen to predict behavioral consumption to earn economic benefits or profits. Beginning around 1960 year, psychology became to be dominated by the brain as an information-processing device replacing the behaviorist conception of the brain as a stimulus-response machine. The information-processing permitted a fresh study of neglected topics like memory, problem solving and decision making. These new topics were more obviously relevant to the conception of utility maximization than behaviorism had appeared to be to apply how to predict behavioral consumption in traditional psychological method.

However, behavioral economy and psychological consumption prediction method, psychologists began to use economic models as a benchmark against which to constrast their psychological models. Early research in behavioral consumption methds have followed these steps. First, identify assumption or models that are used by economists, who expected utility and discounted utility. Second, the assumption or model is a rule out alternative explanations (such as subjects' confusion or transactions costs). And third, the assumption or model creates alternative theories that generalize existing models. The final is to construct economic models of behavior using the behavioral assumptions to test them from the third step. This final step of economic models of behavior has only been taken more recently to be applied to predict why the consumer prefers to choose to do this behavioral consumption of decision finally.

In behavioral economy method, what is the standard economic model? It is the standard economic model, the way most economists think about consumer welfare and consumer choice. What is the rationality in the standard economic model? The standard economic model relies heavily on the assumption that consumers are rational. Standard economic model assumes that consumers are fully aware of all the options who have, who can always and consistently , rank whose options in accordance with their preferences, and always choose the option, who like the best option. Thus, what the assumptions of the standard economic model of consumer are? The assumptions include consumers act with full information, consumers have known preferences, consumers choose the best option available. In behavioral economic view point, It concerns consumers will compare cost to make decision to choose to buy which kind of product which can satisfy whose needs among of similar products of comparision.

The standard economic model of consumer behavioral prediction method advantages includes: A logically consistent theory of consumer behavior can be built, that theory can be used to make predictions about consumer behavior and those predictions can be compared with reality and those models often correspond to actual behavior of consumption reasons. What is the inconvenient truth? It includes clear evidence from psychology has shown that the rationality assumptions of standard economic model are wrong. Evidence from psychology has shown that consumers often are irrational and also who are predictably irrational. So these are wrong view point to influence how economists judge what cause consumption of behavior. Thus, it beings this question? What is mean of predictably irrational? It means that of irrational consumers were irrational in random ways, who would cancel each other out, leaving the overall outcomes determined by the behavioral consumption of rational consumers. As that case, behavioral economic theories that ignored irrational behavioral consumption would work just fine. But, psychology has shown that consumers are irrational in similar and predictable ways. Therefore, irrationality doesn't cancel out and can't be ignored to judge why the behavioral consumption has been caused.

How can behavioral economists judge each behavioral consumption cause? Economists will see evidence that consumers often are unable to make use of what consumers know about whose available options and whose preferences to figure out the best available option. However, although economic theory doesn't always assume self-interested behavior to any consumers, as a practical matter, most applications of economic theory assume that consumers act according to self- interest to decide every behavioral consumption of choice. For insurance industry is one good behavioral economy market example, insurance market competition can make rational consumption. Such as competitive market in auto vehicle accident insurance will charge very high rates to some insurance buyers who might to drive a fast speed, but unsafe motorbike, this one might argue will protect the driving insurance buyers from taking stupid risk. So learning can make rational consumers. Even if consumers are predictably irrational, who can learn from their families and other consumer' or friends behavioral mistakes, therefore, over time irrational consumers will learn to be rational to make the most irrational consumption. As a result, there are few opportunities to learn from consumer individual mistakes of any consumption of decision. Finally, if there are many potential; bad choices and one good consumption of choice, it might take a lot of costly experimentation to figure out the right consumption of choice. Thus, the standard economic model of behavioral consumption of prediction method, which is standard economic theories assume that consumers are rational, strong-willed , and self-interested, but evidence from psychology shows that who are not and that evidence also shows that consumer individual irrationality has predictable features. So, it seems behavioral economic model can make economic predictions more accurate by using the evidence on consumer individual predictable irrational behavioral prediction in any kind of the similar products in competitive market nowadays.

How to apply psychological method to predict consumption of behaviors

The methods how to predict to cause the (consumer's) person's consumption of behavior are the same as those in other areas of behavioral economic and psychological methods. In fact, behavioral economics relied heavily on evidence generated to predict behavioral consumption by experiments. More recently, however, behavioral economists have moved beyond experimentation and the full range of methods are employed by economists. The experiements played a large role in the initial phase of behavioral economics because experimental control is exceptionally helpful for distinguishing behavioral explanations from standard ones.

Suppose we observed this phenomenon in these any one of cares, in the form of failures of legal cases to settle before trial, costly divorce proceedings, and labor strikes. They are phenomenons of human' behaviours are caused by costs and benefits measurement of result. It implies the married people or the legal compensatory amount or labor strikes compensatory benefits will evaluate whether thier economic benefit is more or loss is more to decide divorce behavior or legal trial behavior or labour strikes compensatory behavior . So, consumer individual psychological behavior and economic benefits has close relationship to cause how consumer who prefers to make any consumption of choice every day. As the failures of legal cases to settle before trial , the behavioural economy concept would be difficult to tell whether rejection of offers was the result of reputation-building in repeated games, agency problems (between clients and lawyers) confusion why the lawyer' client (appellant) who choose to continue to attempt to pay legal fee to find the lawyer to appellate the case if the case is fail at the first time . However, in these game experiments of failures of legal cases to settle before trial, costly divorce proceedings, and labor strikes. These explanations are ruled out because the experiments are played once, have no agents, and are simple enough to rule out confusion. Thus, the experimental data clearly establish that subjects are expressing concern for fairness.

Other experiments have been useful for testing whether judgment errors which individuals commonly make in psychology experiments also affect prices and quantities in markets, such as shareholder's individual investment behavior. The lab is especially useful for these studies because individual and market-level data can be observed. Although behavioral economists relied on experimental datato predict shareholder's individual investment behavior, however, behavioral economics subject is seen as a very different method from experimental economics. As noted, behavioral economists are methodological profession. They define themselves, not on the basis of the research methods that who employ, but rather their application of psychological insights to economics.

Experimental economists, on the other hand, define themselves on the basis of use of experimentation which is as a research tool. Also, economists have made a major investment in developing experimental methods that are suitable for addressing economic issues, and have achieving among themselves on a number of important issues. For example, experimental economists often make instructions and software available for precise replication, and raw data are typically shared for reanalysis. Experimental economists also insist on paying performance-based. However, experimental economists have also developed rules that many behavioral economists are likely to find excessively . For example, experimental economists rarely collect data like demographics, self-reports, reponse times and other cognitive measure which behavioral economists have found useful. Descriptions of the experimental environment are usually abstract rather than which are carried on experiment in the outside world because economic theory rarely makes a prediction about how a happen would matter, and experimenters are concerned about losing control over incentives if choosing strategies with certain labels is appealing because of the labels themselves. Finally, economic experiments also typically use "stationary replication", in which the same task is repeated over and over in each period. Data from the last few periods of the experiment are typically used to draw conclusions about equilibrium behavior outside the lab. When economists believe that examining behavior after it is of great interest, it is also obvious that many important aspects of economic consumption of individual behavior to every individual consumer. The consumer's individual consumption of behavioral choose is like the first few periods of an experiment rather than the psychological methods to predict behavioral consumption.

Supposing if we need to make decision of marriage, educational decisions, and saving for retirement, or the purchase of large durables like houses, sailboats, can cars, which happen just a few times in a person's life, a focus on behavior is clearly not warranted. All said, the focus on psychological realism and economic applicability of research promoted by the behavioral-economics perspective suggests the usefullness research outside the lab and of a broader range of approaches to laboratory research. So, economists realize that who have ideal opportunity to learn by trial-and-error, in a stationary environment, and uses the opportunity to learn how to carry on experimenting any psychology and behavioral researches in lab experiment environment.

● What is psychology of consumption behavior?

Psychology is the science of human behavior and mental consumption processes. In consumption process behavior, it is any consumption behaviors as well as consumer mental consumption process is consumer individual internal experiences, comparison with alternative products, products choice of the best, making decision to consume or not consume for the product. So, advertisers often persuade to influence consumers' behavior to attract them to choose to buy whose products.

Why businessmen need to learn consumer psychology? Because psychology can help businessmen scientifically to evaluate common consumer beliefs and misconceptions about consumption behavior and consumption decision making mental processes. Consumption scientific psychology has four basic goals: To describe , explain, predict and change consumption behavior and consumption decision making mental process. Consumption psychological information is based on evidence, this is information based on direct observation and measurements with consumption behavior with scientific method. How are typical images of psychology? Consumption psychologists need to use scientific method to help businessmen to think what predicts who own, make a list of words would who use to describe a psychological scientist and what use to describe a psychological scientist and what images the businessmen have. However, consumption psychologists have difference ways of looking at the same problem for the businessmen, which is why there are so many sub-fields of consumption psychology. Consumption psychology's roots began in philosophy, but the focus changes to a scientific focus consumer.

Behaviorism is focused on consumer buying behavior that can be measured and observable. This returned the scientific approach to consumption psychology. Consumption behaviorist's believe consumers are controlled by their environment. Consumption behaviorism focuses on consumption observable behavior. However, consumption cognitive psychology believes that consumption behaviors are preformed because of the product ideas and thoughts. The cognitive perspective focuses on such consumer decision making and choice processes, such as perception, memory and thinking to the product.

The two categories of consumer's behavioral consumption of decision

The field of consumer's behavioral consumption of decision research, on which behavioral economics has drawn more than any other subfield of psychology, typically classifies research into two categories: judgement and choice. Judgement research deals with the processes people use to estimate probabilities. Choice deals with the processes people use to select among actions, considering of any relevant judgements who may have made. Everyday, we, such as consumers need to make probable judements. Due to judging the likelihood of events is central to economic life. For example: Will you lose your job in a poor economic environment? Will you be able to find another house you like as much as the one you must bid for right away? Will the government raise interest rates in this year or next year? Will a merger strategy increase profits? These questions are answered by some process of judging likelihood. The standard principles used in economic to model probability judgement in economic are concepts of statistical sampling, which are concerned probabilities in the face of new evidence. However, it requires a separation between previously judged probabilities and evaluations of new evidence. However, (consumers) people often overestimate the probability who previously attached to events which later happened. This leads to "secondguessing". For example, Monday morning quarterbacking and may be partly responsible for lawsuits against stockbrokers who lost money for their clients. (The clients think the brokers should have known). For example, anybody has tried to learn from a computer distance learning manual has seen the classroom learning of knowledge in action. Another example for making probability judgements is called "representativeness": People judge conditional probabilities like P(hypothesis /data) or P(example/class) by how well the data represents the hypothesis or the example represents the class. Representativeness is an economical shortcut that delivers reasonable judgements with minimal effort in many cases. For example, in judging whether a certain student (University customer) described in a profile is, say, a psychology major or computer science major, the student decides how well the profile matches the psychology or computer science career to the student generally. So, University can read the student profile to predict whether the student will choose to study psychology subject more prefer or computer subject more prefer to predict whose computer or psychology student numbers more accurate in the year.

Many studies show how this sort of feature-matching can lead people to underweigh the "base rate", in this example, the overall frequency of the two majors. Another byproduct of representativeness is the "law of small numbers": Small samples are though to represent the properties of the statistical process that generated them (as if the law of large numbers, which guarantees that a large sample of independent draws does represent the process, is in a hurry to work). Field and experimental studies with basketball shooting and betting on games that people believe that there is positive attitude that players experience the "hot hand", when there is no evidence that such an effect exists.

For example, how the government tax department can judge whether the company's financial report has not been misled from accounting auditor's moral behavior, how to predict consumer's brand choice behavior and how to control students' learning behavior in classroom . It is important to judge whether it is either a good attitude or bad attitude from the consumer's personal behavior in the past. A consumer's good attitude to the product or the service consumption provides good consumption experience, close to optimal, answers when time or capabilities are limited, but it also needs logical principles and leads to situations. So, optimal is largely a critique (a reasonable one) of the later applied research. Otherwise, a consumer's bad attidude to the product or the service consumption provide poor consumption experience to buy the product or use the service again. Thus, the consumer's good or bad past buying experience to the product or to use the service will have help to assist the businessman how to predict whose consumption behavior next time.

Assume that people misspecify a set of hypotheses, or encode new evidence incorrectly. For example, assuming that people believe hypothesis A is more likely than B will never encode pro-A evidence mistakenly, but will sometimes encode pro-B evidence as being supportive. For another example, investors will think there is wide variation in skill of, say, mutual-fund managers, even if there is no variation at all. (A manager who does well several years is a surprise if performance is mistakenly thought due to nonreplacement, so concluding that the manager must be really good.) A question concerns stock market, such as: Overreacts in the long term. In their model, earnings follow a random walk but investors believe, mistakenly, that earnings have positive attitude. After one or two periods of good earnings, the stock market can not be confident that exists and hence expects, but since earnings are really a random walk, the stock market is too pessimistic and is underreacting to good earnings news. After a good earnings, however, the stock market believes many investors are increasing. Since, it is not the stock market is too optimistic and overreact. So, investor's past experience to earn or loss from the share, which will influence whose invetment behavior to choose to buy the share next time.

For another example, valuable consumer products (A $100 wireless keyboard, a fancy computer mouse, bottles of wine, and a box of chocolate) are sold to postgraduate (MBA) business students. The students were presented with a product and asked whether who would buy it for a price equal to the last two digits of their own social security number (a roughly random identification number required to obtain work in the United States) converted into a dollar figure, e.g. , if the last digits were 99, then the postgraduate business students will accept the hypothetical price was $99 to buy any of it for a price to the last two digits of their own social security number . After giving a yes/no response to the question. Would you pay $99? subjects were asked to state the most who would pay (using a procedure that gives people an incentive to say what who really would pay). Although subjects were reminded that the social security number is essentially random, those with high numbers were willing to pay more for the products. However, many studies have also shown that the method used to elicit preferences can have dramatic consequences.

Nevertheless, when required to make an economic decisions-to-choose a brand of toothpaste, a car, a job, or how to invest, people do make some kind of decision. Behavioral economists refer to the process by which people make choices with ill defined preferences as "constructing preferences". So, psychologic methods can be used to predict why the consumer choose to buy the product as well as any consumer seems who needs to evaluate whether who will earn more benefit or low to choose to buy the brand of product or use the service to achieve the best benefits. However, in classical consumer theory, preferences among different commodities are assumed to be invariant with respect to an individual's current consumption. Specifically, people seem to dislike losing commodities from their consumption much more than they like gaining other commodities. For example, the research of "contingent valuation" studies that attempt to establish the dollar value of products which are not routinely trades. Contingent valuation is often used to do government cost-benefit analysis or establish legal penalties from environment damage. These surveys typically show very large differences between buying prices (e.g. paying to clean up oil of beaches) and selling prices (e.g. having to be paid to allow beaches to be ruined) to reduce environmental pollution from the low cost method for government spending.

Nowadays, there are many USA manufacturers use behavioral economy methods to predict consumer individual behavior, a quarter of the wealth in the USA has more interesting opportunities to do behavioral economies. They find that motivated sellers should regard the price who paid as a sunk cost and choose at a nominal loss from the purchase price. Sellers' listing prices and subsequent selling behavior reflects to nominal losses. There are some cases in which no effect would be expected, such as when products , such as house or antique dealers' products are purchased for resale rather than for utilization. For example, Do art or antique dealers like with pieces who buy to resell? What about surrogate mothers who agree to bear a child for a price paid in advance? Reference points can also serve as social focal points for house or antique products or surrogate mothers whose behavioral judging performance.

For an interesting example from corporate finance. In general, when managers whose firms face possible losses (or declines from a previous year's earnings) are very reluctant to report small losses. As a result, the distribution of actual losses and gains show a very large at zero, and hardly any small reported losses (compared to the number of small gains). A manager who does not have the skill to shift accounting profits to erase a potential loss (i.e. has some earnings in his pocket.) is considered a poor manager. It seems that the bad performance manager whose behavior is bad to mislead public to believe his firm have better performance in this year. Hence, in the mental accounting view, people(accountants) set up mental accounts for outcomes which are psychologically separate, much as financial accountants lump expenses and revenues into separated accounts to guide managerial attention. Otherwise, mental accounting stands in opposition to the standard view in economics that it predicts, accurately , that people will spend money coming from different sources in different ways. So, a generalization of the notion of mental accounting (the accountant's mislead financial report performance) , which aims to let investors and consumers have more confidence to choose to invest or to choose to buy it's products or consume its service more easily. So, it explains why the accountant needs to mislead to report it's earns are more than loss in every year.

Explanation what are of Preferences over risky to behavioral consumption and utility function concept to company profit intention or government tax income intention

What is preferences over risky to behavioral consumption. Such as prospect theory is experimental choices more accurately than (EU) because it gets the psychological of judgement and choice right. It consists of two main components, a probability weighting function, and a "value function" which replaces the utility function of (EU) to any consumer when who needs to choose to buy any product or consume any service by more than one choice. The weighting function P(P) combines two elements: (1) The level of probability weight is a way of expressing risk and (2) Captures how sensitive people are to differences in probabilities. New information of any products can help any decision maker to feel better to make better final purchase decisions. These theories effect may explain demand for information in settings like medicine or personal finance, where new information usually does not change choice, but relieves anxiety people have from knowing there is something who could know to choose to buy the medicine or borrowing loan of low interest payment. So, new information of any products can reduce consumer individual risk to choose to buy.

However, the planning problem for economic agents who would like to behave in fashion and discussed the important time discounting for choice. Most big decisions, e.g. savings, educational investments, labor supply, health and diet, crime and drug etc. decisions use have costs and benefits which occur at different point in time. Thus, time discounting is basically standard time discounting plus an immediacy effect, a decision discounts delays in equally at all moments except the current one, caring differently about well being. This functional form provides one sample and powerful model of the taste to individual to make right or reasonable behavior economic decision. However, most analyses of choice assume that people integrate new consumption with planned consumption. It is infeasible and perhaps for this reason, descriptively inaccurate. When people make decisions about new sequences of payments or consumption, they tend to evaluate them in isolation, e.g. treating negative outcomes as losses, rather than as reductions to their existing money flows or consumption plans.

How to decide fairness and social preferences. The assumption that people maximize their own wealth and other personal material goals just self-interest is a correct simplification that is often useful in economics. However, people may sometimes choose to spend their wealth to punish others who have harmed them, reward whose, so who have helped, or to make outcomes more fair. Just as understanding demand for products requires specific utility function. So. on economic view point, utility function concept can influence consumer choice. if the consumer feels the product has more utility, then who will prerfer to choose to buy the product. Otherwise, if who feels the product has less utility, then who will not perfer to choose to buy the product.

Behavioral economy can also use to assist firms to choose right behavior to decide to do any matters. I show hypothesis to establish any reference level of consumer surplus and product profit. Both sides are entitled to any firm's levels of profit, so price changes which threaten any matter are considered unfair. So raising any product price, it will reduce consumer surplus and is considered unfair. But the cost of a firm's inputs rises, subjects said it was fair to raise prices. Because not raising prices would reduce the firm's profit (compared to the reference profit). Everyday observation that firms don't change prices and wages as frequently commonly.

For example, when the fourth hary potter story book was released in summer 2000 year, most stores were allocated a small number of books that were pre-sold in advance. Why not raise prices or auction the books off? It is possible that it concerned about customer goodwill and excess demand to cause book stores limit such book price increases. Offended consumers are often able to affect firm behavior by media attention or provoking legislation. For example, scalping tickets for popular sports and entertainment events (resulting them at a large premium over the printed ticket price) is constrained by law in most countries. For example, some countries have "anti-laws" penalizing sellers who take advantage of shortages of water, fuel and other necessities by raising prices after natural disasters. So, the countries' governments can protect which citizen benefits to balance the natural resource supply and demand to sell in the reasonable price fairly after the natural disaster occurrence. This is utility function concept. Because the book store believes the fourth hary potter story book will be excess demand and reader goodwill is good. So the books' utility function is enough to prepare to sell to readers, which do not need to raise price to attract readers to read.

Also, scalping tickets for popular sports and entertainment events will rise ticket price to be limited level because the popular sports and entertainment players believe who have attrative ability to attract full ticket buyers and whose numbers will exceed seats demand. So, the ticket numbers utility are enough and which are not need to raise ticket price too much. Also, shortages of water, fuel and other necessities by raising prices after natural disasters, because government make whose citizen has limit number of water, fuel and other necessities supply to keep enough utility function to satisfy whose needs. So, the nature resources do not need to raise price when natural disaster occurs.

A few years ago, responding to public anger at rising CEO salaries when the economy was being restructured through downsizing and many workers lost their jobs. Otherwise, some countries passed a law prohibiting firms from deducting CEO salaries for tax purposes beyonded $1 million a year. However, because some countries need to earn much tax income from these high salary CEO income every year. So, these countries do not suggest to pass a law to probibit firm from deducting CEO salaries for tax purpose. So, utility function can be applied to company benefit. If the company hopes to limit the CEO salary, then it will limit whose CEO 's duty (reducing utility funtion to whose duty). Aim to avoid to pay more salary expenditure to the CEO , when the country's economy is poor and it believes there are less consumers prefer to consume more. Otherwise, if the company does not hope to limit the CEO salary, then it will not limit whose CEO'duty (increasing utility function to whose duty). Aim to hope who can help whose company to earn more profit, when the country's economy is good and it believe there are many consumers prefer to consume. On the other side, if the country tax department hopes to earn more salary tax income, it will choose not to pass a law prohibiting firms from deducting CEO salaries for tax purposes beyonded $1 million a year. In the behavioral economy concept, the government tax department hopes to earn more salary tax when the economy environment is not good or it is worse to compare last year's economy environment. Thus, behavioral economy concept will be applied to company profit intention or country income intention or individual consumption intention.

How can behavioral game theory apply to company income intention?

How can behavioral game theory apply to company income intention ? Behavioral game theory has rapidly become an important foundation for many areas of micro economic theory to any organizations, such as bargaining in decentralized markets, outsource contracting and organizational structure. The descriptive accuracy of game theory in these application can be questioned because equilibrium predictions often assume strategic reasoning and direct field tests are difficult to any organizations. In fact, behavioral game theory uses any experimental evidence and psychological research to generalize the standard assumptions of game theory to any organizations how which choose to make profit intention.

One component of behavioral game theory is a theory of social preferences for allocations of money to oneself and others. Another component is a theory of how people choose in one shot games or in the first period of a repeated game. For example, in share buying and selling market, shareholders shall buy or sell shares from their judgement in the economic cycle market everyday. So share investment is seemed as allocation of game to these shareholders.

Also, shareholders whose mind can influence whose psychological behavior to decide how to invest whose shares in their share investment economic activities. The component of behavioral game theory can include a model of learning to either individual or a population. Also, game theory is one area of economy in which serious attention has been paid to the process by which can equilibrium comes about. Many learning theories have been proposed and carefully tested with experimental data. Theories about population never predict as well as theories of individual learning through who are useful for other purposes. So, behavioral game theory can be applied to these complex environments. e.g. consumer supermarket purchase, share market etc. for these business organizations research.

How to apply behavioral game theory to macroeconomics and saving aspect? Many concepts in macroeconomic probably have a behavioral style that could be influenced by research in psychology. For example, it is common to assume that prices and wages are in nominal terms, which has important implications for macroeconomic behavoir. Behavioral economics suggests some ideas for among consumers and workers, perhaps it is influenced by workers' concern for fairness.

An important model in macroeconomics is the life cycle model of savings or permanent income hypothesis. This theory assumes that people make a guess about their lifetime earnings profile, and plan their lifetime earnings profile, and plan their savings and consumption in each period has diminishing marginal utility; and preferences for consumptions streams are time-separable (i.e. overall utility is the sum of the discounted utility of consumption in each separate period). The theory also assumes people lump together different types income when they guess how much money who will have (i.e. different sources of wealth are different). So, why many young people won't spend too much money for unnecessary expenditure, e.g. entertainment easily. Because who plan to save for their old age to use in their long time life time.

A behavioral life cycle theory of savings in which different sources of income are kept track of in different mental accounts. Mental accounts can reflect natural perceptual or cogitive divisions. For example, it is possible to add up the travellers' paycheck and dollar value of whose frequent flyer miles, but it is simply unnatural to do so. It is important to note that many key implications of the life-cycle hypothesis have never been well supported ,e.g. consumption is far more closely related to current income than it should be according to theory. However, predictions can be improved by introducing utility functions with habit formation in which utility in a current depends on the reference point of previous consumption, and by more carefully accounting for uncertaining about future income.

For example, in the accountancy (economic) professional view point mental accounting is only one of several behavioral approaches that may prove useful. Economics is money illusion, it is the tendency to make decisions based on nominal quantities rather than converting those figures into real terms by adjusting for inflation. Money illusion seems to be pervasive in some domains. So, it appears that employees don't seem to mind if their real wage falls as long as their nominal wages doesn't fall.

How can behavioral game theory apply to company income intention? Labor macroeconomics is involuntary unemployment. Why can some people not find work beyond of switching jobs, or a natural rate of unemployment? A popular account of unemployment pushs that wages are deliberately paid above the market clearly level, which

creates an excess supply of workers and hence unemployment. But why are wages too high ?
As efficiency wage theory shows that paying workers more than who deserve is necessary to ensure that who have something to lose if they are unemployed, which motivates them to work hand and economizes on monitoring.

How Another viewpoint indicates that employer and worker is such as into a gift exchange relationship. Employers pay more than who have to as a gift and workers repay the gift by working harder than necessary. They show how gift exchange can be an equilibrium and show some of its macroeconomic implications. In labor economics, gift exchange is clearly evident of experimental labor markets. In practical working environment, firms offer wages; workers who take the jobs than choose a level of effort, which is costly to the workers and valuable to the firms.

For example, firms and workers can enforce wages, but not effort levels. Since workers and firms are matched for just one period, and do not learn each other's identities, there is no way for either side to build reputations or for firms to punish workers who chose low effort. However, self interested workers should shirk, and firms should anticipate that and pay a low wage. In fact, firms deliberately pay high wages as gifts and workers choose higher effort levels when they take higher wage jobs. It seems that it has strong relationship between wages and effort is stable over time.

For another example, standard life-cycle theory assumes that if people can borrow, they should prefer wage profiles which maximize the present value of lifetime wages. Holding total wage payments constant, and assuming a positive real rate of interest, present value maximization implies that workers should prefer declining wage profiles over increasing ones. However, in fact, most wages profiles are clearly rising over time which is such as a phenomenon. Rather, workers derive utility from positive changes in consumption, but have self-control problems.

If any company has any good wages profiles would prevent them from positive changes in consumption, but have self-control problems that would prevent them from saving for later consumption of wages were more front-loaded in the life cycle. In addition, workers seem to derive positive utility from increasing wage profiles, it is perhaps because rising wages are a source of self-esteem and the desire for increasing payments is much weaker for non wage income. The standard life-cycle of labor supply also implies that workers should substitute labor and leisure based on the wage rate who face and the value who place on leisure at different points in time. If wage fluctuations are temporary workers should work long hours when wages are high and short hours when wages are low. However, because changes in wages are often persisting and because work hours are generally fixed in the short-run. So, it is difficult to tell whether workers are substituting. So, if the company can have good method to decide when to rise salary or wage level , even reduce salary or wage level, as well as how much rising or reducing salary or wage level is the suitable in different time. If the wage fluctations are reasonable in the most suitable time, the labor turnover numbers will not be reduced easily.

How can behavioral game theory apply to individual business income intention? For example, taxi drivers who target daily will drive longer hours on low income days and will drive less hours early on high income days. This behavior is exactly the opposite of substitution. Also inexperienced taxi drivers support the daily targeting prediction. But experienced taxi drivers don't have negative elasiticies, either because target minded drivers earn less and self select or taxi drivers learn over time to substitute rather than target. Perhaps the simplest prediction of labor economics is that the supply of labor should be upward sloping in response to a increase in wage. Suppose to the inexperienced taxi drivers will attempt to drive long hours if who can feel or predict the taxi passengers number will reduce on the low income day. Otherwise, the experienced taxi drivers will attempt to drive less hours if who can feel or predict when the taxi passengers number will increase on the high income day. So, these experienced or inexperienced taxi drivers whose decison of driving long hours or less hours is depended on whose feeling of taxi passengers number who is high or low.

How, behavioral game theory applys to investor behavior. In finance, standard equilibrium models of asset pricing assume that investors only care about asset risks if who affect marginal publicly available information to forecast stock returns as accurately as possible the efficient markets hypothesis. When those hypotheses do make some accurate predictions and some investors in assets have limited rationality of behavioral finance. Also, in share stock market, it is common, shareholders should not want to trade with them, but the volume of stock market transaction is large. So, it presents data on individual trading behavior which suggests that the extremely high volume may be driven, in part, by overconfidence on the part of investors. Thus, if the company's share numbers buying and selling transactions are very large in the year. Then, it will influence many investors have more confidence to be encouraged to choose to buy the firm's shares in the year. Otherwise, if the company's share numbers buying and selling transactions are less in the year. Then, it will also influence many investors have less confidence to be encouragd to choose to buy its' shares in the year.

For another example, behavioral game theory applys to property agent's behavior. Property agent's individual behavior is similar to share agent's individual behavior. In the economy view point , property agent bases a list price for a house on the selling prices of nearly houses that is similar ("comparables"). Every nearest neighbour techniques bases on similarity is also used in credit scoring and other kinds of evaluations. Also, one firm whose every share sale on the selling price is comparable to its similar firms whose every share price in its same business industry. The shareholder will evaluate whose every share issued sale price in the stock (share) market. Otherwise, in behavioral economy view, for example, property or share buyer who has risky choice to decide to buy in the property or share market. It is a process of comparing the similarity of the probabilities and outcomes in two gambles and choosing on dimensions which are dissimilar.

As we mentioned above, behavioral economics simply includes an interest in psychology. In fact, we believe that many familiar economic distinctions do have a lot of behavioral content, they are implicitly behavioral, and could surely benefit from more explicit ties to psychological ideas and data. However, some people do not feel psychology and economy which have close relationship. Such as, substantial debate is ongoing in psychology about whether knowing the precise details of how the brain carries out computations is necessary to understand functions and mechanisms of driving car skill at higher levels, (knowing the mechanical details of how a car works may not be necessary to turn the key and drive it). So, the drivers who concerns more safe to their families and themselves, who will prefer to pay more money to buy the more safe vehicle to driver. Otherwise, the drivers who disconcern safe and concern money save, who will choose to pay less money to buy the less safe vehicle to drive.

Behavioral game theory can apply to price behavioral elasticity for how firm's price decision. For example , it is the distinction between short run and long run price elasticity which concerns behavioral economy. In fact, economy needs have theories concepts to support any evidence to prove any matter has happened. Concerning short run and long run price elasticity cause and effort issue, with a casual suggestion that the run is the time it takes for markets to adjust, or for consumers to learn new prices, after a demand or supply stock. Adjustment costs undoubtedly have technical and social component, but probably also have some behavioral factors influence in the form of gradual adaption to loss and learning. So, if there are many consumers who believe the product is reliable to use and the brand is famous, the product's price won't be push down often and it has less price elastic. Otherwise, if there are many consumers who do not believe the product is reliable to use and the brand is not famous, the product's price will be push doen often and it has more price elactic tendency.

Another macroeconomic model which can be interpreted as implicitly behavior is that business cycles can emerge if it is not general price inflation, so why the consumers shall not decide to buy this kind of product in the competitive market. So price when the market price inflation, consumers will not choose to prefer to spend to buy more food to eat or products to use. Otherwise, when the market price is stable, consumers will choose to prerfer to spend to buy more food to eat products to use. So, inflation will influence consumption of behavior.

Behavioral economic simply includes an interest in psychology. In fact, we believe that many familiar economic distinctions do have a lot of behavioral content, they are implicitly behavioral and could surely benefit from more explicit ties to psychological ideas and data. However, some people do not feel psychology and economy which have close relationship. Such as psychology is about whether knowing the precise details of how the brain carries out computations is necessary to understand functions and mechanisms at higher levels. (knowing the mechanical details of how a car works may not necessary to turn the key and drive it.)

Most psychology experiments use indirect measures like response times, error rates, self reports and natural experiments due to brain has been fairly successful in codifying what we know about thinking. However, pessimists think brain scan studies won't add much. The optimists think the new tools will lead to some discoveries and the potential is great that they cannot be ignored. However, economy needs have theories or concepts to support evidence to prove why any matters had happened. An example, is the distinction between short term and long term price elasticity. This distinction, mentions between of them, with a casual suggestion that long run is the time it takes for markets to adjust, or for consumers to learn new prices, after a demand or supply shock. Adjustment costs undoubtedly have technical and social components, but probably also have some behavioral factors influence in the form of gradual adaption to loss and learning.

However behavioral economy theory can be applied to organizational behavior, organizational behavioral theory concerns that organizatonal contracting are shot through with implicitly behavioral economics. Some economists motivate the incompleteness of contracts as a consequence of rationality in foreseeing the future, but do not tie the research directly to work on memory and imagination. For example, agency theory begins with the presumption that there is some activity the agent doesn't like to do. Why markets are better at making dramatic changes than managers influence cost. So, influence costs are the costs managers preform for projects who like or personally benefit from like promotion or raises. A lot of influence costs are undoubtedly inflated by optimistic, each division manager really does think their division desperately needs funds and social comparison of pay and benefits. Otherwise, why are salaries kept so secret? In all these cases, conventional economic behavior has deeper psychological questions of where adjustment costs, effort and influence costs come from. So, it beings these questions: Could these phenomena surely produce surprising testable prediction? Is psychology regularity an assumption or a conclusion?

Behavioral economics generally begins with assumption rooted in psychological regularity and asks what follows from those assumptions. An alternative approach is to work backward, regarding a psychological regularity as a conclusion that must be proved an explanation that must be derived from deeper assumption before we fully understand and accept it. The alternative approach is caused by a fashionable new direction in economic theory and psychology too, which is to explain human behavior as the product of evolution. However, we may not believe that behavior of intelligent, modern people lived in socialization and cultural influence can only be understood by guessing what their lives were like and how their brains might have adapted generally. There are other models that treat psychological regularity as a conclusion to be proved rather than an assumption to be used. Such models usually begin with an observed regularity. However, I think economic factor can influence consumers to make who feel the more reasonable psychological decision to make the more right behavior. Thus, economy and psychology has close relationship to influence consumer individual decision.

Economists have for deriving behavior from first principles and rationalizing apparent irrationality. Theories of this sort are useful behavioral economics and what fresh predictions do they make. However, critics have pointed out that behavioral economics is not a unified theory, but is instead a collection of tools and ideas. This is true. However, some economists believe that economic models do not derive much predictive power from the single tool of utility maximization. The goal of behavioral economic is to develop better tools that, in some cases, can do both jobs at once.

Economists like to point out the natural division of labor between scientific disciplines: Psychologists should concern to individual minds, and economists to behavior in games, markets, and economies. But the division of labor is only efficient if there is effective coordinaton, and all too often economists fail to conduct intellectual trade with those who have a comparative advantage in understanding individual human behavior. The only question is whether the implicit psychology in economics is good psychology or bad psychology. We think it is simply unwise, and inefficient to do economics without paying some attention to good psychology.

● Can predict consumer behavior with web search?

In behavioral economy view point, it can be applied to predict why consumers buy products from internet. Recent work has demonstrated that web search volume can "predict the present", meaning that can be used to accurately track outcomes, such as unemployment levels, auto and home sales and disease prevalence in near real time. Consumers are searching what for online can also predict their collective future behavior days or even weeks in advance. For example, specifically businessmen can use search query volume to forecast the opening weekend box-office revenue for feature films, first month sales of video games and the rank of songs, finding in all case that search counts are highly predictive of future outcomes from online google research. Finally, businessmen can reexamine previous work on tracking trends and show that, perhaps surprisingly, the utility of search data relative to a simple auto regressive model is modest.

Nowadays, people increasingly use the internet for news, information and research purposes. From this perspective, it is a short step to conclude that what people are researching for today is predictive of what who will do in the near future. For example, consumers may search to prepare to buy a new camera, moviegoers may search to determine the opening date of a new film, or to locate cinemas showing it and individuals planning a vacation may search from a places of interest, to find airline tickets, or to price hotel rooms. So online can aggregately count of search queries related to retail activity. Movie going or travel might be able to predict collective behavior of economic, cultural, or political interest. Determining the nature of behavior that can be predicted using search, the accuracy of such predictions and the time scale over which predictions can be usefully made are therefore all questions of interest.

Researchers have focused on the observation that search " predicts the present". For example, Ettredge et al (2005) found that counts of the top 300 search terms during 2001 to 2003 year were correlated with US Bureau Of Labor statistics Unemployment Figures; Cooper (2005) et al found that search activity for specific cameras during 2001 to 2003 year correlated with their estimated incidence and Eysenbach (2006) found a high correlation between clicks on sponsored search results of flu-related keywords and epidemiolopical data from the 2004 to 2005 year Canadian flu season.

Thus, motivated , I indicate one example how investigates whether search activity is a systematic leading indicator of consumer activity by forecasting. For first example, supposing to opening weekend Box-office revenue for 119 feature films released in the united States between Oct. 2008 year and Sept. 2009. For second example, supposing to first month sales of video games across all gaming platforms, e.g. Xbox, Play station etc.) for 106 games released between Sept. 2008 and Sept. 2009 year. These search data can be collected from yahoo using research rank from the current and previous weeks.

Can online search also predict the near future? A finding that may apply usually to a wide range of consumer behaviors , e.g. airline travel, hotel vacancy rates and auto sales and economic indicators , e.g. real-estate prices, credit card and confidence indicators. It seems all research based predictions simply models to build on publicly available information. For movies, baseline predictions can be used a linear model that includes production budgets, the number of screens on which each movie opened and box office projections from the Hollywood Stock Exchange (HSX) (hsx.com) on online, play money prediction market that is known to generate information prediction. For video games, many of the key indicators of revenue, including production budgets and initial available. Thus, it seems that businessmen can attempt to use internet (online) search technological method to search past information to concern whether what number of customers will be estimated.

● Can firm's conduct and behavior factor influence consumption of behavior ?

In behavioral economy view point, it can explain how firm conduct and behavior factor can infuence consumption of behavior. The usual assumption about the objectives of firms made by economists is that firms seek to maximize profit. The means that firms feel that who are protected against the possibility of new entrants, and proceed to maximize short-run profits. Firms feel that the barriers against new entrants ensure that their profits won't induce new firms to enter the industry and to reduce competitors enter to industry to raise consumers' choices to buy any similar products.

A major challenges to the profit maximization objective has come from proponents of the view that modern larger corporation are under a managerial control, which it is argued leads to the pursuit of other objectives, such as growth. The pursuit of non-profit objective is not unique to managerial-controlled firms, although the growth of such firms and of theories about than have emphasized these types of objectives.

Another view has focused on the controllers of the firm, whether owners or managers, having a wider range of objectives and that the achievement of profit maximization and the cost minimization requires considerable time and effort by the controllers. Thus, the controllers have incentives to forge profit maximization, unless who are forced to do so. Under oligopoly, firms can earn profits above the normal level, e.g. one country has only two electricity power companies are existing in the country's energy supply market. They may change a profit maximizing price, but actual reported profits may be less than potential profit.

This could raise from technical inefficiency or from higher than necessary payments to the factors of production. The technical inefficiency can arise since it takes effort by the controllers to reach full efficiency and which may be willing to make necessary effort. The higher payments can involve higher salaries to the controllers of the firm. For either reasons, company needs to concern how to report profit fall below true profit of the firm, with the difference used to finance inefficiency and higher factor payments in fair business conduct behavior. Particularly, company also need to concern how to carrying on fair business conduct behavior, e.g. none mislead advertising information, correct profit differentiation financial information, product reputations of the existing products presentation, none mislead consumption motives performance (which favor the established over the unestablished) and lower trade-in values of second –hand products of entrants (particularly in the car market). So, it seems that any one firm none mislead conduct behavior factor can influence consumer choices to increase or decrease to buy the firm's products in fair buying and selling transaction.

Another view point, for same products differentiation none mislead conduct factor is also important to influence each consumer behavior. For example, cars don't have a common prototype and each manufacturer must design its particular model. In constant , for a product like sugar , there is a common prototype, and differentiation through branding is within the discretion of the firm involved. This for some good product differentiation may be benefit whereas, for other products differentiation depends upon the activities of the firms involved, although the costs and benefits to the existing firms varies between profits. However, the height of the barrier to entry by product differentiation is likely to be influenced by the conduct and behavior of the firms involved, and thus in the case , there is an element of firm's behavior and conduct can influence any consumer buying behavior of choice to its products.

How to apply behavioral economic principles to assist policy makers or decision makers to make more reasonable decision.

Behavioral economics theories can also apply to assist any policy makers to make right and reasonable decision in right time. I shall indicate new principles to recommend and I also shall give any psychological cases to explain how policy makers can apply behavioral economic theories to judge how to make their any decision is the most right and the most reasonable.

Behavioral economy is an independent and demonstrates real economic well-being. It aims to improve quality of life by promoting innovative solutions that challenge mainstream thinking on economic, environment and social issues. Also, behavioral economy is different branches of more alternative economies into a form that is useful primarily for policy-makers. I think behavioral economy can be given an aid to policy makers how who use economic tools to the broader policy making community by providing a theoretical behaviour for many policy approaches to be used. The standard economic analysis assumes that humans are rational and behave in a way to maximize their individual self-interest. This rational man assumption indicates a powerful tool for analysis. However, it has many shortfalls that can lead to unrealistic economic analysis and policy-making. Also, I think behavioral economics and psychology has these principles to influence human behaviour. These principles include, such as below:

In common, people do many things by observing others and copying; people are encouraged to continue to do things when they feel other people approve of their behaviour. People do many things without consciously thinking about time. These habits are hard to change. There are cases where money is de-motivating as it undermines people's intrinsic motivation. People want their actions and commitments to be values usually. People put undue weight on recent events and who can't calculate probabilities well and worry too much about unlikely events and who are strongly influences by how the problem/information is presented to them. People need to feel effective to make a change, even just giving who the incentives and information is not necessarily enough in any environment usually. So any policy maker ought concern about what the acceptable degree is when who choose to decide to make any new policy in whose country. If who can predict whether whether whose country's citizen will or won't accept whose new policy implement and know why some won't accept whose new policy implement and why some accept whose new policy implement, then who can decide to do any economic activities more reasonable, e.g. investment to build public hospital or public school in the location; spending this expenditure to education or medical more.

In fact, much of our behaviour is strongly influenced by other people's behaviour. Social learning is a process by which we take in the behavior of others to learn how to behave. In more complex situations with which we are unfamiliar, we consciously watch and learn from the behavior of others. For example, when use a new library for the first time. When we make a conscious decision on how to behave, our sense of social identity is important, we think: how would other from my group behave in this situation? So, the policy marker will need to make to compare the economic benefits to choose to build either library or public school between of them to satisfy readers need or students need more in the location.

In situations where there is high social capital. i.e. where there are strong networks between people and a high level of mutual trust, so its seems other people's behaviour and our sense of social identity may be extremely important in influencing our own behavior and policy makers ought need to know how to judge their behaviour whether their behavior is either right and reasonable or wrong and unreasonable in any learning process of environment. The standard economic theory is tried to explain where people's preferences come from, so it does not take account of the direct influence of the people's behaviour and social norms on our behaviour. The theory assumes we independently know what we want and that our preferences are fixed. This standard theory is very good at explaining short-term decision making for policy makers only. In decision marker view point, for example, I want green vegetables and choose fruits as they are on special offer in short term, but it cannot explain longer term changes in preferences. Now, I only choose organic food for long term because orgnic food can have more clean and no pollution to compare general green vegetables and fruit. Thus, the learning process environment will influence the food consumers who prefer to choose to buy organic food more than general green food in supermarket.

For driving example, it would require too much effort to look up all the rules when driving in a new country, to find out all the fines/punishments for failing to meet the rules, to work out the probability of being caught and the possible costs, before deciding how to drive there. Instead we just copy other people, and perhaps adjust our behaviour according to the feedback we receive. However, some psychologists indicate to see people how to behave, especically in crises situations and when others are experts. These psychologists have identified that we are open to influence from people in authority or people we like. When we are influenced by authority, an expert, someone with legitimate power to direct our actions, someone who can either reward or punish us. The effects are less likely to be lasting than we are influenced by someone we like. Thus, learning process of environment can influence any person's psychological behavior change easily. However, some people's psychological behaviour is similar to economic behaviour to judge to make any decision. For example, why do you wear a seatbelt in your car? Most of us wear seatbelts as it has became normal behaviour, everyone does it. We neither evaluate the likelihood of having an accident, nor the chance of getting caught without our seatbelt on and incurring a fine. The enforcement of seatbelt wearing is now hardly necessary, as it has become a social norm.

What does this mean for policy makers? Policy makers focusing only on economic analysis may often devise a system that has an immediate effect. In psychologists view this issue point, knowing that there is a fine for speeding and a high likelihood of getting caught, the driver will probably drive more slowly, but who will drive just as fast one who realise the chance of being caught is low. However, of policy makers can change the social norm, perhaps in this case by encouraging us to frown on others who drive dangerously fast with campaigns against dangerous driving, then less enforcement will be needed after the change. In other words policy makers might want to take preferences as fixed in the short term, but they should consider shifting preferences in the medium term.

An example where policy appears to have successfully changes people's preferences in the US and Singapre and Hong Kong is banning smoking in public places. This change appears to reduce the social proof of the amount people smoke in private places and public places both also. It seems that government policies can influence the decreasing numbers of consumers require to buy cigeratte to smoke habitually, due to fine and punishment is regulated to be ban effectively. Such daily routines quickly became habits. Even when we consciously think about what we do, it can be difficult to change our behaviour. Perhaps I think it is a good idea for people to use public transport, but I do not know where the bus stop is or when the bus runs. I think to use private car to drive to work place is more preference choice. The reward feeling , my journey by car was easy and free to reinforce my old bad habit. Psychologists theories on changing habits generally involve raising it to a conscious level where we can consider the merits of alternative behaviour.

In our learning process in environment, this is followed by adopting the new behaviour, which, with time, becomes frozen as a new habit. Thus, I think that we need have regulation to control my behaviour, then we can change my behaviour to be new habit from old habit of behaviour easily, such as consumption behavior. For example, human blood sale is an economic product, due to paying donors for blood would increase supply. Supplies would be provided at a cost advantage in the future, if demand continued to rise. Such as supplies to hospitals for blood will has cost from donors when there are many patients need much blood to use to treat any diseases in any hospitals. Otherwise, if there are not many patients need much blood to use, but there are many donors have effort to provide blood to any hospitals, then it will be economic inefficiency and it is highly wasteful of blood. Thus, the hospitals need to predict when there are many patients need much blood or there are less patients need less much. Then, hospitals can pay cheap cost to donors for blood supply. Thus, the learning processing for donors for blood supply is needed for hospitals.

For shareholder behavioual learing process in share investment environment example, if you hold some shares in a firm that has gone down in value. What do you do? Many people hold on to their shares in this situation, in the hope that they will recoup their losses. Conversely, when shares have gone up in share, people are happy to sell them to realise their gain, A similar behaviour is also observed for professional traders who tend to hold on to shares with a loss for longer than those with a gain. The traders who exhibit this type of loss to a lesser degree tend to be the more successful ones.

For another learning process environement example, this is a case where the theory is directly applicable within economic cost-benefit-type analyses that include valuations of no-market products, such as valuations of pollution damage. Policy makers have a choice as to whether-to-accept, and as these may vary by up to a factor, the outcome of such an analysis many well depend on which value is chosen. When a policy maker reasonably has a right to something that might be taken away from them, the willing-to-accept value would be used. On the other hand, when the policy maker only reasonable has a right to the status quo and an improvement is proposed, then the willingness-to-pay is the correct value to use. Thus, for valuations of pollution damage, policy makers need to learn whether pollution damage cost is higher or pollution bringing benefit is higher to make reducing pollution decision for long term. In generaly, people are expected to rationally make the best choices given their preferences, independent of how these choices are presented. Therefore more information and choice is always considered good. Using this theory, policy makers should ensure that people always have as much information and as many things to choose between as possible, the process of introducing policy is irrelevant. Thus, gathering information can assist policy makers to choose right decision for pollution damage benefit or cost behvioral choice to their society for economic benefit.

So, a participatory approach not only improves policy, it also makes to any policy makers more happier. In most cases these principles cannot be used directly as part of any mathematical economics analysis, but highlight situations where this standard analysis will not accurately describe human behaviour and therefore might have unintended consequences when implemented in policy. However, that the policy implications could be quite powerful as the behavioural approach provides quite different lines of analysis to the standard economic model. It is heartening to see policy makers focusing more on the psychology of behaviour when devising policy. So behavioral economics is a relatively new field of economics that attempts to incorporate insights from psychology into economic models and analyses. As above cases seem any policy maker's economic activities which are relative to whose psychology's decision.

However, psychologists are often interest in understanding at the level of individual or social group of behaviour, the primary interest in economic is usually in understanding how behaviour and interactions play out in a system to shape economic outcomes. Economists are interested in system-level outcomes, such as the level and path of wages, the effect of taxes on economic output, how rates of savings respond to interest rates etc. However, those economic outcomes depend on complex interactions of individuals. So, behavioural economy concerns to how to judge individual to do the reasonable or right behaviour to hope to get the reasonable economic result as well as it's goal rather to help improve any policy makers to understand their behaviour in ways that allow economists to make better predictions and suggest better economic policies. However, new elements about information processing or individual preferences might impact economic models and analyses in any learning process environment.

Is psychology influencing all field of economics? It is possible that behavioral economy needs theoretical contributions and laboratory evidence to support to make any reasonable or right decision to any policy makers. This type of work generally uses existing observational data and estimates relationships between variables of interest by either using naturally occurring variation in the data i.e. natural experiment.

Perhaps more than any other field, behavioral economics has had a large impact on finance to the point that behavior finance is often considered a separate field as opposed to being of behavioral economics. Also, public economic is the study of how government policies in fluence economic markets. A primary emphasis of public economic involves the topic of taxation. Otherwise, the biggest impact that the behavioral approach has had in economic is the analysis of retirement saving to influence any employees' decisions about their retirement savings. However, when employees can do make any active savings choices to prepare their retirement. If employers can assist whose employees to design any methods to allocate fund, then accumuates interest and is tax free until the retirement funds are withdrawn to every retirement employee. The tax advantage make effort to save for retirement.

Behavioral economic is in understanding how individuals do or do not smooth consumption over time. Smoothing consumption is a standard economic models. It suggests that individuals should borrow or save in order to consume a similar amount throughout one's lifetime. For example, a teacher who is paid a salary 12 months a year, who should not spend all whose salary within one year. Rather, the teacher should smooth whose consumption over the 12 month period. How to allocate to spend paychecks, food and social security payments which concerns the teacher decide to spend whose salary efficiently. Hence, who needs to plan how he shall spend whose one year salary to be reasonable use in the future.

Public economic is to understand how people respond to taxation and social benefit programs. This has been an area that has seen an explosion of behavioral work in recent year. i.e. how taxpayers can experience over-withholding and receive tax refunds from tax department. Policymakers and insurers are also increasingly turning to psychology for approaches to improve health behavior. Traditionally health-policy focused largely on information provision, assuming that as long as individuals were well informed, their decisions would maximize their health choices. For example, influential work on the effects of smoking taxes, however, well being of smokers appears to increase with higher taxes to influence health behaviours are not completely rational.

Behavioral economic has also had a small impact on the study of criminal behaviour. For example, individuals are not less likely to commit a crime when who are 18 age and the pubishment of doing so increases dramatically. However, some economists explain the motivations people have for giving to charity and who understand the psychological motivations for charitable giving. So, it seems that charity award giving has probable to reduce 18 age people who choose to do crime behaviour easily because who feel who have effort to assist charity in their life time.

Industrial organization economists study why firms exist and how which function and compete with each other. Insights and psychology and behavioral economics have made a significant contribution to develop that model the interactions of profit maximizing firms with their customers. In fact, firms often need to evaluate whether their products if prices are needed to set what of price of level is the most reasonable and attractive to customers to choose to buy their products.

For cell phone plan sale example, individuals choose cell phone plans with fixed minute allotments and steep charges for going over the minute limits, but frequently exceed their plan limits. This behavior is the best explained by a model in which people overestimate the precision of their demand forecasts. So, cell phone firms need to research how cell phone plans with fixed minute allotments and steep charges of cell phone call fee charge plan is the most acceptance method to cell phone clients generally. However, cell phone call charge plan and various cell phone product features and the way cell phone clients allocate their limited attention affects cell phone products markets which are external important factors can influence any cell phone clients why who will choose to use the cell phone call plan because any cell phone will be very large durable product to any cell phone consumer after who choose to buy the cell phone product. Hence, who will not often choose to use the old cell phone firm call charge plan if who feel it provides the excellent cell phone call service and reasonable phone call plan to use to compare other cell phone call plans in the cell phone call market.

Hence, the cell phone call firm needs to make marketing research why consumers need to choose to use which cell phone call plan among of other cell phone call plans in the cell phone call market. Also, researching the cell phone buyers' choice behaviour why who choose to buy the cell phone to use issue, which will have influence to the cell phone buyer why who choose to use the cell phone call charge plan because expensive cell phone is needed to use excellent quality of cell phone call service usually. Otherwise, cheap cell phone is needed to use poor quality of cell phone call service usually. So, cell phone call plan is needed to follow the cell phone quality and price to be used and they ought have direct relationship to influence why the cell phone buyer who chooses to use the cell phone call plan.

Finally, behavioral economy can also apply to be used to labor supply as a motivating in negative or positive labor supply elasticities in taxi driving example. For example, it is possible that taxi drivers work fewer hours when wages are high-consistent with a model of daily income targeting. This finding is that when wages are high (perhaps it is raining and thus it is easy to find people who want a taxi ride), taxi drivers are able to hit their daily target quickly and then go home. However, when wages are low, taxi drivers are not able to hit their target quickly and thus work additional hours in order to hit their target. It means taxi driver's behaviour produce the effect that taxi driver works more when wages are low than when wagers are high. This work has resulted to analyze taxi driver of labor supply decisions with daily reference points in non taxi domains. So, instead of the weather and client numbers and taxi charge factors, the factors of taxi drivers' hours worked and the quality of service is produced is another important factor to influence any taxi drivers' numbers to supply to the taxi market.

Behavioral economic has also influenced the understanding of how staffs can impact worker productivity and job satisfaction. For example, it is possible that poor cooperation can cause worker productivity decreases and it can also cause poor job satisfaction to the worker. So, when working environment can impact productivity, social comparisons can have an impact on job satisfaction as well as the worker's job satisfaction and search intentions are affected by knowing about the salaries of their peers in whose firm. Hence, the worker's positive or negative psychological feeling to whose employers which will have effort to influence whose working performance and productivity to whose firm in possible.

Behavioral economic is increasingly being used in the field of development economics or low income countries. Such as, how Philippines can offer commitment to individuals who wanted to save money in whose country or how Philippines can change to smoking behaviour when commitment devices were offered to Philippine smokers. So, Philippines policy makers need to concern resource scarcity and resource allocation issue to solve how to let its low income level householders can raise to the middle income level to achieve the high income level householders and the low income level householders whose income level is not distant very much.

Have behavioral economy and psychology methods close relationship.

Finally, I shall analyze whether it has close relationship between the discipline of behavioral economy and psychology which two branches are totally opposite or if the behavioral theories is only complement that mainstream economics. I think study of economy is the behavior of the complex human beings; this science examines how people choose to act and allocate resources in different market situations. So the economic analysis, is based on the implications that arise from a series of simple assumptions (which are sometimes cited as unrealistic) regarding the human nature. However, in psychological view, the individual is characterized by unlimited rationality and by the ability to follow time consistent, in every situation, his self-interest. In these conditions, behavioral economic attempts to consider a field of analysis in the study of economic phenomena.

Because economics deals with the study of human behaviour on the market, it highlights the human character of the science and the fact that, besides of all the patterns and models, the analysis refers to the real individual. It is also behavioural because it attempts to combine approaches from several sciences mainly from economics and psychology, and also from sociology, philosophy, anthropology or biology. This is not an easy mission, in the conditions in which these various disciplines have adopted in time different approaches that became, in many ways, contradictory. So, behavioural economics is that a multidisciplinary approach will increase the explanatory power of economics.

On one hand, there are specialists two argue that behavioural economic is a field of economics that continues the hand, there are others who see it as a distinctive school of thought, which proposes a new paradigm. However, behavioural economists propose a multidisciplinary study, criticize certain assumptions on which the traditional model is built (such as rationality and self-interest, in their unlimited form), resource to experiments (the classical method of psychology) to validate some assumptions, propose new theories (such as the prospect theory) and advance different interpretations of the economic behaviour, e.g. how to maximize consumers satisfy their needs. This issue is concerned to concern consumption of psychology and social economic situation research aspect.

Also, I think that behavioural economics can help the economic science by describing more realistically the utility functions of the individuals. This field of study is based rather it is a natural extension of the basic approach. However, it is can be claimed that behavioural economics is also built on the premise that psychology methods and assumptions are equally important. Also, models of behavioural economics, allow the utility to depend on the differences between one's own level and a reference level. People are sensitive to changes and preferences are not stable in time. The vision of behavioural economics concerning the inter-temporal choice (which assumes that individuals prefer immediate gains and delay unpleasant activities) seems to be more appropriate to the human behaviour that the one of the traditional model (which assumes that utility is updated over time). I shall give below suitations to explain how to apply behvioral economy method to predict consumption behavior.

- How can consumer debt management psychological factors influence consumption behavior?

In behavioral economy view point, it can be applied to explain why consumer debt management psychological factors can influence consumption behavior. Some consumption psychologists had investigated several psychological variables which have been suggested as causes or effects of debts. Economic and demographic factors can predict debt category well to support this influence of factor. How can consumer manage money skills to pay debt which can influence when who plan to consume? Debtors were more likely to buy cigarettes and Christmas presents for children than non-debtors. Conclusions must be qualified because of low return rates, but the results suggest that a complex of psychological and behavioral variables affect debt and are affected by it. It is argued that these variables are linked to the psychology.

In general, economical environment is poor, it will cause many unemployed people, even some people will loan debt to pay daily essential expenditure from banks. If those debtors can't manage whose debt to be better to spend. Whose behavior will cause who do not have more spending desires often. Because these debtors will feel themselves as being in a community where debt was more common and more tolerated than non-debtors. The whole question of the classification of products a necessities or luxuries and its consequences for purchasing behavior is of current interest in economic psychology. Since debt is associated with poverty and poor people tend to give external reasons for economic phenomena, such as poverty and unemployment, causality may run the other way. In either case, however, there should be a positive correlation between external control and debt. There have different variables offer explanations of debts at different levels. One factor may be a consequence of another, or the mechanism by which it takes effect (for example, different patterns of economic socialization might generate different attitudes towards debt).

Some debtors need to borrow debt (loan) for house purchasing need. So, if the house loan debtors who need to pay back whose house loan to bank for long time. It is possible that their house loan will influence to reduce to spend much of daily consumption behavior to buy non luxury and daily essential products for long time. Thus, the result is these house loan debtors will reduce every day essential expenditure, such as food and soft drink, entertainment etc. to consume too much to compare to non house loan debtors for long time. It seems that retailers can attempt to apply debt management behavior to predict consumer shopping of desires.

In conclusion, I shall indicate two theories to explain why economy and psychology has close relationship to influence human do any behavioural economic activities daily. For example, through the prospect theory, behavioural economics adds new parameters to improve the mathematical modelling method, which was advanced by economists for decisions taken under uncertainty. However, the theory also proposes a slightly different interpretation. The results are interpreted by the individual as positive or negative deviations from a reference point, which has a neutral psychological value. Last but not least, in addressing social preferences, behavioural economics adds parameters that increase the concern of decision-makers to also assess their utility function in relation to others. For another example, the choice theory; secondly there is not a common consensus between the specialists of behavioural economics regarding the variables that should be included; and finally, many variables that affect the behaviour are not quantitative, but qualitative, and cannot be precisely measured. The findings of behavioural economic are relevant and can help the mainstream theory by providing a more realistically base of study. However, this argument has contributed to the development of behavioural economics, because there are a large number of phenomena that cannot be entirely explained by the mainstream economics.

So, why in the beginning, I indicated why behavioural economics does not imply the totally exclusion of the neoclassical approach and the most studies in this area try to provide a more realistic base of the standard theory. In the concluding, I believe that in time, behavioural economic models will replace the simplified ones, based on unlimited rationality. Also, economists have provided a great importance to the quantitative structures, departing from the human nature. However, behavioural economics can become truly revolutionary only it will always be receptive and will provide a critical insight to their own theories and perspectives, and especially the ones regarding the aspects that they reproach to the traditional economic theory. However, I also feel that the individual's behaviour on the market is determined only be economic factors. In brief, individual choices and, by this, the demand variation are explained only and the variations in the prices of products/services and the available personal income. Am important discussion in the field of determine directly the economic behaviour of an individual (like the sociological and psychological of factors) are actually active elements in the process the reshaping of the utility functions. Finally, in my view, I believe that the conduct of the market phenomena, as it occurs in reality. In this sense, the research of behavioural economics aims to see how the neoclassical model could be improved, using mainly psychology concepts. Although, there are some specialists who argue that behavioural economics can be an alternative to the neoclassical theory.

Finally, most findings, of my study conducted in this book, modify some of standard economical assumptions, in order to provide a greater psychological realism. However, the additions proposed by behavioural economists simply recognize the human limitations on (mentally) calculations, will and self-interest. So, I think psychology and economy has close relationship to assist any policy makers or decision makers to do any economic psychology daily. Because the purpose of economics is to better understand and explain the conduct of the economic activities as which occur in reality. Otherwise, human being is complex and its behaviour and constitution is studied by all the social sciences. Consequently, multi and interdisciplinary approaches can bring real benefits to the economic science, by providing a more realist foundation to cause any policy makers or decision makers how to decide to make any behaviours or economic activities by behavioural economic activities support daily.

● Can price change influence consumer behavior?

In behavioral economy view point, it can explaine why price change can influence consumer behavior. In general, under short –run profit maximization,

the price was seen as a mark –up marginal cost with the marketing determined by the elasticity of demand. However, economists have used these methods to determination of how prices change behavior. The first is the indicated prices are determined relative to costs by firms in the pursuit of objectives. In the view point, the first is firms are price-makers and let prices in a way which think will achieve these objectives. Subject to constraints arising from demand and cost conditions. The second is theory of perfect competition, firms are effectively price-takers and the interaction between demand and supply in the market set price. So, firms are regarded as price-takers, and hence not in position to set prices, such as price-adjuster . The third is the idea of observing the process of price decision-making and seeking observation is on the prices of price determination. Their view is expressed as price is based on full average cost , including a conventional allowance for profits and full average cost . Is determined as follows? price or direct cost per unit is taken as the base, a percentage addition is made to cover overhead or on cost or indirect cost, and a further conventional addition of percentage is made for profit. This, it seems price change behavior can influence consumer individual consumption behavior to any products.

● Can constructive consumer choice processes influence consumption behavior?

Consumer decision making has been an interest in consumption behavior research, e.g. how technological changes, an information explosion factor can influence consumer individual choice decision to buy any products. Due to limited processing capacity, consumers often don't have well-defined existing preferences, but construct them using a variety of strategies contingent on task demands. Rapid technological changes for instance, has led to multitudes of new products and decreased product lifetimes. In addition, new communications media, such as the world wide web have made amounts of information on options potentially available (Alba et al. 1987). It seems time pressure, such as fast product lifetimes and new communications, media, internet advertisement can influence consumers how to make decision to buy any thing which is the best to them, e.g. choice of gathering products of advertisement information to buy products from internet (electronic shopping) instead of traditional visiting shops consumption behavior. So, new information advertisement media, e.g. internet advertisement consumer information media will influence consumer individual decision tasks. For example, a consumer may be fairly certain about the values of some of the attributes to choose to buy which kind of mobile phone from electronic shopping easily at home. However, the consumer may not have information for all of the mobile phone options on some attributes (e.g. reliability information would not be available for a new mobile model) from internet advertisement. In addition, some attributes, such as safety may be difficult for consumer to trade off; making trade off requires possibly accepting a loss on such an attribute with potentially threatening consequences.

What is characteristics of consumer decision strategy in product choice process? It includes the total amount of information processed, the selectivity in information processing, the pattern of process, (whether by alternative brand or by attribute). First, the amount of information processed is very a great deal. For example, a mobile phone choice may involve detailed consideration of much of the information available about each of the available mobile phone, as implied by more rational choice models, or it may have a consideration of a limited set of information (e.g. repeating what are choices last time). Second, different amounts of information can be processed for each attribute or alternative (selective processing), or the same amount of information can be processed for each attribute or alternative (consistent processing). For example, suppose a consumer considers the mobile phones to decide that life time is the most important attribute, processed only that attribute and chooses which mobile brand, with the famous brand value on that mobile phone attribute. Third, choice process would involves on that attribute. This choice process would involve highly selective processing of attribute information (since the amount of information examined differs across attributes), but consistent processing of alternative mobile phone brand information, since one piece of information is considered for each mobile phone. The fact that working memory capacity is limited effectively requires selective attention to information, e.g. internet advertisement media.

In general, the more selective consumers are in processing information, the more susceptible their decisions may be to factors that influence the salience of information, some of which may be irrelevant, such as different mobile phone brands of product life time comparing information. Information may be processed primarily by alternative, in which multiple attributes of a single option are processed before another option is considered, or by attribute, in which the values of several alternatives on a single attribute are examined before information on another attribute is considered. For example, a consumer might engage in attribute processing by examining the price of each of the mobiles, concluding that mobile brand (A) was the most expensive, another mobile brand (B) was the least expensive, and the another mobile brand (C) had a very good price . However, the consumer could process in an alternative-based fashion or is design by examining the reliability, price, safety of mobile phone brand (A) in order to form an overall valuation of that mobile phone brand (A).

Finally, an important distinction among strategies in the degree to which are compensatory. A compensatory strategy is one in which a good value on one attribute can compensate for a poor value on another. A compensatory strategy thus requires explicit trade off among attributes. Deciding how much more one is willing to pay for very good rather than average reliability or long useful life time in a mobile phone involves making an explicit trade -off between reliability long useful life time and price for examples. Thus, in general, constructive consumer choice processes attribute , such as the product's price, quality, life of time , reliability, design , brand information of media sources as well as electronic internet shopping or visiting shopping buying channels of these factors will influence the consumer to do the final decision to choose to buy which kind of product in the consumption market. Also, any retailers need to concern whether which is the major influence of attribute to the product. Because wrong evaluation of the major attribute of the product will influence the consumer to make final buying decision when who compares the retailer's product to other retailers whose similar products in the consumer's choice process.

● How can economical environment factor predict consumers consumption?

The dominant approach to industrial economics is
the one which is usually described as the structure-conduct-performance approach. So, predicting the performance of an industry in terms of profitability and advertising growth can predict consumer consumption in possible. The structure of an industry covers factors like the relative and size of firms, involved the ease of entry into the industry and the elasticity of demand for the output of that industry. The conduct of firms covers the objectives of the firms, price setting behavior, and attitudes to competitors (actual and potential), and from that the performance of that industry predicted, particularly in respect of profitability.

What are the main features of the structure of an industry? Many consumption psychologists discuss on the structure-conduct-performance topic, the number and relative size of the firms and the extent of barriers to entry into the industry to influence the product suppliers to consumption choices in the market. The number and relative size of firms is usually placed under either the size distribution of firms or individual concentration. Most industries don't fit into the category of a large number of small firms or of one firm.

Barriers to entry into an industry comprise all the factors which lead to new entrants into the industry being at a disadvantage to the existing firms because consumers have more choices to buy the similar products from the competitors . The first factor is the existence of economies of scale which means that a new entrant would have to produce on a relatively large scale increasingly. The second factor, the brand of products are supplied by a significant amount and thereby depressing price a significant amount , differentiation and advertising, so that a new entrant has to incur costs to overcome the loyalty of consumers to existing products. A third factor is the ability of existing firms to produce and distribute at lower costs than new entrants. Although, for example, access to cheaper new materials, accumulated knowledge of the industry etc. So, these external marketing environment factor will influence consumption behavior choices. For example, if the industrial structure determines or influences performance, the governments concerned with aspect of industrial performance (particularly aspects like price changes, technological progress and employment levels).

Consumption psychologists have often been assigned that the level of concentration in an industry is largely technological determined and that increases in concentration reflect impact of technological advance with increase the desired size of factory or firm. For example, mobile phone manufacturing industry, if the brand of mobile phone manufacturer had technological advance to manufacture any new model to attract consumers have more buying choices from their mobile products. Then, technological factor will influence consumers have more choices to buy the brand of mobile phone products. Other some psychologists believe the way in which unit costs change with the scale of production (cost conditions and economies of scale) factor which can influence consumers choice behaviors. When public policy favor active industrial intervention to change industrial structures, some indication is required as to whether the minimum efficient scale is small or large relative to the total market to supply their product numbers to influence consumers' behaviors. In the former case a policy favoring small units would be indicated, whereas, in the latter case large units may be favored.

Increasing returns to scale and economies of scales are usually defined as a situation when all inputs into the productive process are increased in the same proportion the volume of output increases in a greater proportion . How can economies of scale influence products supplying numbers? For example, that is the scale of output increases the degree of capital intensity rises. But within that change the type of the capital equipment is likely to be varied. Further, the balance between skilled and unskilled or between manual and non-manual labor may change. Thus , it is necessary to adopt a view of both increasing and decreasing returns.

The definition of unit costs of output declining with increased output. This must refer to all costs(including capital costs, and can only relate to a particular set of relative prices for inputs from which the unit costs are calculated. It would include any change in the price of input usage, such as mobile phone products which need to use different materials to manufacture any mobile phone products Thus, if a mobile phone firm had to pay more wages as its use of labor increased, that would have to be included. It is generally assumed that, for any scale of output, the firm is combining the impacts in an efficient manner. This efficiency includes economies efficiency (choosing the least cost combinations of inputs) and technical efficiency (producing the maximum feasible output from given inputs). The measurement of returns to scale under this definition may be only relevant to a particular economy, as it depends upon the particular relevance prices used.

Such as, each mobile phone product price will influence consumer individual behavior of choice to buy only one among the different brands of model mobile phones. So, mobile phone manufacturers need to concern how to reduce cost to gain economies of scale input to raise mobile phone output. For example, from a reduction in the effective price of an input to the model of mobile phone, as the volume of the styles of mobile phones purchases increased arising from an increase in monopsony power. For example, three mobile phone plants, A, B, C are assumes to have a fixed mobile phones output, and initially produce with unit costs A1, B1, and C1. Respectively. Supposing plants A and C would make subnormal profits and plant B super-normal profits, when capital costs are based on the historical cost of the mobile phone plant. Now the capital values of plants A and C are, it is argued, unlikely to fall and that of plant B to rise , for the amount which another mobile phone firm could be prepared to pay for a plant will reflect its profit prospects. If the decline in capital value fully reflects the initial deviations for normal profits, unit costs shift to A2, B2 and C2 respectively. Thus, there is a tendency at work towards mobile phone constant unit costs being observed. How far this tendency operates depends upon the based on which mobile phone firms value their assets. When the value is based on historic cost, the tendency does not operate. But the tendency does operate when the value is based in some way on the assets' profit prospects. Thus product manufacturers need to concern how to earn economic of scale to cost to avoid each product price will be changed often to influence consumer choices to other competitors more easily.

● How can auctions or online experimentation respond to predict consumer behavior and sale forecast accuracy?

Nowadays, in UK suggests that consumer buying behavior has changed significantly. Consumers caan buying different things, at different times and through different channels. As a result, forecast accuracy is very poor and many companies feel automated forecasting systems can not predict buying behavior more accuracy and relying on analysts to predict buying behavior by psychological methods. Automated forecasting systems weaknesses are such as: Historical data alone can't be used to predict feature sales in times and drawing together a wider range of internal and external data would help improve forecast accuracy. The impact on revenue manager varies widely. When sales forecasts are important, adjustments to revenue management system outputs are needed to retain credibility. When customers' behavior are poor to understand, there may be a need to sell from auctions or online experimentation to predict the market response. So, these automated forecasting system have these weaknesses to cause companies feel technological method can not be better than psychological method to predict further consumption behavior for whose products.

In psychological consumption of prediction view point, learning how to predict changes in consumers' attitudes and behaviors which is important to any companies. For example, in part behavior has changes as a result a recent major disruptive events, such as recession and exchange rate changes etc. economic factor, but there are other non economic factors to change consumers' attitudes and behaviors. For example, consumers are becoming smarter in their use of the internet to research products based on previous customers' view, seek out the best, deals and offers and then buy online, with a corresponding increase in the number of price comparison sites. So , companies are percentage seeing the rise of the strategic consumer who observes the dynamic of supplier pricing and adapts their buying strategy in response. However, some observers suggest that these changes to consumers' attitudes and behaviors are fundamental long, lasting and likely to continue to be disruptive.

Some consumption psychologists feel sales have become less predictable. In general, sales forecasts based on historical patterns in time series have become less accurate and hence less useful in the past year in many industries, not just these traditionally served by revenue management. Does forecast accuracy easily? For some revenue managers may be not too much, in some businesses prices are set by reference to the main competitors and forecasts have limited impact on operating and decisions about capacity. Marketing forecasting is aim to setting prices, maximizing revenue and managing operations.

However, forecast accuracy is very important to find why changing consumer attitudes and the implications for customer segmentation and forecasting of buying behaviors are not just relevant to revenue management. They are also fundamental to sales, marketing , brand management, customer loyalty, product design and beyond. Perhaps it has an opportunity for revenue managers to take a lead in influencing thinking of their colleagues in these areas. Some consumption psychologists forecast the future, who concern the historical data of companies collection before the recession, it can no longer be applied to forecast consumer behavior during the recession or after. At the opposite extreme, companies can simply continue to between auto prediction system to predict when the market stability will return soon and how to influence consumer behavior.

Sales are likely to depend on the economic situation, the competition and consumer behavior. However, these are external environmental factor to influence consumption of behavior. If it is possible to separate out these effects, then the forecasting model can take account of them by either building the economy/market into the model or segmenting consumers in an economy/market invariant way. External data, for example on the economic situation can also provide a good indicator of future sales. For example, internet (online) web site research technology is one possibility for combining and processing data from different sources on the web using automated tools. If buying behavior is changing and every consumer demand is becoming elastic, not only to increase revenue, but also to improve knowledge of the customers. For example, online auctions are mainly used in the travel and hospitality industries for offloading surplus capacity have been shown when facing only uncertain consumer demand. However, analyzing external economy environment factor is not effective to minimize risk to the sellers. Because sale forecasts are never going to be completely accurate and there is an argument for moving the focus away from being smarter with existing data towards making the business less dependent on sale forecasts. For example, taking close look at increasing flexibility in the supply chain or operations or re-examine the strategy for setting price.

What the current situation really emphasizes however is that there is certainly a need for forecast accuracy to be taken seriously by revenue managers and reported on by revenue management system. Thus, revenue managers need to concern how to predict whose consumers' psychological emotions to find why the reasons can influence whose consumption attitudes and behaviors changing to cause their product sale numbers had been falling. So, it seems that consumers' emotions can be influenced whose buying behavior by online auctions factor.

How to predict passenger individual consumption choice for airline industry

How can airline gas or oil price influence passenger individual airline choice?

For airline industry, if the airline firm can predict global economy trend how to influence oil or gas price, then it can predict its passenger consumption of choice more easily. Due to we are entering globalization. In Special, airline transportation demands are also increasing, due to many travelers need to catch planes to travel as well as many cargoes need to be carried to planes to transport to different countries to sell. It seems aviation transportation industry is important to influence the health of the global economy growth nowadays. However, ignorance of internal or external market dynamics, catching travelers business can be detrimental to airline profitability more than carrying cargoes business. Because the demands of travelling different countries' travelers' consumption are still more than the demands of businessmen carrying cargoes in any countries every year. So, the passenger income sector is still have the important position to compare to cargo income sector in global airline transportation industry any countries nowadays.

How can negative social change influence any airlines' air ticket prices to be risen to influence cost raising? In fact, the increase in petroleum price can have chance to affect airlines in a negative manner because increased oil prices have resulted in the reduction of services operations, the number of airline schedules flights, even airline bankruptcies. Whether inflation, terrorism, oil price, bank interest rate etc. external factors have the most influential to cause the bad effects to cause airlines need to raise air ticket price to influence traveler numbers to be decreased.

SEVEN

HOW SOCIAL FACTOR INFLUENCES CONSUMER BEHAVIOR

Human Behavioral network job brings social economic benefits

What does human network job mean ? Why may human network job be popular? Why human network job behavior may influence economy ?

Nowadays internet is popular to use. We can apply internet to find data , search any new things, even earn money. Why does internet

may become huma network job source. For example, e-publish may be one kind of new human network job. Any authors may apply internet

channel to help them to sell electronic or paper books from e-publisher web store. They may apply facebook, you tub etc. any online

channel to promote themselves new books to let new readers to know whether when they may buy themselves favourable new topic books to read

from electronic publisher web store.

Thus, future electronic publisher industry may help any authors to build internet network platform to help them to sell and promote

ot advertise their any one new electronic or paper book topic to let global any one reader to choose to buy their any new topic books from electronic publisher web store easily and conveniently. However, it implies that electronic network platform author may be one kind of future new human network job in our societies.

How electronic network platform author job may bring economy benefit in macro economy view? A person can have few friends, contacts and still be very influential if these few
friends and contacts are themselves highly influential, e.g. one author must not need to know any one reader in global society. When they like to choose any electronic books from electronic internet network platform. They may become the author's any one topic book buyer, when they feel the author's any one topic book is fun and attract they make decision to buth the strange author whose the topic book from electronic book publisher's platform web store conventiently in short time. Although, they are strangers, they do not know themselves , but the reader can understand what it way that made Google from writing platofrm to create new creative mind and typing network job method to replace traditional hand writing book method for global authors. It will be one kind of new human network writing job.

Hence, global any one reader can apply an innovative search engine , such as google.com to find whether whom author personal new topic books are value to read from internet.
Then, the electroniuc publisher's web store may be new book store platform sale network to help the author to sell many electronic or paper books from electronic network platform
in short time. So, internet may be future new network plaform to help global any one author to create network writing job absolutely. Furthermore, internet may be popular social media
to help any one author to build goold relationship between his/her readers. It is one kind of new network, human network job. New authors do not need to buy many paper books to prepare to put in any one book shop warehouse. Their every book can print on demand to reduce out of book stock in any one book shop. They may choose to sell either electronic books or paper books both from any one book publisher web store. So, electronic network platform may be one kind of good writing channel to help human authors to create income and it can also help authors to bring new creative mind and new topic fun content books to let readers to know and buy to read from electronic publisher network platform.

Why does human behavior may be one kind of new human network job to bring global economic advantages. ALthough, it may be free income or without inocme, but the person does the network behavior, his/her behavior may be bring advantages to influence many other people's health. For this case, when a worker in a coffee shop in an airport gets a vaccination aganinst the flu, it does not only helps him or her stay healthy, but also helps the many travellers who might otherwise have been inflected if that workers caught the flu. So, the externality , the result implies the vaccination of even a part of a community conveys benefits to the whole community. For example, governments pay special attention to the vaccinations of school children, teachers, health mothers, and the elderly, categories of people particularly susceptible not only to catching, but also to transmitting a disease.

It is not accidential that governments are heavily involved with vaccination . When there are externalities, free market, fail to persuade individual incentives with society's
their the worker's decision of whether to get a vaccine ends up attracting whether other people get sick. The workers might not fully take all these other people's potential suffering into account when making her or his vaccination

decision.

As Stanford University does many suggestions, understand this and tries to help them make the right decisions and so providers free flu vaccines for its staff and students.

Small pockets of unvaccinated individuals can allow a disease to gain a spread more widely well-being. For example, parent weighing the costs and benefits of a vaccine for their child is not always thinking of the consequences of that vaccination to other people. THese are markets in which subsidizing or regulating behavior can make everyone better off. Because the reason for requiring that a child be vaccinated before enrolling in school is not just to protect that child, because each child's vaccination affects others via potential contagions.

Robots take our jobs behavioral and economy influences

Robot job behavior brings economy influences

If one day robots can replace human to do simple, even complex jobs. They will bring what influences to our global societial economy.The popular economic refrain declares that the global middle class is dying and robots will soon take our jobs, e.g. shopping center customer service jobs, library service jobs, cinema ticket sale jobs, restaurant kitchen cooker jobs, even, bus drivers, taxi drivers etc. public transport driving jobs, accountant, doctors etc. professional jobs. Whether it is beautiful or petty matter if our future societies have many human jobs can be replaced to do from robots. Businessman must may reduce to employ employees and reduce to pay salary or wage, when robots can be replaced to do their employees tasks. But, societies must bring unemployement rate rises , due to societies will have many people loss jobs when their employers choose to buy robots to serve their clients or do any office tasks or customer service or cleaning etc. tasks.

In micro economy view, employers may save money in long term, but in macro economy view, it will cause unemployment ratio rises , even crime rate rises when there are many people lose jobs in societies. These models of doom, though, fail to account for the hundreds of businesses riding the waves of change in their industries when robots may be invented to replace human to do many simple , even complex tasks in our future societies.

WE may image that one small factory needs to manufacture fishes canes to sell to supermarket, the small , cheaper stuff and higher margin parts of the fishes manufacture industry. Before, this factory needs to employe many human factory workers need to help every fresh customer makeing the perfect fishing gear, designed for performance, durability, and cost in order to achieve to manufacture every fish cane in whole fished processing manufacturing stages. Every worker needs to spend about 15 to twenty minutes to finish every fish cane , till to delivery to any supermarket to sell. If this fish canes manufacturing factory can apply manufacturing robots to help them to finish any one working tasks , every robot can only spend five minutes to finish whole fresh fish cane manufacturing process. Thus, every robot can help this factory save 10 to 15 minutes time to finsh every fish cane manufacturing process. IN fact, time is money,

because when every robot can help this factory to reduce 10 to 15 minutes time to compare human worker. Then, this factory can finish about 20 fish canes in one hour if it can use robot to help it to manufacture fish canes. Otherwise, if this factory still use human workers to help it to manufacture fish canes, then it can finsh about 3 to 4 fish canes in one hour. SO, the manufacturing efficiency ensures that robots must help this fish manufacturing factory to raise fish canes number more than human workers. So, in robotic behavioral economy view, manufacturing robots must help this fish canes manufacturing factory to raise fish canes manufacturing number and deliver increasing number to supermarkets to prepare to sell every day. Robots can help this fish canes manufacturing factory bring manufacturing time saving, rising manufacturing efficiency, improving performance and reducing wages expenditure long time advantages in micro economy view. However, manufacturing robots can also bring disadvanages to society, e.g. increasing unemployment ratio, increasing crime rate,
this factory workers will lose jobs and income, they need earn social welfare from government and increasing government finance pressure in short time, even long time in macro economic view.

Stanford University graduate program in economics, Scott lecturer explained that "in demand and supply economic theory for robots supply and demand case, robots supply number increasing may influence human workers demand number decrease. It sometimes calls " the efficient frontier".
No specific human beings were mentioned in any of economics classes. As robots supply and demand in market case, They (robots) may be purely theoretical " agents" who reached to the most reasonable sale prices in order to persuade any one businessman buyer to make manufacturing robot buying decision whether robots can help him / her to bring how much saving time , saving money, saving cost, improving performance, efficiency economic benefit before he/she plans to reduce workers number when he/she decides to apply robots to replace human workers in his/her factory or office or any service department, e.g. cinema ticket sale service, shopping center customer service, shopping center cleaning , supermarket customer service etc. service or sale tasks. When robots can replace human to do any one of these tasks in any organizations. So, robots may be human worker agents who reached to prices the way robots would react to a software
command. There was nothing that explained why some people thrived and others did n't or why truly brilliant, hardworking people could fail when much lazier folks succeeded." Having been admitted to the Stanford University graduate program in economics, Scott lecturer hoped to get his answers there.

How robots influence our future social changing? Using the right technology can be a boon to your business in this economy. For internet example, it is easier than ever to find well-matched customers all around the world, to stay in contact with them, and to more quickly design the products they want. If you focus solely on being cutting -edge, though you risk letting the technology
take over what should be very robust relationships with your customers , employees, and colleagues. IN nowaddays society, technoligical advances and cutomation, personal
relationships in business are more crucial than ever. I mean that robots can not replace human to serve clients to let them to feel more comfortable and passion more easily. For shoe shop case example, if the shoe shop apply one

robot to serve its clients to replace human shoe salesperson to serve its shoe customers. Robots ensure that they can not persuade every shoe potential buyer to make shoe buying decision more easily when robots need to contact every shoe potential buyer. The reason is simple, because robots can not touch any one shoe buyer individual emotion very easier.

If the shoe buyer needs the robots to help him/her to choose any right shoe styles when he/she can not feel himself / herself can make the most right shoe style choice decision. The robots can not replace human shoe salesperson to make shoe style choice judgement more easily. They must need longer time to analyze whether which shoe style may be the most suitable to the shoe buyer. Otherwise, human shoe salesperson may attempt to make the most right shoe style choice decision to help any one shoe buyer to chooce the most right style shoe because he/she owns shoe style sale experience, shoe style knowledge, the most important reason is that they can feel every shoe customer individual emotion to touch whether he/she will feel comfortable or happy when they attempt to help every shoe customer to seek the most right shoe style in every shoe customer whole shoe searching processing. Othwerwise, serving robots are only one machine, they can not touch or feel every shoe customer individual emotion whether he/she feel comfortable or unhappy or happy when they need to contact them in whole shoe searching processing. Hence, I believe that some tasks robots can

not repalce human staff to do very easily. Otherwise, robots may bring disadvanatges to let any one businessman to loss his/her customers, due to robots can not touch every customer

emotion to compare human staff in service tasks more easily. Robots serving customer behaviors may cause money lose and customers number lose to the shop in micro economic view.

Intellectual human economic behaviors

What does intellectual human economic behaviors mean ? I believe that when we choose or decide to do intellectual behaviors, then our societies will be influenced to bring economic growth in consequence.I shall attempt to indicate pollution case to explain how and why eithet our intellectual or foolish behaviors may bring economic growth or recession in consequence as below:

On one hand, for air pollution social case aspect example, if we only consider to buy cars to drive for working aimr or holiday leisure aim. Then, our societies air will be polluted. Our health will be influenced to bad. Our car driving behaviors may cause global environment air pollution serously. In long tiem, global air pollution will bring our bodies health to be bad. Although, ourselves car driving behaviors may bring our driving travelling leisure enjoyment and comfortable feeling in short time, also we so not need to pay public transport fare often, but we need to compensate ourselves health economic intangible loss due to air pollution , when cars number increases, dirty air will cause ouselves health to become bad.

In the result, we will need to pay more medical expenditure when we are old age, due to ourselves bodies will become bad, due to we breathe global dirty air every day, due to ourselves cars pollute air in long time, e.g. 10 to 20 years, even 30 more without limited air pollution environment. So, driving cars behavior may be one kind of human foolish behavior and our foolish behavior may bring ourselves future long time medical expenditure absolutely.

One the other hand, water pollution social aspect, if we often keep much rubblish to pollute sea, oil exploration porcessing pollute ocean , ships gas pollute ocaen, then fishes will eat polluted food and drive dirty water, due to global ocean is polluted.

In fact, because human only to conside how to buy boats to carry on leisure enjoyment activities, or catch cruises to travel on the sea. Also, oil manufacturers only consider researching anywhere to find new oil exploration places to manufacture oil product, when their oil exploration processes pollute ocarn . Consequently, global fishes drink polluted warer or eat polluted food. They will have poison. SO, human will have high chance to eat poison polluted fishes, due to fishes are poison or are polluted.

So, human is doing foolish activities, we only hope to find oil exploration places to pollute ocean or we only spend money to buy ticket to catch ships to travel anywhere in global ocean. All of these human foolish behaviors will bring pollution to global ocean. On consequently, we will need to compensate to eat polluted or dirty or poision fishes, ourselves bodies health will be bad. In long time, we need have high chance to pay medical expenditure when we are old. So, pollution case may be one good example to explain how and why human foolish behavior may influence ourselves future need to compensate serious medical loss.

All of these human foolish behavior will bring pollution to global ocean. On consequently, we will need to compensate to eat polluted or dirty or poison fished , ourselves bodies health will be bad. In long time, we will have high chance to pay medical expenditure, when we are old. So, pollution case may be one good example to explain how and why human ourselves intellectual or foolish behaviors may influence future long time economic loss or economic growth or recession in micro and micro economic view.

On another water pollution aspect hand, if we often keep rubbish to sea, oil exploration processing pollutes ocean and ships' gas pollute ocean, then fishes will eat polluted food and drink dirty water, due to fishes will eat polluted food and drink dirty sea water because the global ocean is polluted seriously.

In fact, because human only consider how to buy boats to carry on any leisure water activities, or catches cruises to travel on the sea. Also, oil manufacturers only consider any where to find oil exploratin places to manufacture oil products from ocean, when their pol exploration processes can plooute ocean. Consequently, global fishes drink polluted water or eat direty food. They will have poison. So, human will have high chance to eat poison fishes.

Otherwise, such as pollutin case, it can infuence inflation or deflation. Consequently, the reason indicates supply and demand theory. If air pollution is serious, then we will consider health issue, global cars demand number may be influenced to reduce, when global cars number demand will reduce, global car prices and supply number will need to change to fall down in order to attract or persuade global car consumers choose to make car purchase decision.

Hence, global car manufacture number and car price will be influenced to reduce, due to global air pollution issue. Consequently, deflation will occur because when the country citizen usually does not spend much extra saving money to buy car expensive goods. Money value will be low. Otherwise, if global cair pollution is not serious, human considers to buy cars to enjoy driving leisure lives. So, global car demand is influenced to increase , also global car price will also influenced to increase.

Consequently, gobal human will choose to buy cars to drive. Due to we accept to spend extra saving to buy expensive car goods. Car sale price and supply may be influenced to rise up. Money value is influenced to reduce. Inflation may be influenced, due to global car consumers number increases, we would not have extra money to spend easily. Car expensive goods expenditure influences our spending habit to avoid to make car purchase decision more easily. So, human intellectual or foolish activities may bring inflation or deflation consequency in possible indirectly in macro economic view.

On conclusion, above pollution case explain that how and why human intellectual or foolish economic behaviors may bring inflation or deflation consequency as wll as economic growth or recession consequency as well as any goods demand and supply increasing or decreasing consequency. It implies that human behavior may have indirect relationship to influence any goods demand and supply number to either increase or decrease result as well as any goods price will be influenced to increase or decrease in micro and macro economic view.

The relationship between social change and human behavior

Why does economic changes may influence human individual behavioral change? I shall attempt to indicate shopping behavior and staying at home behavior to explain their case and effect relationsip as below:

Human behavior can be influenced by economic change or economic change can be influenced by human behavior? Why does recession may influence consumers reduce shopping desire? In social recession suitation, it is possible that many people lose jobs suddenly, due to businessmen lose many customers. They need to make decision to reduce employees number in order to continue to keep businesses. Consequently, many firms (organizations) their employees may lose jobs. When they have much time, due to lose jobs, they will feel to avoid to spend too much time and money to go to shopping often. Many losing jobs people, they will often stay at homes.

So, they will reduce time to go to shopping, then non essential products won't their preferable choice purchase products. Hence, recession will change many losing jobs people their shopping or consumption desires to avoid to buy non essential products often . Usually when economic boom, many people have jobs to do because consumers number must increase when many people have jobs to do. Then, many people can accept to spend money to buy non essential products often. Many people feel spend time to go to shopping can satisfy their purchase of any kinds of new products useful psychology or desire. So, recession is one good example to explain it can influence many people do not like often to leave homes to go to shopping easily. Many people like to stay at homes, becaue they feel worry about spending too much shopping time when they leave homes. Their staying home time is one good negative shopping behavior example. So, economic change may influence human individual behavior changes , they have direct cause and efect relationship in behavioral economic view.

May human behavior influence economic change? Is it possible that human behavior may bring the country social economic change in macro economic or micro behavioral economic view ? I shall indicate publishing industry example. Do you feel that if there are many students feel learning is very important when they read many books or many of students feel interesting to read or they have reading new books in habit, then it is possible that the country will have many students like to spend time to go to any book shops to choose the books, they feel that they can help they learn new knowledge. Then the country will increase students number, they often spend time to visit any one book shop every week. Their visiting book shops behavior which may become their habits. So, the country will increase students number, they often spend time to visit book shops. Also, it implies that visiting book shops behaviors may be their behavioral habits.

So, when the country has many students often spend time to visit book shops , their visiting book shops behaviors may help any one book shop to raise books sale chance. So, the country's student individual often visiting book shop behaviors, their habitual visiting book shops behaviors must may assist help any one book shop to increase books sale number absolutely.

Consequently, any one book shop , its books sale bumber must be influenced to increase to increase because the country will have many students like or feel need visit book shops habit in order to choose any suitable books to buy to read at home in order to raise themselves learning effort. When the country has many bok shops often have many students visit their book shops, then their books sale number may be influenced to increase. It explain why student individual visiting book shop behavior may help any one book shop sale number increases also.

How human productive behavior may influence economic development

May any country which citizen behavior assist themselves country development? It is one cause and effect economic question. I mean that if the country itself citicen can not concentrate mind or energy to choose to do one kind of industry in order to let themselves country can bring the most benefit, then whether the counry itself economy can bring the most serious economic benefit. I shall attempt to indicate these countries themselves indistry choice to explain whether these countries themselves citizen productive behavior may help themselves countries to achieve the largest economic benefits. I shall indicate as below:

New Zealand farmer individual wine productive behavior

For New Zealand country example, this country concerns itself effort is foucs on farming agricultural aspect. So, this country has many farmers concentrate on farming agricultural aspect. May New Zealanders choose to spend time to produce different kinds of wines, e.g. wine or red grape wine is for the people are eating meat, or they are eating dinner.

When these New Zealanders their behaviors choose to do farming or agriculture to grow and produce different kinds of taste of white or red grape wine drinking products job. Themselves grape agriculture behavior will influence these New Zealanders themselves, they can learn how to improve different kinds of grape wine drinking products in order to achieve every kinds of white or read grape wines taste improving aim during their white or red grape producing process.

Why can New Zealander every individual white or read grape wine producers improve their white or read grape wine taste more easily? In behavioral economic view, it can explain that why any one New Zealander white or read grape wine producer can be encouraged or excited or persuaded to concentrate nervous and energy and effort to learn how to improve their white or red grape wine products easily.

In fact, New Zealand is one agricultural food export country. It has good natural environment resource , e.g. land, seed to provide any one farmer to produce themselves any kinds of agricultrual food products, e.g. fruit, or wine food products. Because New Zealanders know themselves country has enough natural resource . So, in common, many New Zealanders choose to attempt to do farming agricultural jobs in order to export themselves any kinds of fruit or meat or wine products to overseas or sell to domestic in order to earn profit.

So, when these New Zealand farmers number has been increasing every year. This country farmers will feel themsleves competition between this New Zealand farmers themselves are serious due to they may feel New Zealanders choose to do agriculture businesses in order to export themselves different kinds of farming food to overseas or sell to local to earn profit.

Hence, when many New Zealand farmers feel that farmers number has been increasing every year. They will feel themselves competition is serious. They must need to spend much time and nervous and effort to research what method is the best how to produce the best taste of white or red grape wine products in order to let local or overseas wine buyers to choose to buy his/her producing white or read grpae products to drink.

Hence, in competition psychological view, may influence many New Zealand white or reaad wine producers had been beginning to change their learning behavior on researching what method is the best in order to produce the best quality of taste red or white wine products to sell in order to attract overseas or local white or read grape wine drinkers to choose to buy his/her wine products. Their behavior will focus on learning how to raising or improving white or read grape wine taste method more than only focus on producing a large number white or red grape wine products. They believe wine quality is more important to compare wine producing number. So, New Zealand wine producers themselves wine producers behaviors have been changing on concentrating on researching wine quality method aspect more then wine producing number aspect in behavioral economic view.

America high technological productive behavior

For America example, US is one high technological country, it owns many high technological knowledge talent inventors, e.g. computer science inventors. Hence, US must attract many diferent countries owning high technological computer inventors choose to go to US to develop their computer science profession career. Also, it seems that when many computer science inventors or professions choose to go to US to develop themselves computer science new career. In behavioral economic view, due to their leaving themselves countries choice, which may bring influence themselve country job behaviors need to be changed. They must need to adapt US new live. Because they will forgive their past computer science job. These computer science professionals need to spend time to adapt US new lives. They " past computer science job behaviors" will need to be changed to their new US any computer employer's new computer science job model.

Because their traditional computer science jobs needed to be forgot in their themselves countries. They will feel their old computer science job knowledge and behavior needed to change in order to let their US any one new of computer company employer feels satisfactory to accept their new working behavior in any one US computer organization.

So, on the other hand, many US computer company employer will feel that they must need time to accept any one new overseas computer science professions their working behaviors, their working attitude daily, because these foreign comouter science professional, their past computer working behaviors and working attitude must be different to US domestic computer science professions.

In behavioral economic view, these overseas computer science professions, their working behaviors and attitude must be needed to change in order to adapt any one US new computer company itself domestic or local computer science professional stafs themselves daily working behaviors and attitude because these overseas and local computer science professionals must need to team work together.

In behavioral economic view, it is only one way that foreign computer science professionals must need to change themselves past country traditiona daily working behaviors and attitude in order to cooperate with these US local computer science professionals in teams more easily.

Consequently, if these foreign compute science professionals can change their past working behaviors and attitude to let any one US local computer science professional feels to cooperate with them easily in short time. Then, the US computer company itself whole computer professional teams themselves efficiencies will be influenced to raised or improved by the changing past working attitude and working behaviors of these foreign computer science professionals. So, in behavioral economic view, only if US any one computer company hopes itself computer teams themselves efficiency can be raised or improved when it decides to employ foreign computer science professionals and US domestic computer science professionals. They need to work in teams together. They must need to let these foreign computer science professionals to know how to change their working behaviors and attitude to let their domestic computer science professionals feel easy to work together. Then, the US computer company itself whole team efficiency must be rasied or improved easily in short time.

- China share market investing behavior

For China share market example, economic development depends on financial market. Because if many Chinese have interest to invest to carry on shares buying and selling activities in orde to learn how to earn shares interest and share profit when the China shareholder can make decision to sell himself/herself shares in the the high price, then he/she can earn money when he/she can sell the China company's shares in the high sale share price position.

If China has many Chinese like to spend time to carry on investing shares activities. Themselves shares buying and selling behaviors will influence China has many companies can increase fund from many Chinese shareholders in order to have enough money to expand or develop themselves businesses in China in long term.

Consequently, when China can have many Chinese like to attempt to carry on buying and selling shares investing behaviors in China share market. Themselves buying and selling shares behaviors can help many Chinese companies have effort to increase enough money or capital in order to continue to do their businesses in long term absolutely. So, it explains why when many Chinese become shareholders , they can assist China will have many companies continue to develop their businesses if many Chinese like to carry on shares buying and selling investing behaviors in long time in China financial investment market nowadays in behavioral economic view.

Why has any individual country have many people invest share behavior which can influence the country's macro consumption desire?

I shall apply shares market buying and selling investment behavior to explaiin why shares investment behavior which may impact the country's overal consumption desire as below:

In behavioral economic view, I assume that when the coutry has many people have interest to attempt to carry on shares buying and selling investment behavior, then their frequent shares buying and selling behaviors which may bring negactive consumption desire or shopping desire of these shares investors their consumer behavior.

The reason is simple, when the country has many share buyers number suddenly been increasing rapidly. Consequently, these large group share investors must need to spend much time to research any kinds of company shares variations, whether when their share prices will rise up of fall down in order to achieve buying the company's shares in the lowest price and selling the company's shares in the highest price level in order to earn profit.

Basic on this reason, they must need to spend much extra time to research share prices changing behavior every day, e.g. one working person will wait to leave his/her job, after he/she can spend time to gather data to research the day's share price changing behavior after dinner. So, the working person's right time may be his/her share price market research behavior. Before he/she may spend his/her night time to go to shopping after dinner, but nowadays, he/she will fogive to do his/her shopping behavior before dinner or after dinner at hight sometime. He/she will make decision to spend much night time to turn on computer to click on share market website to research his/her share purchase choice to investigate whether his/her share price whether it rises up or falls down at the moment in order to make his/her share buying or selling decision at ever night time.

I mean the when the country has many people are share investors, their shares investment behavioral spenging time which will influence many shops lose customers at might often because the country will have many people feel need to spend night time to turn on computer or watch television to investigate share price variation. So, the country will have many people / share investors choose to stay at home in order to carry on share price variation investigation behavior, they need to listen share market update news from radios or watch the share market update news from computer or TV at home every night. Consequenly, they must reduce times to leave themselves homes at night. So, their shopping behavior also will be reduced. Because these share investors feel need to spend time to investigate share price variation news at homes which can bring economic benefits (high opportunity benefits) when they choose to forgive to leave homes to go to shopping times (opportunity cost) every night.

On conclusion, it seems that when the country has many people are share investors, then their share price investigating behavior may bring negative shopping emotion at night. Consequently, the country's any one shop may lose many customers from this share investor consumer group in behavioral economic view. Hence, when the country's share investors number had been increasing rapidly, it will influence any shops lose many customers from this share investing customer group at night frequenly in short time, even long time in behavioral economic view, because their shopping desires or shopping emotion will be brought negative feeling when they make decisions to spend much time to listen radios or watch TV or computers share price update nes at night. Hence, share market will bring negative impact to influence consumer shopping desire or negative shopping emotion in behavioral economic view.

Can technology influence human shopping behavioral change?
Nowadays, technological development has reached mature stage, whether technological mature stage may bring positive or negative shopping emotion influence to global consumers. I shall aplly internet inventin or ecommerce shopping channel tool to explain whether internet technology can bring postive or negative influence to global consumer behavior in behavioral economic view.
Internet is a good technological tool, it brings e-commerce business chance. In fact, commonly, global has have many businessmen choose to use internet channel to carry on their products transactions between global online-buyers and their electronic websites. So, global many shoppers had begun to feel online shopping is more convenient to compare visiting shops shopping. Their shopping behaviors have been changed from internet technological tool. Global has many shoppers choose to buy any products from any overseas or local businessmen their web stores. They only need to spend time to find any businessmen their webstores to choose the most suitable products to pay visa to buy from their webstores. at homes. So, in general, global had have may shoppers had changed their shopping behaviors from visiting shops to visiting webstores at homes often.
So, it seems that internet technological tool had influenced global many shops disappear, but internet webstores will be replaced their actual shops on streets. Some of businessmen either they choose webstores to replace shops or choose websotes and shops both or still keep shops only. Hence, internet tool influences global businessmen have three kinds of products sale channels to let globa local and overseas consumers to choose how to buy their products.
However, in fact, many of global shoppers, youngers and olders had begun to accept to buy any products from webstores. They feel to spend time to leave homes to visit shops , their shopping behaviors will be wasted time to not essential part to their daily lives. Hence, since internet technological invention, it had changed many consumers their traditional visiting shops shopping habit to change to buying products from webstores channel.
However, on the one hand, internet creates webstores ecommerce shopping channel to let global many consumers do not need to leave homes to go to shopping. It brings negative visiting shops shopping emotion to global general consumers nowadays. But on the other hand, it also brings positive visiting internet webstores shopping emotion to global general consumer nowadays. So, it seems that global many consumers feel that they often do not need to spend much time to go out shopping. Many global consumers feel convenient and enjoy to choose any products to buy from different internet webstores, when the online buyer chooses the most suitable product, he she only needs to pay visa card to buy the product from the online seller's webstore conveniently at home.
Hence, online shopping can bring economic benefit to online buyers, e.g. avoiding walking time or spending transport fare to visit the shop to go to shopping, shortening or reducing shopping time to do another important matter.
On conclusion, global many consumers began feel online shopping can bring more economic benefits on shortening shopping time, avoiding transport fare spending aspect. So, online shopping will be popular shopping behavior for future long time. It may encourage global many shoppers can make rapid shopping decision in short time in order to carry on any products buying transaction to global any one online shopper in short time easily in behavioral

economic view. So, global many businessmen had begun to build themselves one attraction webstore in order to persuade different countries consumers to choose to click themselves webstores from internet channel to buy any kinds of products in short time easily.

So, internet technology had changed consumers traditional shopping behaviors to build positive online shopping emotion as well as raise online sellers' any products sale chance easily in behavioral economic view.

Why and how human behavior may influence the country's economic growth or recession?

When one country has many people choose to do the same matter for one period, whether their behavior may influence the country's pvera; economic growth or recession . I shall attempt to indicate cases toexplain their relationship as below:

For flowing rubblish behavioral case example, do you feel that when the country has many people often flow rubblish on the streets, instead of their flowing rubblish behavior may bring streets dirty? But, their flowing rubblish behavior may explain that this country has people may have enough money to buy food to ear, or enough cloths to wear, enough bottles of water to drink, even they may have enough money to buy new television, radio, refrigeraters , washing machines, desktops or laptops electronic home products from old to new to use in order to satisfy their living needs. So, when they flow old electronic home products, their flowing old home electronic products behaviors may seem that they have enough money to buy other new home electronic products to replace old home electronic products to use at homes.

However, it seems thaat this country ought have many people have jobs to do. So, many of them, they can easy to make purchase decison to flow any old home electronic products and buy any new home electronic products to use . Because this country has many people have jobs to do. So, they can often not use old home electonic products to become rubblishs to flow on streets after they had bought any kinds of new home electronic homes.

In fact, it also implies that this country's economy grows rapidly. So, many businesses can glow up rapdly. When they expanded their businesses, they must need to increase employees number in order to let they help themselves to raise productivity or serve their clients absolutely. So, when the country has many businesses can grow up, it seems that its economy must be better or it is improved to compare past. Due to many different kinds of home electronic products had been often bought to use by this country people in this period. So, this country's any streets can be observed that expensive electronic home products were flowed on streets anywhere. then, this country will have many electronic home products sellers can sell their home electronic products very easily. When this country has many people can find any kinds of jobs to do easily. So, due to unemploymen rate had been decreasing.

In behavioral economic view, as this many electronic home products rubblish country case, we can observe this country may have many people have jobs to do. So, consumption number has been increased long time. So, cheap food, or expensive home electronic products may be rubblish on any streets. This country's people , their flowing rubblish behaviors may be explained that many of people have enough jobs to do, so they have ability to buy any good taste food to eat or buy any kinds of expensive electronic home products to use. So, this country's economy may be improved for this long period. So, in behavioral economic view, when this country can have many electronic home products rubblishs are flowed on anywherer in streets frequently. It seems that this country will have many people have jobs to do, so it causes they often change old home electronic products or replaced them easily, when they have enough income to spend to buy any kinds of new home electronic products to use at homes easily. Moreover, their flowing old electronic home products behaviors also indicate that this country has many people their salaries may be increased in possible from their emplyers. When this country can have many different kinds of home electornic products are sold. It means that this country's electronic home products needs or demand had been increasing, due to many people have jobs to do and income increases to excite their living of needs also improve. Consequently, this country may seem have better economic improvement. We can observe from this country's electronic home products rubblish increasing income in theis period.

On conclusion, this country ought experience economic growth at this period. So, " flowing expensive electronic home rubblish increasing number " may seem that this country's economic growth is rapidly in this period, due to many people have jobs to do as well as salaries increase in this period.

Technology how impacts human behavior changing?

Technology how influences human behavior to bring changing? For example, online share purchase and sale transaction from smart phone brings share investor can do share buying or selling transation in any where and any time conveniently, non manual driving auto vehicle, bring car owner feels comfortable and spends free time to do other matter, e.g. reading, listening mucis in himself or herself car freely. electrical energy vehicle can help car owner to reduce air polluton and it can brings the drivers do not feel drive long time in any journeys in order to avoid air pollution for environmental protection responsible car drivers in our societies. Thus, they will drive long time in any journeys when they can drive electronic energy cars to replace oil energy cars.

However, online technology can also bring consumers can choose to stay at homes to buy any things from seller individual online webstore conveniently. Such as online technology can bring shoppers do not need to spend much time to visit shops to buy any things. They can choose any kinds of products from any online sellers individual online webstores conveniently at homes. Online technology excite busy consumers can make purchase decision easily as well as it can help online sellers sell any kinds of products from internet easily.

In behavioral economic view, technology can change human behavior to be improved, it can let human feels comfortable, more free time ro use, rapid making any decisions, such as apply smart phones to make share purchase or sale transaction decision, online shopping decision, even travelling any where decision in short time, when the traveller finds the most cheap hotel accommodation room price and air ticket price frm any travel agent online tourism webstore, then the potential travel customer can follow the online hotel accommodation price and air ticket price data to make decision when to buy the air ticket from the airline travel agent or make decision when to prebook which hotel accommodation room to go to the country to travel from online travel agent tourism webstores. So, technology can encourage global any country travelers to make anywhere to trvel rapidly. If the traveler can find the country's general hotel rooms and airline tickets prices had been decreasing more sightly. The traveler may make travel decision to choose the country to travel in short time, then he/she can prebook the country;s any hotel room and airline ticket to pay by visa fraom the country's any hotel and airline travel agent webstores., before one week, even one month or more easily. Hence, online technology can also encourage traveler individual frequent travel times to be increased, due to global travelers can find any hotel rooms and airline tickets prices from internet conveniently at homes. They do not need to spend time to visit any airline travel agent to enquire travel choice country's hotel rooms prices and airline ticket prices. They can compare global travel of countries choices ' all hotels rooms and airline agents air tickets prices to make prebook airline seat and hotel room decision before one week, one month even six months early.

On conclusion, online technology can encourage global travelers can make travelling any where and when traveling time desicions easily. It can excite tourism industry develops in long time. Also, such as electricity cars invention can encourage environment protection car owners do car purchase decision easily, because they can choose to drive electronic energy cars to replace oil energy cars in order to avoid air pollution occurs easily. So, electronic cars can increase electronic car purchasrs number, due to many of environmental protection attitude of car owners can choose to drive electricity cars to bring air cleans, even non -manual driving cars can encourage lazy driving and free time driving car owners to choose to buy non-manual (artificial intelligent) cars to drive , because they can spend much free time to read, listen music or do any matters in themselves cars, they do not need to drive cars, robotic (AI) auto driving machine is such one non-manual driver to help them to drive themselves cars confidently. So, non-manual driving cars can attract lazy and enjoying free time driving car owners to choose to buy to replace traditional manual cars to drive easily. Moreover, online share transaction can help any share investors to make share buying and selling decision in short time easily. When they can apply smart phones technological tool to carry on share buying and selling activities easily. They can observe any share rising or falling price suitation from smart phones in any where any any time easily. So, smart phone technology can help global any shareholders to make share purchase and sale transaction easily. So, technology can encourage human makes decision in short time rapidly.

Printed by Libri Plureos GmbH in Hamburg,
Germany